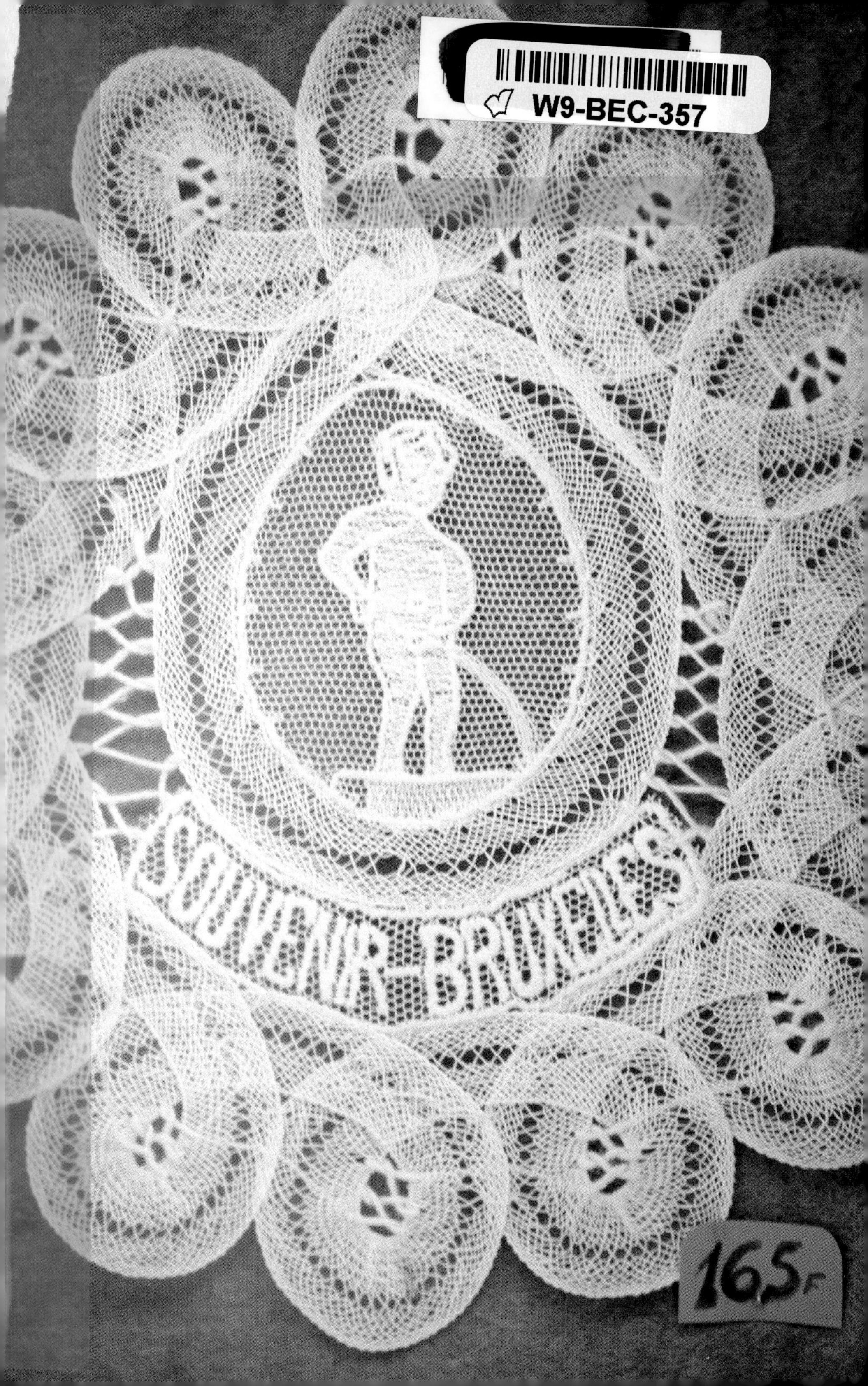
SOUVENIR-BRUXELLES

INSIGHT GUIDES

The world's largest collection of visual travel guides

BRUSSELS

Original edition by Kristiane Müller
Updated by Rachel Parsons
Managing Editor: Dorothy Stannard

Editorial Director: Brian Bell

Discovery
CHANNEL

APA PUBLICATIONS
Part of the Langenscheidt Publishing Group

INSIGHT GUIDES

BRUSSELS

CONTACTING THE EDITORS: Although every effort
is made to provide accurate information in this
publication, we live in a fast-changing world and would
appreciate it if readers would call our attention to any
errors or outdated information that may occur by
writing to us at Apa Publications,
P.O. Box 7910, London SE1 1WE, England.
Fax: (44) 171-403-0290.
e-mail: insight@apaguide.demon.co.uk.

First Edition 1992
Updated 1999

Distributed in the United States by
Langenscheidt Publishers Inc.
46–35 54th Road, Maspeth, NY 11378
Fax: (718) 784 -0640

Distributed in Canada by
Prologue Inc.
1650 Lionel Bertrand Blvd., Boisbriand
Québec, Canada J7H 1N7
Tel: (450) 434-0306. Fax: (450) 434-2627

Distributed in the UK & Ireland by
GeoCenter International Ltd
The Viables Centre, Harrow Way
Basingstoke, Hampshire RG22 4BJ
Fax: (44) 1256-817988

Distributed in Australia & New Zealand by
Hema Maps Pty. Ltd
24 Allgas Street, Slacks Creek 4127
Brisbane, Australia
Tel: (61) 7 3290 0322. Fax: (61) 7 3290 0478

Worldwide distribution enquiries:
APA Publications GmbH & Co. Verlag KG
(Singapore branch)
38 Joo Koon Road, Singapore 628990
Tel: 65-8651600. Fax: 65-8616438

Printed in Singapore by
Insight Print Services (Pte) Ltd
38 Joo Koon Road, Singapore 628990
Fax: 65-8616438

This guidebook combines the interests
and enthusiasms of two of the
world's best known information pro-
viders: Insight Guides, whose range of titles
has set the standard for visual travel guides
since 1970, and Discovery Channel, the
world's premier source of nonfiction television programming.

The editors of Insight Guides provide both
practical advice and general understanding
about a destination's history, culture, institutions and people. Discovery Channel
and its Web site, www.discovery.com, help
millions of viewers explore their world from
the comfort of their own home and also
encourage them to explore it firsthand.

Brussels plays a key role in Europe
today; it has always done. In the days
when the Low Countries were in
French hands, then in Spanish, then in Austrian, Brussels was always the chosen capital of "the Netherlands". Even since
becoming the capital of the independent Kingdom of Belgium in 1830, the city has maintained its European identity. And, although
the poets and thinkers, artists and merchants
it once attracted have been largely super-
seded by the planners of the European Union and NATO, it remains a thriving place where
not only Europeans but the world can feel at
home. After all, almost one-third of its inhabitants are foreigners.

But there's more to Brussels than the
bureaucrats The city possesses what many
consider to be the world's most beautiful
market square, the Grand' Place. Another
famous symbol of Brussels is the statue of
Manneken Pis, which embodies the citizen's
ungovernable spirit.

It is in Brussels – which lies only a few
kilometres north of the French linguistic
boundary – that the clash between Belgium's
Walloons and Flemings can be most clearly
seen. It is a conflict that manifests itself not
least in the language rivalry. The visitor will
immediately notice that signs and street
names, as well as all city districts, are labelled in both Flemish and French.

Müller

Even if Flemish and French are the official languages, most people here actually speak French. And another aspect of the city with a decidedly French accent is the cuisine. Brussels is a gourmet's delight; the repertoire consists of much more than just the legendary "*moules et frites*".

I t is partly the cuisine of the city that motivated **Kristiane Müller** to edit *Insight Guide: Brussels*. For this book, she explored Brussels and Brabant with **Eberhard Urban**, a writer and calendar maker from Frankfurt. Here, he takes a look at some of the famous names to have been associated with the city – clergymen and philosophers, artists and writers, movers and shakers from Erasmus of Rotterdam and Karl Marx to Peter Paul Rubens and Pieter Brueghel the Elder. His daughter **Susanne Urban**, who studied politics and history in Frankfurt, provided the article about one of the darker chapters in Belgian history – the acquisition of the colony of the Congo.

Urban

Hartmut Dierks works as a journalist and radio producer in northern Germany. Here he gives us an insight into what the king of Belgium actually does, and also provides the shopping and entertainment chapters.

Freelance journalist **Nina Köster** describes the origins of Brussels, the fortunes of the city from the Habsburgs to the 1830 revolution. She also describes the city's lacemaking tradition. **Kirsten Kehret** wrote on the "Kingdom of Belgium".

Dierks

The author and journalist **Rosine de Dijn** hails from Antwerp, and was responsible for tracing the fate of Jewish children during the war. **Joseph Lehnen**, a journalist from Brussels, looks at the development of the country after World War II. He also explores Brussels' fascinating Marolles district and describes some of the local personalities who have left their indelible mark on the city.

Gisela Decker reports on the problems of the continuing language dispute between the Flemings and the Walloons. **Helmut Müller-Kleinsorge**, who refers to himself as an "all-weather journalist", also looks beyond the

Lehnen

boundaries of the city as such and explains why it is that the Belgians have only ever produced one sportsman of truly international standing, namely the cyclist Eddy Merckx.

Wolfgang Schmerfeld, who has also contributed to a number of Insight Guides, looks at the way of life in Brussels' Upper City and examines what's on offer at some of the city's bustling markets. Every day is market day in Brussels. A journalist who reports a great deal about food and drink, Schmerfeld also samples what's on the menu in the city's best restaurants. It is not known whether he managed to taste all of the astonishing variety of beers available.

The chapter on the Royal Greenhouses was based on the work **Edgar Goedleven**. The historian and author **Dr Barbara Beuys** gives a guide to the battlefield of Waterloo, reliving the events of Wellington's finest hour and Napoleon's final defeat. Frequent Insight contributor **Lisa Gerard-Sharp** provides a sceptic's eye-view of the Capital of Europe.

T he photographs are the work of a variety of specialists, including the portraits of Cologne photographer **Bodo Bondzio** and the best shots of **Wolfgang Fritz**, who explored Brussels and Brabant extensively. Further images came from **Henning Christoph**, **Thomas Mayer** and **Jörn Sackermann**. Thanks also to **Marion Schmitz-Reiners** and **Ingeborg Knigge**,.

Of great help to the original editors were **Cécile Pierard** of the Vlaams Commissariaat-Generaal voor Toerisme and **Annette Beautrix** from the Office de Promotion du Tourisme de la Communauté Française de Belgique, both based in Brussels.

The original German text was translated by **Jane Michael-Rushmer** and **Susan Sting**, under the supervision of **Tony Halliday**. It has since been updated by a Brussels-based journalist, **George McDonald**, who is author of *Insight Pocket Guide: Brussels,*

This update to the book was researched by **Rachel Parsons**; the managing editor in Insight Guides' London office was **Dorothy Stannard**.

CONTENTS

Preceding pages: the Flower Market on the Grand' Place; the craft of lace-making brought wealth to the city's merchants; a souvenir of the Mannekin-Pis.

TRAVEL TIPS

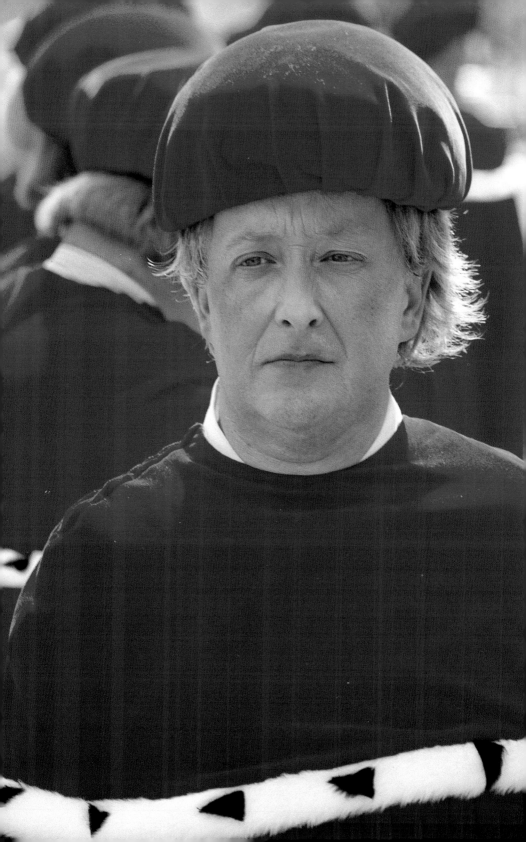

THE FOURFOLD CAPITAL

Opinions vary about Brussels. The 19th-century English poet Matthew Arnold called it a "white sparkling, cheerful, wicked little place". The American Herman Melville, on the other hand, sourly remarked "a more dull, humdrum place I never saw".

What isn't disputed is its key role in modern Europe. A comment by another English writer, William Thackeray – that it had "an absurd Lilliput look with it" – belongs firmly to the 19th century. Today, about 1 million people live and work in the city. It is the capital of Belgium and Brabant and headquarters to thousands of European Union and military personnel. A wide variety of high-technology industries mean that Brussels, a former weavers' town, is well equipped to march into the 21st century as a modern, cosmopolitan metropolis.

The city has a colourful history, and its fair share of legends. The man who planted Brussels at the centre of Europe is said to have been St Gaugerich; according to the story, he carried Brussels here as a seed in his bishop's mitre in the 6th century. In the course of time, both town and country were ruled by Burgundy, Spain, Austria and France. Its inclusion in the Netherlands in the 19th century was only briefly tolerated. A performance of Auber's opera *Masianello* – which in Act IV contains the exhortation "No tyrants, no slavery; all power to the citizens!" – triggered the revolution which put Leopold of Saxe-Coburg on the throne as the first King of the Belgians in 1830.

Not to be forgotten are the darker chapters in Belgian history – the acquisition of the colony of the Congo under Leopold II and the German invasions during two world wars. A tribute to the struggle of the Belgian Resistance is included in this guide, as is an account of the rescue from the Nazis of hundreds of Jewish children.

Visitors will enjoy getting to know all aspects of Brabant and its capital. There is plenty to see and experience here: the Grand' Place, the glittering Upper City, the historic Lower City, its top restaurants and humble snack bars, the colourful markets and the luxurious shopping arcades, the Heysel Park and the Atomium, the Botanical Garden, the Museums of Ancient and Modern Art, the Comic Museum, the Stock Exchange, the theatre and the capital's surrounding countryside, from the idyllic towns of Leuven and Tervuren to historic Waterloo.

Preceding pages: a modern-day 'soldier' reliving the Battle of Waterloo; richly-decorated and gilded façades recall the wealth of the city's merchants; the Atomium, from the 1958 World Exhibition; flags of the European Union nations; an artist captures the Grand' Place by night; club members celebrating – a favourite pastime. **Left**, a robed guild member recalls the traditions of the past.

According to legend, it was St Gaugerich, Bishop of Cambrai – also known as St Géry – who was responsible for the founding of Brussels. It is said that he carried the seed of the city here in his mitre and planted it like a flower. At least, that is one version of the story. According to a more plausible version of events, the bishop fell ill here while travelling across his diocese and had a chapel built on one of the islands in the Senne. A settlement rapidly developed around the chapel. Opinions vary as to the exact date that this took place, but it is generally thought to have been some time between AD 580 and 695.

Brussels was first mentioned in records in the year 966, under the name *Bruocsella*, which means something like "The House in the Swamp." In 977 Charles of France, Duke of Lorraine, built a fortress here. Two years later he made it his residence. For this reason, 979 is regarded as the year in which the city was officially founded.

With the river – today completely built over – providing additional natural protection, craftsmen and merchants soon settled around the castle. The new town expanded rapidly when Count Lambert II of Leuven moved into a new fortress on the Coudenberg in 1041. In an unprecedented move, he ordered the building of a rampart to separate the classes of townsfolk. His knights and stewards and local merchants built their homes within its walls while humble craftsmen and peasants had to remain outside. This strict segregation of the classes was to sow the seeds for many a future conflict.

The weaving industry: During the following century, Brussels profited from its location on the trading route between Cologne and Bruges and rose to prosperity and renown. Artefacts of worked gold and silver from Brussels became desirable trading items.

The town spread from the valley to the slopes of the surrounding hills.

During the 13th century the weaving industry flourished. Wool was imported from England and processed here. Nowhere else did the manufacture of cloth match the quality of the cloth-making industry of Belgium. Colourful fabrics from Flanders and finely woven material from Brabant were in demand as far away as the Orient. The beneficiaries of this development, however, were the cloth merchants rather than the weavers,

dyers and fullers. The craftsmen were relegated to the position of humble employees, earning pitiful wages.

The worst incidences of exploitation involved the Beguine communities, in which women lived and worked together as if in a convent but were not tied by lifelong vows. They sewed, wove and embroidered for the "Glory of God" – a privilege which again benefited the cloth merchants rather than the women themselves because it reduced still further the abysmally low wages of the industry. Some Beguine convents have survived until this day.

Preceding pages: Leo Belgicus. Left, the Cathedral of St Michael and St Gudula, the city's patron saints. Above, a refuge for women: the ancient Beguine Convent.

The city soon began to express its burgeoning prosperity in fine building. In honour of St Michael and St Gudula, the town's two patron saints, the construction of the Cathedral was begun in 1225. The remarkable building with its twin towers was not completed until the 16th century, and naturally incorporates features of many different architectural styles. It is known unofficially as "St Michael and Gudula's".

Class war: At the end of the 13th century the craftsmen revolted against the supremacy of the merchants and cloth manufacturers. Tired of having to labour on behalf of the privileged few whilst they themselves con-

tinued to live in poverty and without civic rights, they joined forces in an attempt to improve their lot.

Initially their efforts backfired, and their right to form a guild was made subject to the agreement of the town council. Their second offensive was more successful; in 1303, following the example of their fellow guildsmen in Bruges – who had ejected their French rulers in the "Battle of the Golden Spurs" – the oppressed masses of Brussels rose up openly against those in power and the patrician minority were forced to give way. The guild of weavers, fullers and dyers was awarded the right of representation on the Town Council.

The peace following their hard-won victory was short-lived. In 1306 Duke Jean II, backed by the patricians' mounted troops, took up arms against the "Plebejer". The rebels were defeated in a bloody battle at Vilvoorde; their leaders were buried alive before the city gates.

From then on, craftsmen were forbidden to carry weapons and weavers and fullers, who had been at the forefront of the unrest, were subjected to a curfew and forbidden to leave their homes after nightfall. Nonetheless, the forces of change had been set in motion and the grim determination of the guildsmen enabled them to win progressively more civil rights.

To protect their city against foes from far and near, the upper classes of Brussels built a second defensive wall, 6 km (4 miles) long and enclosing some 450 hectares (1,100 acres). Entry was via seven fortified gates and drawbridges. The position of the ramparts roughly corresponds to the inner ring of avenues encircling the city today.

By this time, Brussels was gradually eroding the position of Leuven as the capital of the Duchy of Brabant. In 1402 the foundation stone of a magnificent Town Hall was laid. Miraculously surviving virtually unscathed the artillery bombardment of the Grand' Place by Louis XIV of France in 1695, its 90-metre (200-ft) tower still dominates the market place today.

The building of the Town Hall coincided with the start of a new stage in the city's development. At the beginning of the 15th century the powerful Dukes of Burgundy assumed power in Brussels, a position they were to maintain until 1477. Their regency marked the beginning of an era of prosperity for the city. The local citizens – or at least, the wealthy upper classes – were able to enjoy life to the full.

The manufacture of artistically worked wall hangings replaced the cloth industry, which by this time was no longer able to compete with its English counterpart. Brussels tapestries became famous all over the world. Many of the redundant weavers were able to redirect their skills and make a livelihood in this sphere; those who could not left the city.

The Burgundian Court: In 1430 Philip the Good became the ruler of Brabant and Brussels became the favoured residential city in his powerful kingdom. As a result of a number of cleverly arranged marriages and fortuitious land acquisitions, by the middle of the 15th century his territories included Brabant, Flanders, Limburg, Holland-Zeeland, Hennegau (Hainaut), Namur and Luxemburg as well as Burgundy. Philip, like his son, Charles the Bold, who succeeded him in 1467, had a fondness for ostentation, luxury and elitism. To celebrate the occasion

its service. Jan van Eyck, for instance, painted the portrait of Philip's future wife, Princess Isabella of Portugal, and Rogier van der Weyden worked for many years as the official artist of Brussels.

The city became the arena for magnificent jousting tournaments and festivals, and an ambitious building programme was embarked upon. The Church of Notre-Dame-de-la-Chapelle, which had been destroyed by fire, was promptly rebuilt. The remarkable Church of Our Lady of the Victories was built at the behest and expense of the city crossbowmen, who decided to replace a smaller place of worship built in 1304. Pros-

of his marriage, he founded the Order of the Golden Fleece, a knightly order for the aristocracy of Europe.

The glittering lifestyle at the Burgundian court attracted large numbers of famous artists and craftsmen. Philip was the richest man in Europe and his court became a focal point of European civilisation and culture. Famous Flemish painters were employed in

Left, Philip III ("the Good"), Duke of Burgundy, amassed great luxury and power. **Above**, weaving brought prosperity, at least until the revolt (painting by Isaac Clacsz, around 1600).

perous burghers surrounded the market square with dignified guildhalls reflecting the ruler's love of pomp.

The fall of the House of Burgundy was ultimately due to its over-ambitious aspirations. Charles the Bold's attempt to create an extensive, independent Kingdom of Burgundy, at the expense of his archrival, the King of France, including the province of Lorraine foundered in 1477 in the Battle of Nancy. Charles himself was killed in the battle. His body was discovered many days later, naked and bearing the marks of attack by wolves.

The death of Charles the Bold in 1477 brought to an ignominious end one of the great periods of European history. His daughter Mary's marriage to Maximilian I of Austria was the only thing which could save the Burgundian possessions in the Netherlands from French attack. There was, however, a heavy price to pay: the acceptance of the Habsburg yoke. When Mary died young following a nasty riding accident, the Netherlands sank into war and civil unrest. At one stage Maximilian himself was held prisoner in Bruges.

In 1494 Maximilian handed over the Netherlands to his 16-year-old son, Philip the Handsome. By virtue of his marriage in 1496 to the Spanish princess Joanna of Castile, Philip laid the foundations for what would in the future become the world empire of their son and heir, Charles V, born on 24 February 1500 in Ghent.

At the age of 15, Charles V took up residence in Coudenberg Castle. Although he spent little time in the Netherlands, travelling constantly in his capacity as King of Spain and Holy Roman Emperor (from 1519), he regarded Flanders and Brabant as his home throughout his life. In 1531, Brussels was declared capital of the Netherlands. It is to Charles that Brussels owes its cultural and political importance in 16th-century Europe. No other city within his vast empire profited more from his reign.

Trade in luxury goods flourished and Brussels lace achieved world fame. In Paris it was the height of fashion to wear pillow lace from Brussels. Equally coveted were weapons forged by the city's smiths; Henry VIII of England tried in vain to persuade some of them to work for him. With the completion of the Willebroek Canal between Brussels and Antwerp in 1561, the city acquired a direct link to the North Sea.

Left, a knight in shining armour: Charles V, German Emperor and King of Spain (copy by Peter Paul Rubens, 1603, after the original lost painting by Titian, 1548).

Poets and philosophers, artists and merchants all revelled in the city's lively atmosphere. The great philosopher Erasmus of Rotterdam lived for a few months in Anderlecht. Returning home to Rotterdam, he looked back nostalgically on his visit. "Oh... if only Brabant were not so far away!" Pieter Brueghel the Elder, the most famous 16th-century artist in the entire Netherlands, left Antwerp in 1563 and settled in Brussels.

Science also flourished in the city. Charles V's personal physician, Andreas Vesalius, who was born in Brussels in 1514, boldly disregarded the taboos of the time and dissected human corpses in the course of his studies. His discoveries revolutionised medical practice and formed the basis of modern anatomy.

Religious unrest: But dark clouds were already looming on the horizon. When Charles V abdicated in 1555, he was succeeded by his son, Philip II, who proceeded to rule the Netherlands ruthlessly from Spain. His father's means of preventing the forward march of the Reformation had been to have Calvinists beheaded or burned at the stake as heretics; Philip took even firmer action and sent in the Inquisition. When the religious struggle developed inexorably into a popular uprising against Spanish rule, the troops of the Duke of Alva set out for the Netherlands.

The duke established the "Bloody Council", intervening mercilessly and suppressing the revolt with great cruelty. In 1568 Counts Egmont and Horn were executed on Brussels' Grand' Place for demanding greater sovereignty for their country.

After Egmont's death – recorded for literary posterity by Johann Wolfgang von Goethe's drama – aristocratic leadership of the rebellion was assumed by Prince William I of Orange (William the Silent). A skilled negotiator and fundraiser, he succeeded in breathing new life into the struggle for civil rights and freedom of religious practice throughout the Netherlands and finally forced the Spanish to give way. In 1576 he entered Brussels at the head of a triumphal procession; and in 1579 he established the independence from Spain of the Seven United Provinces. But conflict continued. This time it was the turn of the Catholics to be persecuted.

Philip's desire to concentrate all power in himself led to a policy of repression, intrigue and a series of military campaigns. The ill-fated Armada which set sail from Spain in 1588 was to form part of an attempted invasion of England by a Spanish army from the Netherlands. Having previously sent the Duke of Parma, Alexander Farnese, to the Low Countries at the head of a large army,

sels, which remained capital of the Spanish Netherlands, returned to a peaceful existence. The economy boomed again, the gallows and scaffold disappeared, and courtly pomp prevailed once more.

Brussels' citizens rediscovered their taste for celebrations. At no other time were there so many processions and banquets as during the ensuing years. Peter Paul Rubens, the most famous baroque artist in Europe and, during his youth, Albert's court painter, captured the spirit of the era in his paintings.

The peace, however, was short-lived. In 1695 Brussels was drawn into the conflict between France and Spain which had flared

Philip had been able to force the rebellious southern states to capitulate one by one; in 1585 Brussels, too, was retaken by Farnese. In the meantime, however, the northern provinces had broken away from Spain and asserted their independence following the ceasefire of 1609. In the South, a mass exodus got under way; some 100,000 Flemings emigrated to the republic of the United Netherlands (the Netherlands of today).

In 1598 Philip transferred his power over the Spanish Netherlands to his daughter Isabella and her husband, Archduke Albert of Austria. During their reign life in Brus-

up at intervals throughout the century. Louis XIV's artillery bombarded the city for two days. Thousands of buildings were destroyed. The Grand' Place was reduced to rubble; only the tower of the Town Hall remained standing.

Within the space of a few years, the citizens of Brussels completely rebuilt their city. The Grand' Place acquired its present character, which has won universal acclaim as an architectural masterpiece; the harmonious fusion of Gothic, Renaissance and baroque elements has made it famous throughout the world.

The death of Charles II in 1701 marked the end of the Spanish branch of the Habsburg dynasty. After years of fighting, the Spanish possessions were divided between Austria and France. Then in 1714 the Spanish Netherlands were ceded to Austria. Brussels was torn apart by unrest caused by the new foreign rulers. The revolt was led by François Anneessens, the leader of the guilds. His execution in 1719, however, put an abrupt end to the uprising.

Under the Empress: A more settled era dawned in 1744, when Charles of Lorraine arrived in Brussels as governor on behalf of Empress Maria Theresa and quickly set fanned the smouldering resistance to Austrian rule. Although Joseph's attempts to curb the influence of the Church of Rome left most citizens apart from the Catholic clergy indifferent, he aroused unpopularity at every level with his range of administrative and judicial reforms. In particular, his plans for a centrally-run German-speaking empire met with universal opposition. Encouraged by the revolutionary turn of events in France, the citizens of Brabant successfully revolted in 1789. They evicted the Austrians, and a United Belgium was proclaimed.

In 1792 the Austrians succeeded once more in winning back power, but just two

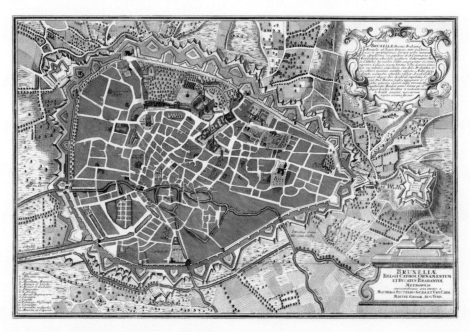

about improving the city. The Place Royale and the Forêt de Soignes – the capital's green lung – both date from this period. The dignified style adopted under Charles's aegis is typified by the exquisite Place du Musée close to the Place Royale.

However, the hasty reforms of Maria Theresa's son, the Emperor Joseph II, who became sole regent of the Spanish possessions in 1780 following his mother's death,

Left, the city is dominated by the spire of the Town Hall. **Above**, a solid wall protected the citizens from the enemy outside.

years later they were forced to withdraw once and for all in the face of the French revolutionary army. Belgium now became French; and Brussels became the capital of the "Département de la Dyle".

The hopes cherished by its citizens – especially those from the poorer classes – in these new rulers were to be unfulfilled. A series of reforms was undertaken, but the misery of the masses scarcely improved; in fact, the Napoleonic Wars drained the city of its few remaining resources. As usual, only the wealthy benefited in any way from the new regime.

In 1803 Napoleon himself visited Brussels for a reunion with Josephine. During his stay he attempted to ingratiate himself with the populace; the fountains gushed wine, and craftsmen were inundated with contracts. Nonetheless, few tears were shed in Brussels when Napoleon's empire came to a bloody end in 1815 on the battlefield of Waterloo, 18 km (11 miles) from the gates of the city.

Unification at last: At the Congress of Vienna (1814–15) the major powers decided to link Belgium with the neighbouring republic to form the United Kingdom of the Netherlands under William I of Orange. After more than two centuries of separation, the dream

of a single country finally came true – albeit only for 15 years. It was attended by a new flare-up of the old conflict between the Walloons and the Flemings, at the root of which lay the boundary between German and French spheres of influence, which divided the land in two. Brussels and The Hague were nominated joint capitals, but the northern half of the country, economically the stronger, set the tone. The constitution received no majority vote in the South, but was put into force by virtue of a trick.

William introduced Dutch as the official language in both halves of the country. Much to the annoyance of the citizens, even in Brussels itself – for many years a French-speaking city – he ruled that Flemish was to be spoken in the schools and courts, and by all official bodies. Unrest was also provoked by the King's interference in the training of priests and the curriculum. Catholics and liberals alike felt themselves badly treated.

The slogan for the revolt against the loss of Belgium's autonomy first went up on the evening of 25 August 1830, during a performance of Auber's opera *Masianello* (*La Muette de Portici*) in the city opera house, the Théâtre de la Monnaie. The audience became increasingly restless during the aria *Sacred love of our Fatherland.* "Far better to die than to live a wretched life in slavery and shame! Away with the yoke before which we tremble; away with the foreigner who laughs at our torment!" These words perfectly expressed the feelings of the majority of the citizens of Brussels under Dutch rule.

The finale of Act III heightened tensions in the theatre: "Bring your weapons! Bring your torches! Courage! We shall fight now for the victory of our cause!" And during Act IV, as the cry went up, "No, no more tyranny! No more slavery! Power henceforth to the citizens!", the audience rose from their seats and stormed onto the streets, where a workers' demonstration was taking place. Together, the insurgents stormed the Palais de Justice. The revolution was triggered.

The troops of the Netherlands army were successfully beaten back. On 25 September 1830 a provisional government was established; it declared the independence of Belgium on 4 October. Brussels became the capital of the new kingdom; the throne was offered to Leopold of Saxe-Coburg (1790–1865), who at this time was living at the English court and who entered Brussels in triumph in July 1831. He married one of the daughters of Louis Philippe of France. Leopold ruled the country strictly according to the constitution, and managed to safeguard and strengthen Belgium's neutrality.

Left, the 1830 uprising brought Belgium liberation and independence. Right, Charles V abdicated the throne in 1555 in favour of his son Philip (a 16th-century etching by Hogenberg).

EMPEROR CHARLES V

Charles V, Holy Roman Emperor and King of Spain lived in the saddle of a fast horse or on the creaking deck of a sailing ship. His territories and responsibilities were vast. Despite his sickly constitution, the last emperor of the Middle Ages made nine journeys to Germany, seven to Italy, six to Spain, four to France, two to England and two to Africa.

Flanders and Brabant were the nearest thing to home that Charles ever knew. He was born on 20 February 1500 in Ghent, the son of Philip the Handsome, King of Castile, and Joanna the Mad. His childhood was spent in Mechelen, but it was in

Emperor's crown. In 1522 Charles returned to strengthen his hold on Spain, which was torn apart by rebellion.

He had no chance to settle down. The Spanish and Habsburg empire he had inherited extended across Europe from Spain and the Netherlands to Austria and the Kingdom of Naples, stretching across the Atlantic Ocean to Spanish America. Time and again he was forced to take up arms – to put down his archrival, François I of France or to quash the infidels (Turks and Protestants) within and without his realm.

In the final analysis, he failed on both these counts. By the end of his life he had managed to prevent neither the schism within the Christian church nor the fragmentation of his empire. Charles's fortunes waxed and waned as King

Brussels that he was declared of age, being nominated Duke of Brabant and King of Spain (as Charles I) in 1516. He returned again and again to his native land; and at heart he remained a Netherlander all his life. He shared with his compatriots a love of good food, riotous feasting and fine art. As an old man he referred to the Netherlands in a letter to his son Philip as "Our Father Burgundy".

And yet, he never had the chance to settle there. His life of travelling began when he was only 17. After the death of his grandfather, Ferdinand of Aragon, he sailed to Spain in order to take up the reins of government there. But, three years later, in the summer of 1520, before he had a chance to win over the proud southerners to his cause, he had to hurry to Germany to receive the Holy Roman

Henry VIII of England and the popes transferred their allegiance between his cause and that of François I and back again.

In 1553, old, sick and disillusioned after a lifetime of almost continuous war, he returned to the Netherlands. It was here that he made his last public appearance in October 1555. In a moving speech given before the assembled estates of the 17 provinces in the Great Hall of his castle in Brussels, Charles V renounced the throne of the Netherlands in favour of his son Philip. At the beginning of 1556, he also relinquished the Spanish crown; and shortly after that he abdicated as Holy Roman Emperor in favour of his brother Ferdinand. Divested of power, he left the Netherlands for ever, retiring to San Geronimo de Yuste in Spain, where he died in 1558.

THE BATTLE OF WATERLOO

About 18 km (11 miles) south of the Belgian capital lies Waterloo, where Napoleon, following his period of exile on Elba, attempted to return to the political arena of Europe. It was here in June 1815, in an area of countryside just 2 km square, that 45,000 men died in agony or were seriously wounded and 15,000 horses were slaughtered.

From 2.30am on the night of 15 June 1815, the French army could be seen marching northwards in two columns – a total of 125,000 men and 25,000 horses. The next day, at noon, Napoleon, mounted on his dainty grey, rode through Charleroi. Leaving the town behind him, he rode on to a rise where the road forked left towards Brussels and right towards Fleurus. Here the Emperor came to a halt. Back on the road, the endlessly winding procession was veiled in dust; the tramping of thousands of soldiers mingled with the rhythmical beating of drums, the shrill blasts of bugles and the echoing cries of *"Vive l'Empereur!"*

Battle tactics: A short time later, Napoleon explained his war strategy to his field marshals and commanders. The English soldiers, under the command of the Duke of Wellington, had stationed themselves around Brussels; the Prussian troops, under Field Marshal Blücher, were approaching from the Rhine. It was essential to French success that these two armies should be prevented from joining forces.

It was not until 26 February 1815 that Napoleon had been able to leave his place of exile on the island of Elba. But he wasted no time in re-establishing his power. On 20 March he had entered Paris in triumph. Within just five days, an alliance had been formed by Austria, England, Prussia and Russia with the objective of waging war and defeating him once and for all.

On Friday 16 June 1815, Marshal Blücher set up his command post in the windmill at Brye. Only a few kilometres to the south as the crow flies Napoleon had installed himself in a windmill near Fleurus, from which point he could observe the troop movements of his opponent through a telescope. At 3pm he gave the signal to attack.

The Prussian army had lined up a force of 84,000 men and 216 cannon, and were dug in at Ligny; they hoped that Wellington's troops would reach them during the course of the afternoon. Napoleon had 67,500 men and 164 cannon.

Ligny was soon engulfed in a sea of flames under the carefully aimed gunfire of the French. The Prussians waited in vain for reinforcements from the English. By 10pm that night it was clear that the French would emerge from the bloodbath victorious and Prussia, having lost the battle but not the war, beat an ordered retreat. That same night they marched off in a northerly direction with the intention of joining the English forces in the final struggle against Napoleon. Almost 20,000 dead and wounded remained on the field of battle.

Napoleon failed the next day to reinforce the advantage he had gained at the battle of Ligny. Wellington and his troops, who had left Brussels the previous night, took up battle positions on the hill known as Mont St-Jean on the road between Brussels and Charleroi. Their plan was to ward off the French army until Blücher arrived. Wellington himself established his headquarters three kilometres to the north, in the old posting station of the village of Waterloo. During the afternoon of 17 June there was a sudden thunderstorm.

Napoleon reached the Belle Alliance inn, 9 km (5 miles) south of Waterloo on the Brussels road, shortly after 6pm. He watched Wellington's troops setting up camp across the valley on the Mont St-Jean, only 1.5 km (1 mile) away, then took up quarters himself in the dairy farm Le Caillou.

The rain looked as if it would never cease. The cavalry soldiers sat huddled in their saddles trying to snatch some sleep. The foot

Preceding pages: a modern re-enactment of the Battle of Waterloo. **Left**, a more contemporary view of the decisive battle.

soldiers searched in vain for dry patches in the trampled fields of corn. The camp fires had to be stoked continually with wood. They produced clouds of acrid smoke, but very little warmth. It had been a wasted day, a day for reflection.

The protagonists: The three leading players in the battle of Waterloo were no strangers to each other. For 20 years, Europe had acted as a stage for their posturings. Napoleon Bonaparte, a native of Corsica, was the most famous of the three. He had become consul, emperor, ruler of the continent and beneficiary of the Great Revolution of 1789. But Arthur Wellesley, since 1814 First Duke of Wellington, and Gebhard Leberecht Blücher, a Pomeranian landowner and field marshal, were both revered military men.

Wellington, a tall, slim Irishman, was a typical product of the British aristocracy. Cool, almost phlegmatic, he regarded soldiering merely as a job, not a matter for emotional involvement. He rarely wore a uniform; his tailor was considered one of the finest in England. He had been commissioned in 1787, and from 1796 to 1805 had served as a soldier and administrator in India. In 1808 the British government had sent him to Portugal to support the local citizens' guerrilla war against the Napoleonic forces of occupation. In defeating the French, he had allowed their forces to withdraw, a concession for which he was court-martialled but later exonerated. In 1812 he had marched into Madrid, driving Napoleon's forces back into France; two years later, he had reached Toulouse.

What drove Blücher on to the battlefield was hatred; his hatred of Napoleon and his destructive power. The longer Napoleon's rule lasted, and the more oppressive it became, the more Blücher's view was shared by his compatriots. With every battle which Napoleon won, and with every corner of Europe he seized, the more Prussia yearned for freedom and unity.

The Germans proved apt pupils when it came to learning the lessons of the French Revolution. The twin ideas of nationhood and democracy were born together. During the struggle against Napoleon, pan-German patriotism arose for the first time, spreading across the frontiers of the many individual German states.

There was a basic difference in the motives of the English and the Prussians. The English were determined to defy Napoleon, but their enmity remained basically dispassionate: they already lived with a confident national identity. However, Napoleon's territorial aspirations had destroyed Prussia, the one state on which German hopes of national unity were based, and the Prussians wanted their revenge. Shrill voices of protest were to be heard from the intellectual élite, whose violent resistance to Napoleon echoed the missionary-like fervour of the

French revolutionaries. When, in 1813, the French tyrant had been defeated near Leipzig by an alliance between Prussian and Russian forces, with the assistance of Sweden, the nationalist movement in Germany, which had steadily been gaining ground, had become full of hope.

But the diplomats at the Congress of Vienna in 1814 were divided as to the best way of resolving the most pressing problems in Europe. The majority remained determined to reinstate the feudal conditions of 1789 and to prevent the rise of a powerful Germany. The Congress of Vienna attempted to set out the framework for the restoration of order in post-revolutionary Europe, but for the Germans it signalled the beginning of a long period of frustration, of the failure of national democratic hopes. Blücher, by this time 73 years old, shouted to the soldiers as they set off westwards from Berlin in June 1815, "Now we soldiers can put right the diplomats' blunders!"

The campaign to defeat Napoleon represented a combined strategy by the Allied Coalition – the seventh formed against France between 1792 and 1815. A total of five armies was involved: an Anglo-Dutch force under Wellington and Blücher's Prus-

Ligny on 16 June, during which Blücher was wounded, the Prussians broke camp at Wavre at dawn on 18 June to continue their westward march. Blücher was in good spirits. He was confident that once they had joined forces with the English army, his soldiers would easily defeat Napoleon.

Napoleon and his troops also rose early that Sunday. The breakfast table was laid before 5am. But, as fate would have it, bad rain impaired visibility, and the attack – planned for 9am – was delayed. The gun crews could hardly move the cannon on the muddy ground even with teams of 15 men and 12 horses per gun. But, despite such

sian regiments were to meet near Brussels and converge on France; the Austrians under Karl Philipp zu Schwarzenberg were to operate along the Rhine, with the Russians led by Barclay de Tolly in reserve; and an Austro-Italian army commanded by Johann Maria Frimont were to block a retreat from northern Italy.

During that June of 1815, the English and Prussian forces spearheaded the attack. Refusing to be discouraged by the defeat at

Left, a smile from a girl dressed as a French sutler. **Above**, into battle with music and wine.

unpromising conditions, Napoleon was sure that victory would be his: "Gentlemen, if you carry out my orders well, we shall sleep tonight in Brussels," he said.

Napoleon's defeat: At 11.30am, from his command post south of the Belle Alliance inn, the emperor gave the signal to attack. The English troops were engulfed in the fire from 120 French cannon. Opposite, in his headquarters at Mont St-Jean, Wellington took shelter under an elm tree, from where he could direct his army.

In the valley between Mont St-Jean and the Belle Alliance lay the ancient manor of

Hougoumont to the west and the farmstead La Haie Sainte to the east, on the road to Brussels; both were occupied by English troops. It was evident that if the French wanted to storm the Mont St-Jean they would need to take both strongholds first.

The attack on Hougoumont started shortly after 11am. At 5pm the French gave up the attempt. Piled up in front of the perimeter wall was a gruesome heap of corpses – almost 3,000 French soldiers lost their lives in the assault. In the meantime, at 1pm, Napoleon had ordered his men to attack the centre of the valley, although he was already aware that the Prussians were approaching.

The French infantry charged down into the valley in columns of 4,800 men in 24 rows of 200 soldiers each. The English forces waited behind the embrasures of La Haie Sainte or behind the hills. A deadly rain of cannon fire engulfed the manor; to the amazement of the French, thousands of English soldiers suddenly rose up from the crest of the hill and fired their muskets.

The French, even more than their opponents, fought as if in a drunken frenzy. Some of their columns did actually manage to reach the top of the eminence, but the task of killing the enemy became progressively more difficult as the growing mountains of dead soldiers and horses hampered their advance. At 6.30pm the French Tricolour was hoisted above La Haie Sainte. Wellington's front at the heart of the Mont St-Jean wavered. He had no more reserves. Hopes for the arrival of Blücher or nightfall was the only comfort he could offer his generals when they demanded fresh supplies.

But Napoleon had only his Old Guard in reserve battalion when, at about 7.30pm, the first brigades of Prussians reached the battlefield. The emperor sent his personal guard charging down the hill of Belle Alliance. The well-aimed fire of the English marksmen hit them fatally at short range. By 8.30pm, Blücher and his entire army had arrived. Shortly afterwards there was no holding the French; they knew they faced defeat. The battle cry went up "Run for your life!" as the Prussians and British careered down the hillside after the fleeing soldiers.

Victory and repercussions: At 9.30pm, Wellington and Blücher embraced each other in the courtyard of the Belle Alliance inn. The Prussian band played "God Save the King" and "*Grosser Gott, wir loben Dich*". News of the French defeat reached Brussels at about 10 o'clock. Four days afterwards, Napoleon dictated his second document of abdication in Paris. In Wellington's words, the outcome of the battle had been "the nearest run thing you ever saw in your life".

It is Wellington who in most British minds was the key figure in the the victory at Waterloo; but in Germany Blücher became an equally popular hero and a symbol of German aspirations, which had been thwarted at the Congress of Vienna. For the Germans, despite their victory in the battle, 1815 represented the failure of their ambitions to achieve nationhood and democracy, a failure which would be repeated in the Revolution of 1848.

On 18 June 1990, the 175th anniversary of the battle was celebrated in colourful costumes on the battlefield of Waterloo. Visitors travelled from England, France and Germany to witness the occasion.

The English infantry (underline: left) lives to fight another day, to the displeasure of Napoleon (underline: right).

THE KINGDOM OF BELGIUM

After the battle of Waterloo in 1815, the country which would later be known as Belgium once more found its fate in the hands of foreign powers. The members of the "Holy Alliance" – Austria, England, Russia, Prussia, France and the papacy – linked Belgium with the Netherlands to form the "United Netherlands". The union took no account of the historical, political and economic differences between the two halves of this uneasy partnership.

Dissatisfaction with the arrangement quickly took root, with the Belgians seeing themselves as victims of discrimination. Catholics, liberals, supporters of the French connection and conservatives all united with the common aim of ridding their land of the rule of the Dutch House of Orange. When a number of petitions sent to the foreign rulers brought about no improvement, social and national tensions increased.

National independence: France became Belgium's role-model. In France itself, the July Revolution of 1830 aimed to revive the ideals of the 1789 French Revolution. For the Belgians this was to prove the signal to rise up against the House of Orange. In August 1830 the War of Independence began in Brussels, actively supported by the French government.

The 4 October of that year went down in the annals of Belgian history. On this day, Belgium officially declared itself to be an independent country. The provisional government demanded instant recognition of the new state by other European governments. A few months later on 26 July 1831, during the London Conference, the European Great Powers confirmed Belgium's independence and guaranteed its neutrality.

This acceptance of the new nation's autonomy marked the first step along the road towards true independence. As the next step, the newly-created parliamentary monarchy

needed a suitable king. In their search for an appropriate sovereign, the political leaders of the country agreed upon Leopold of Saxe-Coburg. By virtue of his blood ties with the English monarchy (he was the uncle of Queen Victoria), his education, diplomatic skills and interest in military matters, Leopold united all the qualities considered to be desirable prerequisites of a representative royal sovereign. In 1831, the national congress voted Leopold of Saxe-Coburg king of

the Belgians, and 21 July was proclaimed a day of national rejoicing.

In 1832, Leopold I married Louise, a daughter of King Louis Philippe of France – an act which strengthened the friendly links between the two countries.

Leopold I's principal successes lay in the improvement during his reign of relations between Belgium and the neighbouring Netherlands and the foundations that were laid for the industrialisation of the country. However, despite such measures, from 1840 an undercurrent of restlessness could be detected beneath the apparently calm surface

Left, the Belgian flag is aired for the national holiday. **Above**, the first king of the Belgians was a German: Leopold I of Saxe-Coburg-Gotha.

and workers began to rebel against their appalling living conditions. Leopold I was unable to live up to his task as mediator and unifier of the Flemings and the Walloons and against the background of the language dispute, initially regarded as a minor problem, violence repeatedly broke out. On his death, in 1865, Leopold bequeathed a range of social problems to the son who succeeded him, Leopold II.

Private colony: The new king harboured various ambitions, determined chiefly by his own personal interests rather than those of the nation as a whole. First of all, he attempted to boost the national economy by

Leopold II's coup in the Congo was sanctioned in 1885 by 14 nations at the Berlin Congo Conference, under the chairmanship of Bismarck. In return, Leopold agreed to allow unrestricted trade and freedom of navigation within the Congo basin. Belgium's economic upswing profited still further from this exploitation of the colony. Meanwhile, in England and Belgium, opposition to this private colony was growing, and in 1908 Leopold found himself obliged to subordinate his sovereignty over the Congo to the Belgian parliament.

Leopold, a man who had repeatedly managed to assert his personal will against the

bringing his influence to bear on Belgian financial policy, and subsequently, having achieved this, he set about realising his long-cherished dream of becoming a colonial power in Africa.

The king's intermediary in the African Congo was an Englishman, Sir Henry Morton Stanley. Through the offices of Stanley and by pursuing a policy of murder, deception and colonialism of the worst type imaginable Leopold II gained control of the entire Congo basin. This vast region, half the size of Western Europe, in effect became his private property.

liberal powers of parliament, died one year later. The next king, Albert I, was his nephew. In 1914 German troops marched into Belgium at the beginning of World War I and Albert declared war. Belgium was defeated later that same year; but at the Treaty of Versailles at the end of the war Belgium gained the German-speaking territories of Eupen and Malmedy.

Albert I died near Namur during a mountain walking trip in 1934. His son was crowned Leopold III at the height of the Great Depression. He had married Princess Astrid of Sweden in 1926 and the royal couple had three children: a daughter Josephine Charlotte (the current Archduchess of Luxembourg) and two sons, Baudouin and Albert, who made their political debuts after World War II.

The German invasion: In the face of the increasing threat from Germany, the king was able to have Belgium reinstated as a neutral country in 1936. Only a few months after the beginning of World War II, German troops again invaded Belgium. Leopold III capitulated in the name of his country on 10 May 1940. Although the government fled to London, the king remained at home. Until 1944 he was interned by the forces of occu-

1950, however, he abdicated in favour of his son, Baudouin, then aged 20. The new king was crowned on 17 July 1951.

One of Baudouin's most pressing official duties was to supervise the decolonisation of the Congo. Before that, however, there were private matters to attend to: in September 1960 he became engaged to a Spanish noblewoman and trained nurse, Dona Fabiola de Mora y Aragon.

Whilst the engagement celebrations were taking place in Brussels, in the Congo Belgian troops were firing on a population which – despite international protest – had been thrust into independence without any

pation in Laeken Castle; then, as the Allied army advanced, he was moved to Germany. He remained there whilst Belgium was liberated, his brother, Prince Charles, becoming temporary regent.

When Leopold III returned, rumours of his collaboration with the Germans persisted, but a referendum as to whether he should continue to reign voted in his favour. In

<u>Far left</u>, Leopold II was notorious for his exploits with the dancer Cleo. <u>Left</u>, Leopold II in a more official pose. <u>Above</u>, King Baudouin on parade in front of the Atomium.

preparation. The royal couple were married in December 1960.

Future hope: The marriage was childless, so when Baudouin died suddenly in 1993, his brother succeeded as King Albert II, with his Italian-born wife Paola as queen. The unity of this divided country depends on King Albert's performance of his duties, following the popular Baudouin. It seems certain that Baudouin's eldest nephew, Prince Philippe, will ascend the throne. He has been prepared for his role: he is an officer in the army, has studied political sciences and has had ample practice at dealing with the media.

THE BELGIAN CONGO

For many years Belgium kept out of the race to acquire colonies. Leopold I, who became the first King of Belgium in 1831, refused to be involved in an official state colonial policy. After his death in 1865, however, his son, Leopold II, made up for lost time.

Sir Henry Morton Stanley (1841–1904), the British explorer and journalist, provided the king with the expertise for such a venture. Stanley's first expedition to the River Congo concluded that the river's wide channel made it an ideal trading route. In 1878, Leopold II commissioned the explorer to undertake a second trip to the Congo. Following the instructions issued by the Belgian monarch, Stanley came to "agreements" with several of the native tribes .

The basis of these contracts was that the Africans would receive fabric and similar items in return for granting the white intruders the usufruct on their land. The wording was such that the terms could be interpreted as "purchase". In this way, by 1884 Leopold II had gained possession of almost the entire area. He named it the "Congo Free State".

The 19th-century colonial powers soon began to demand a formal agreement on the Congo State. The "Congo Conference" was held in Berlin between November 1884 and February 1885. Belgian authority over the Congo was recognised – with the proviso that henceforth in perpetuity there should be freedom of trade within the country.

At the instigation of Leopold II, the Berlin Conference also passed a resolution repudiating the slave trade. In reality, things were very different. Within Africa slavery was at its peak. Natives were unscrupulously sold as cheap labour and porters, or press-ganged as soldiers. Whippings and murder were daily occurrences. Between 1889 and 1890 the "Anti-Slavery Conference" was held in Brussels; once more, lip service was paid to the noble aims of colonialism.

Left, the British explorer Henry Morton Stanley "discovered" the Congo, and "bought" the Africans in the name of Leopold II.

From 1890 the Socialists and progressive Liberals stepped up their protests against the King's colonial policy. In the meantime, the Congolese themselves took up the fight for their own freedom. Between 1895 and 1897 riots were brutally quashed.

In 1908 the criticism openly voiced in Europe concerning the King's authoritarian system of exploitation forced the Belgian government to transfer the monarch's power over the new Belgian Congo to the state.

When Leopold II died in 1909 his nephew, Albert I, became king of Belgium and the Belgian Congo. Between 1912 and 1918, the determined resistance of the oppressed Congolese led to further unrest. Following the arrest of ringleader Simon Kimbanga, the leader of the African National Church and a Congo resident (he was imprisoned until his death in 1959) there was a general strike. The ruling powers replied with a machine-gun salvo from the "Force Publique" and the internment of freedom fighters in so-called "improvement camps".

After the war the Congo experienced an economic boom, and the outbreak of World War II overshadowed the problem of independence. After 1945 the unrest flared up anew. King Baudouin and the majority of Belgians were disinclined to relinquish the colony, whose minerals, rubber, palm oil and ivory had boosted national prosperity.

However, unrest could not be contained. The revolt which erupted after the First African Peoples' Conference in 1958 led to the Belgian government's precipitate agreement to independence on 30 June 1960. Inter-tribal conflict then broke out in the newly-independent state and the breakaway of the rich mining province of Katanga (now Shaba) led to fresh conflict. The superior attitude of the Belgians who had remained led to a desperate rebellion on the part of the Congolese. Once more, Belgian soldiers fired their guns at the native population. The unrest led to the first Congo Crisis. In 1971 the state, still tottering, assumed the name of the Republic of Zaire.

The history of Brussels after the Revolution reflects that of Belgium as a whole. Brussels is the seat not only of the King, but also of both government and parliament. The history of the country is determined from Brussels. Since Belgium became independent, Brussels has also served as the starting point for the country's rapid economic growth.

The years following Belgium's declaration of independence in 1831 were characterised by a gradual overthrow of the foreign domination it had so long endured. The industrial revolution began with the construction of the railway line between Brussels and Mechelen, the first on the continent.

The rail network became steadily denser as the exploitation of the coal mines in the South and the development of the iron and steel industry in the area around Liège raised Belgium to a position alongside the principal industrial nations. This process was supported by a flourishing textile industry centred upon Ghent and Kortrijk.

Furthermore, in 1863 Leopold II was able to buy back from the Netherlands the right to levy customs duties on the River Scheldt, a loss which had severely hampered the expansion of Antwerp. The arms industry was a further source of profit. The country's industrialists used their head start in heavy industry to gain a foothold in new export markets.

Prosperity at a price: Not everybody benefited from the boom; wages were low and working hours long. Female and child labour were commonplace. Social security, industrial safety standards and free Sundays were a long way off the political agenda.

Brussels achieved the dubious honour of having the highest infant mortality rate of all European capitals. The working classes lived in indescribable misery in damp, cramped apartments; their diet consisted

Left, Nippon in Laeken: a Japanese pagoda for the king (coloured postcard from around 1900).
Above, Brussels' lacemaking industry once employed thousands of women.

largely of cabbage, potatoes and bread. Their wretched existence could be summed up in one word: the Marolles. This was the district in the city centre where the poor and the oppressed had lived together for centuries. It was here, too, that the first workers' associations were formed.

As far as the outside world was concerned, Belgium and Brussels enjoyed a reputation for progressiveness. The country's freedom of speech and freedom of the press were

often upheld as examples of what might be achieved in other countries. Brussels became an asylum for persecuted socialists from all over Europe. Karl Marx sought refuge here in 1845. In 1848, when the Paris Revolution was on everyone's lips, he and Friedrich Engels published their joint *Communist Manifesto*. This, however, stretched the liberal attitude of the city fathers too far, and Marx was expelled from the country a few months later.

His ideas, however, did not go unheeded by the citizens of Brussels and at the turn of the century they led to bitter fighting which eventually led to the introduction of universal suffrage and the right to strike.

Colonial power: In the meantime, Belgium had taken its place amongst the world's colonial powers. In 1878, thanks to lack of public interest, King Leopold II had been able to purchase the Congo out of his own private fortune. His one-man enterprise proceeded to flourish. A regime of forced labour and reign by terror in the colony filled his coffers, profiting Belgium in general and the capital in particular.

The king made over part of his income from his colony to the state, and Brussels itself was treated to a facelift. Leopold had a

In August 1914, German troops invaded Belgium, despite the latter's neutrality. For almost four years pitiless trench warfare was fought between the Germans on one side and the English, French and Belgians on the other. Hundreds of thousands laid down their lives on the battlefield. By the end, Flanders was devastated and the town of Ypres had been razed to the ground. The city of Brussels was spared during the hostilities, but was the object of attempts at political occupation on the part of the Germans.

The city courageously continued its policy of passive resistance. At the head of the movement against the forces of occupation

number of magnificent avenues constructed and various fine buildings erected. The Palais des Colonies was built in the suburb of Tervuren.

The import of copper, uranium, diamonds, rubber, cotton and tin increased the general prosperity of the Belgian people. But it was at a heavy price. The merciless exploitation of the Congo, which brought death to hundreds of thousands of Africans – through exhaustion, hunger, violence or merely the whim of the mercenary troops – is one of the blackest episodes in Belgian history (*see chapter on the Belgian Congo, page 49*).

was the mayor, Adolphe Max. Refusing to reveal the names of unemployed workers destined for forced labour in Germany, he was arrested and deported.

King Albert I acquired a glorious reputation during World War I. He had become regent in 1909, and personally led the Belgian army as well as encouraging the country's citizens to resist the foreign invaders. In the autumn of 1918 the country lay in ruins, but at last the trench war was over. In November there was an armistice.

Immediately after the end of the war, the population was rewarded by a number of reforms. Belgium finally introduced universal male suffrage (though women were not given the vote until 1948) and the right to strike. The economy, badly damaged by the war, was slow to recover.

When the Allies failed to enforce the high reparations that the Treaty of Versailles had levied on Germany, hopes of compensation for the devastation wreaked by the war went unfulfilled. During the Great Depression, unemployment rose rapidly. Here, as in other cities across the continent of Europe, Fascists profited from the general unrest.

On 10 May 1940 German troops marched into Belgium once more. Their offensive

Collaboration and resistance: The Belgian Pierlot-Spaak government refused to capitulate and continued the fight from its London exile. Nonetheless, there was widespread collaboration with the occupying forces. Various right-wing groups openly declared their sympathies with Hitler's regime.

On the other side stood the communists, socialists and Christians, who actively fought against the Germans. Many unemployed Belgians joined the Underground because they were afraid of being transported to labour camps.

A Jewish resistance group was also formed. It succeeded in saving 20,000 Bel-

continued unabated until they reached Dunkirk. Unlike his father, who had stood at the head of the resistance movement against the German invaders during World War I, King Leopold III was a great disappointment to his people during war. Leopold's request for a ceasefire on 27 May 1940 served as a prelude to the country's rapid acceptance of German occupation.

Left, German field kitchen on the Grand' Place (World War I). **Above,** young members of the Resistance fought as a "secret army" against the Germans (1944).

gian Jews from Hitler's concentration camps by organising their flight abroad or by hiding them in the homes of non-Jews.

Following the landing of the Allied troops in Normandy, Belgium was liberated in September 1944. Collaborators were brought to trial throughout the land. A total of 57,000 were sentenced; 241 of them were executed. Following a number of bloody riots, Leopold III was forced by the Walloons and the citizens of Brussels to abdicate. He was succeeded on 31 July 1950 by his son, Baudouin. With this, Belgium entered a new era of prosperity.

WHAT HAPPENED TO BELGIAN JEWS?

There are few people who do not know the poignant story of Anne Frank (1929–45), the daughter of a Jewish businessman from Frankfurt, who along with her family fled to Amsterdam early in the Hitler regime. In 1942 she and her family went into hiding. With the help of Gentile friends, they managed to survive for over two years in a secret annex in a warehouse. Then, in 1944, they were betrayed to the Gestapo by Dutch informers and transported to concentration camps in Germany. Anne's father alone survived; her mother died in Auschwitz in 1944, and she and her sister in Bergen-Belsen in 1945.

Returning to Holland after the war, Anne's father found the diary she had kept during her years in hiding. *Diary of a Young Girl*, recording the events of her life during World War II, was published in 1947 and quickly became a classic of its kind. It serves as a memorial to the millions of Jews exterminated in the Nazi Holocaust.

In Belgium, a total of 2,700 Jewish children survived the persecution of the Nazi era. Their escape was thanks to the relentless efforts of a unique underground organisation that hid the children under false names in convents, boarding schools and private families.

But inevitably rescue came at a price to the children. The children had to live under the enormous strain of an assumed identity, a burden later replaced by feelings of guilt associated with being one of the "lucky" ones who escaped.

Now the generation of those who helped them is dwindling one by one. Many members of the underground rescue operation lost their lives at the time, or have died in the intervening years. Most of those who remain are now about 85 years old. Some of them have written accounts of the period of history through which they lived; none of them can free themselves from its shadow.

After the war and its aftermath, the generation of children they saved withdrew into a sort of emotional no man's land. Even today, so many years on, few of them are willing to talk about their years in hiding. This is an account of what happened in Belgium.

From 1 June 1942, Belgian Jews were required to wear the yellow Star of David. When they were called upon to volunteer for the labour camps in the early summer of 1942, many of them actually did so, believing this was their safest course of action. This led to thousands going unwittingly to their death. In the 100 days between August 4 1942 and 31 October 1942, more than 17,000 Belgian Jews were deported from the Flemish town of Mechelen alone. In the two-year period between October 1942 and September 1944 (Brussels was liberated by the Allies on 4 September) the Germans captured 8,000 Jews, less than half the number in that 100-day period in Mechelen. The reason for this was that, from October 1942, those remaining realised the outcome of surrendering. By then, they knew that their only hope of survival lay in flight or going underground and began to organise themselves accordingly.

Their principal aim was to save their children. Adults were in a position to arrange a life on the run, but the question of what they could do with their children was difficult. In this time of desperate need, an organisation of Jews and non-Jews – Belgian resistance fighters, social workers and idealists – joined forces to do whatever they could.

Organisation and co-ordination were vital to their success, but so was absolute secrecy. Maurice and Estera Heiber, a Jewish couple whose child also had to be hidden, set up an illegal coordination centre. Yvonne Rospa, a Jewish social worker and dedicated anti-racist, set out with a group of Belgian supporters to find accommodation and hideouts for the children who were at risk. Under the fictitious name of Madame Pascal, Estera Heiber could be found each morning in the flat of a Belgian opera singer. Here she could be consulted, could receive and pass on information, provide money for accommodation and distribute food ration cards.

The helpers were faced with a gargantuan task, not least how best to persuade loving parents that it was better for all concerned if they agreed to separate from their children. Parents had to accept the fact that they would receive no details of the name and address of the prospective foster parents. The separation of family members in such dangerous circumstances was heart-rending, but knowledge and information represented an additional risk of discovery.

Yvonne Jospa says that not all Belgians were prepared to help, but she refuses to judge those who failed to do so. Some were too afraid; others were unconcerned. She says that assistance came from isolated individuals from every social class. Those who agreed to take a Jewish child into their families were well aware of the risks involved and prepared to face them. The child had to remain as inconspicuous as possible, adopting the customs of the host family, attending the local state or confessional school with the other children in the

dren unscarred. Those children who survived refer only occasionally to their years spent in hiding. The parents on the other hand, especially those who were actively involved, find it easier to convey their experiences. They were able to join the resistance movement, whereas their children were helpless in the face of their fate.

Andrée Geulen, a former Belgian partisan married to a Jew, has six grandchildren. She lives in Brussels. She knows from the annual meetings with "her children", those she helped rescue, just how sensitive these Jews are today. Now in their fifties or sixties, they have made their homes all over the world.

"It is amazing," she says, "to discover that only now, more than 45 years later, are some of my

family and going to church. They had to pray and eat exactly as the family did.

False passports were issued with the help of Belgian officials. Names were changed to disguise Jewish origins – Apfelbaum, for example, became Appelmans – so that a ration card could be claimed. Without one, survival in wartime Belgium was impossible.

The tragedy of being separated from their parents, of having to live with the permanent anxiety of an assumed identity and with the ever-present fear of being discovered, did not leave these chil-

Left, Jewish children murdered by the Nazis in World War II. <u>Above</u>, many Jewish girls were hidden by Catholic schools, thereby escaping the Holocaust.

protégés willing to permit others to see just how deep these unhealed wounds go. Only now have they begun to speak hesitatingly about their repressed, deep-seated fears. How can we possibly comprehend the feelings of a six-year-old girl snatched away from the bosom of her family and burdened with the inhuman knowledge that she must never reveal that her real name is Rachel, must never betray the fact that she is Jewish, for to do so would mean death?

"I knew personally the little girl called Rachel. Throughout the war she was known as Monique. Today she is almost 50 and admits she never answered when called by her assumed name. People tended to think she was retarded, but – as she recently told me in tears – 'I just didn't really know who I was'."

BRUSSELS AFTER WORLD WAR II

The best clue to understanding present-day life in the Brussels metropolitan area can be found by examining the pattern of its development over the years, and the economic and political changes which have shaped how and where people live.

The city centre roughly corresponds to the working-class districts of the 19th century, which until the 1980s were still inhabited largely by the poor and by immigrant guest workers. The social housing programmes of the inter-war years determined the rest of the town's social structure. The garden cities built during the 1920s for the burgeoning middle classes, for example, lie in a green belt around the centre.

The centre and the surrounding districts dating from the 19th century comprise about 75 percent older houses, many of which are in a dilapidated condition and usually divided into privately owned flats. Around this core lies a zone containing somewhat better flats; and in an outer circle lie the luxurious villa districts.

This situation prevailed from the end of World War II until the 1960s and '70s, when the exodus from the city centre gathered speed. The nouveaux riches began to desert the city centre and settle on the periphery of town. This coincided with a wave of new building work, as illustrated by the many concrete tower blocks in the area between the Gare Centrale and the Lower City.

As has happened elsewhere in European cities, this exodus was reversed during the 1980s. Many people, particularly the young, began to seek accommodation in the heart of the city. Reduced purchasing power, increasing unemployment and rising interest rates all contributed to this development, but so did a desire to escape the monotony of characterless suburbia. It seems as if the second generation of suburban dwellers (who are now in early middle age) are anx-

Left, the beauty of the facades around the Grand' Place is enhanced still further by these brightly-coloured standards.

ious to live in the heart of the city again, breathing new life into old buildings and adapting it to suit their own lifestyles.

Until recently, most people in Brussels tended to live in rented flats, and stay in the same place for much of their adult lives, since few were able to raise the capital required for house purchase. However, this has changed as loans have been more widely available and the property market has become more mobile. The presence of a large and affluent expatriate community has undoubtedly increased both rents and house prices, but they are still low compared to London or Paris.

of fine townhouses have been, and continue to be, demolished and replaced by office blocks to house the EU or the organisations which court it. The current vogue for *façadisme*, where the entire structure of an old building is destroyed except the frontage, only pays lip service to the ideal of preserving the city's architectural heritage.

Despite efforts by pressure groups and conservationists whose aim is to preserve the many historic buildings in, for example, the Marolles district for indigent future generations, the process of gentrification somehow seems inevitable. Developers are able to purchase an entire street and transform it into

Changing places: Powerful vested interests have had a major impact on the city's landscape. Certain elements of the urban communities are keen to attract capital-intensive industries and new residents with high purchasing power. Unfortunately the victims of such projects are usually the city's long-standing residents who have to move out to make way for the new money. They cannot afford to buy or even rent an apartment in their old neighbourhood, but are excluded on income grounds from government housing.

This phenomenon is particularly visible in the European quarter, where whole swathes

private luxury flats and elegant offices. As a consequence property prices rise sharply. The Art Nouveau houses of the area are particularly coveted but are well beyond the reach of the ordinary *Bruxellois*.

This trend is quite clearly luxury-oriented; the inner city's new residents are mostly high earners. Grandiose hotels have mushroomed on all sides, and a range of expensive sports facilities and cultural events has evolved along with them.

Capital of Europe: On a more positive note, as the capital of Belgium has moved towards realising its ambitions as the capital of Europe, many improvements have taken place. Brussels is a popular target for investment, and new jobs are being created all the time, notably in the sector which services the European institutions. Environment-friendly industries, development and research institutes are also part of this trend. The city's international transport infrastructure has been greatly enhanced with the expansion of the airport and the completion of the motorway from Calais.

The Brussels Regional Development Agency created four scientific industrial centres to support high-tech enterprise. Each of them is partially administered by one of the

accessible by motorway and underground. Brussels also lies on a canal which links it to Antwerp harbour, one of the largest ports in Europe. The high-speed TGV railway lines link Paris with Amsterdam and London with Cologne. This improved network has brought Brussels within just a few hours' travel of the major cities on the continent.

There are still numerous opportunities for expansion within the service industry sector. Large firms are tending to leave this sphere (office-cleaning, courier services, sales, marketing and legal and management consultancy) to medium-sized concerns. The unemployment rate in Belgium was among

four universities; three are situated in the vicinity of the principal university hospitals. The fourth zone is located in Belgium's so-called "Silicon Valley", near the European Headquarters of NATO on the road leading to the international airport at Zaventem.

The decision to move the centres of academic learning to the city outskirts, near the industrial areas, demonstrates a carefully planned overall strategy: they are all easily

Left, where is the king? A solitary guard protects the palace. **Above**, a summer stroll through the shady Mont des Arts.

Europe's highest for most of the 1990s, and although the mass of unqualified young people and foreigners seeking work provides an inexhaustible reservoir of labour for this sector, there remains the underlying problem of an under-qualified workforce.

Brussels is, however, first and foremost a political switchboard. It is not only the capital of Belgium, but also – since the constitutional reforms and the federalisation of the state – the capital of the Flemish half of the country, of the French community and of the Brussels region. Large numbers of private firms have settled in the vicinity of the administrative capital in order to lobby in the corridors of political power.

Should the European Parliament one day settle exclusively in Brussels, it will be able to make full use of the new Parliament building, a vast and palatial extravagance which can accommodate around 1,000 representatives. The building is currently used for only two parliamentary sessions per year.

The demand for office accommodation seems almost limitless, and likely to be a perennial problem if the EU carries out its plans to expand from the current 15 member states to 21 in 2002 and possibly to 26 in the following years.

The city's business district extends from the North Station (Manhattan Centre, CNN), the Rue de la Loi (Parliament, the ministries) across the Quartier Léopold (site of the new European Parliament) and the Avenue Cortenberg to the E5 motorway (Silicon Valley, NATO), the Boulevard du Souverain and the Boulevard de Woluwé.

Ethnic Diversity: No history of recent developments in Brussels would be complete without some reference to the problems of the city's Maghrebis, Turks and Africans. Although it would be an exaggeration to speak of ghetto-like developments, some quarters certainly contain strong concentrations of

Formerly, most businesses were located on the upper side of the North-South axis. Today, the centre of gravity has shifted more from the Place Rogier to the Place de Brouckère and beyond, in the direction of the Stock Exchange. Increasing numbers of business people are attracted to the Canal district, where shops, leisure centres and comfortable, upmarket flats are being built. The commune of Molenbeek, Brussels' old industrial quarter, is experiencing something of a cultural renaissance, stimulated by a new-found appreciation among *Bruxellois* of their city's past.

these ethnic minorities. Their socio-economic status (they tend to belong to the weakest social groups and thus provide the main pool of unskilled labour in the city) forces them to the fringe of society,

The unemployment rate among these ethnic minorities is high, and risks creating an under-class of disaffected young people. Lack of skills, compounded by racial discrimination, makes them virtually unemployable.

The most recent influx of economic immigrants are the Polish, who lead a precarious life working "on the black" as builders, decorators and cleaning ladies, sending most of their money back home to support their families or buy their own houses.

In contrast, other minorities – for example, the British, American, Scandinavians and Japanese – enjoy a higher social status and hence have experienced no problems with integration.

Brussels is an international metropolis in which the various ethnic groups form their own cultural associations; freedom of worship for all is guaranteed by law. The many foreign restaurants and shops resulting from the rich cultural mix form an integral part of the city's character; the *Matongué* from Zaire at the Porte de Namur, the Chinese restau-

Monnaie – to the almost 100 museums, many of them beautifully restored, and avant-garde theatre. Regular events are staged in the Palais des Beaux-Arts, the Botanique, the Halles de Schaerbeek and the Ancienne Belgique. Festivals of drama, music and film are frequently staged.

Old rivalries: Finally, mention should be made of the tiresome language rivalry between Flemish and French speakers in the capital – the fires of which are frequently fanned by politicians and students. Almost every crisis in Belgium seems to polarise the two communities. For example, the dioxin scandal in 1999, when the government was

rants behind the Stock Exchange, the Turkish establishments in the Chaussée de Haecht, the Maghrebi places in Saint-Gilles, and the Vietnamese eateries near the University in Ixelles. There are French, Greek and Italian restaurants on virtually every corner.

Culture plus: The wide variety of cultural and artistic opportunities available in Brussels is worthy of any capital city and ranges from the Opera – the Théâtre Royal de la

<u>Left</u>, Belgium's motorways are said to be so well-lit that they can be seen by astronauts. <u>Above</u>, enjoying ice-cream on the Grand' Place.

perceived to have concealed a public health risk in order to protect the interests of the largely Flemish farmers, provided an opportunity for the usual mutual recriminations.

In spite of its bilingual status, Brussels is 85 percent Francophone. Since the creation of the Region of Brussels, which has its own government, the Flemish minority has been most assertive in maintaining its identity in the face of French domination. Individuality is the cornerstone of the Belgian personality: the Flemings won't yield to the French-speaking majority without a fight – as violent demonstrations in the past have shown.

WHAT DOES THE KING DO?

King Albert II, Belgium's reigning monarch, ascended the throne in 1993 following the sudden death of his brother Baudouin, who had ruled for more than 40 years as a much-loved sovereign – indeed, who was seen by many Belgians as the glue which held this factious nation together. With Queen Fabiola at his side, Baudouin had been an uncontroversial figure – with the exception of one episode where he briefly "abdicated" to avoid having to sign an Abortion Bill. Throughout his reign he fulfilled his duties diligently and took his role as the representative of his country very seriously.

Baudouin's was a hard act to follow, but King Albert and his Italian-born wife, Queen Paola, have made a good start, following very much the principles Baudouin had espoused. He assumed the monarchy at a critical time for Belgium, when it seemed to many that the progressive federalisation of the state had come perilously close to its breaking up into its component parts: Flanders, Wallonia and Brussels, as well as the small German-speaking community in eastern Belgium.

The royal couple's official residence is the Palace of Laeken, situated in the northern outskirts of Brussels. A black, red and gold striped flag fluttering from the palace roof indicates that they are at home. The official office and audience rooms are in the Palais Royal in the centre of Brussels. It is here that Albert conducts most of his state work, receiving overseas ambassadors accredited to his court, as well as representatives of the various European Union organisations and foreign firms.

The rights and duties of the king of Belgium were laid down by the country's constitution of 1831. A number of modifications have been made to the clauses of that first constitution, but those referring to the sovereign have remained unchanged.

Left, King Albert, who, with his wife Queen Paola, succeeded his long-serving brother, King Baudouin, in 1993.

According to Article 65, the king is responsible for nominating and dismissing his prime ministers. In practice, of course, the choice lies in the hands of the political parties and the king has no real power of his own. However, every day King Albert signs a large number of documents and makes full use of his right to be informed concerning all matters of state. He frequently summons government ministers, representatives of parties, trades unions and other important organisations to his presence, sometimes successively in the course of a single day.

Article 63 of the constitution states that the king's person is sacrosanct. Article 64 rules that all documents signed by the king also require the signature of a minister to make them valid (the minister bears sole responsibility for the content). In addition to attending to paperwork, King Albert represents the state on all occasions, including on an international basis. He frequently sends an envoy to the various celebrations amongst the aristocracy of Europe.

King Albert, who enjoyed something of a playboy reputation in his youth, an image enhanced by his marriage to a glamorous Italian, has taken up his duties in sober fashion, performing the endless round of constitutional and ceremonial offices with ability and grace. He knows he is in the spotlight, facing the difficult question: can he do as well as his brother? And, in the longer run, can he and his son, Prince Philippe, who will succeed him, carve out a distinctive style and mission of their own?

If you wish to see the King Albert in the flesh, your best chance is to visit the city towards the last week in July. On 21 July, the national holiday, he traditionally takes part in a huge military parade held in honour of the nomination of Prince Leopold as the first king of Belgium in 1831. He and the queen often receive guests in their private palace at Laeken, greeting them in the royal glasshouses. Once a year they invite the general public to view the greenhouses (*see the chapter on The Glass City, page 197*).

Brussels is one of the most cosmopolitan cities in Europe. Its reputation in this respect is based primarily on the presence of the various EU organisations.

Over the centuries, the city and its inhabitants were ruled by a succession of foreign powers. Forces from all over the continent succeeded in occupying the city; Burgundy gave way to Spain, and France to the Netherlands, until in 1830 the Walloons and Flemings launched a revolution for independence. By and large, the Belgians are not particularly patriotic; they are more concerned with individual liberty and proud of their country's reputation for freedom of speech and freedom of the individual.

The attitude of the statue of Manneken Pis, known to the genuine Brussels citizen as Menneke Pis, embodies something of the citizens' independent spirit and tendency to complain. The determination of the various ethnic groups to fight for respect for their different cultures is demonstrated not least in the frequently mentioned language rivalry.

It is in Brussels – which lies only a few kilometres north of the French linguistic boundary – that the clash between the contrasting cultures of the Walloons and Flemings is most clearly evident. One result is that all signs and street names, as well as all city districts, are labelled in both Flemish and French, although Belgium actually has a third official language – German.

It may be that the centuries of foreign rule account for the low level of xenophobia. Brussels today has a population of approximately 1 million; every fourth person is not a native Belgian. Even the city's geographical position is interesting, for it lies at the heart of Western Europe. If you were to draw two diagonal lines across the continent, from Scotland to Greece and from Spain to Denmark, you would discover that Brussels lies where the two axes cross.

Left, subjects enjoy a late-afternoon beer in the sun opposite the King's House. **Above**, a face in the city crowd.

The prime reason behind Brussels' internationalism is undoubtedly the presence of NATO and the European Union with its three principal institutions: the European Commission, the Council of Ministers and the European Parliament.

Cradle of a common market: In March 1957 the three associations – the European Coal and Steel Community, Euratom and the European Community – joined together to form the European Economic Community (now

the European Union). Brussels was the obvious choice as headquarters, since in 1956 the negotiations which formed the basis of the founding treaties of the European Economic Community and the European Atomic Authority had taken place in the city. Apart from the city's central location and good transport links with the rest of Europe, the other advantages included its wealth of office space required for the vast numbers of officials.

At the time, Brussels was preparing for the 1958 World Exhibition. Taking advantage of the opportunity, Brussels was able to make a successful bid to be the site of the European Community administration.

Initially the offices of the departments stationed in Brussels were scattered across several districts of town. From 1967 the main Commission building was the Palais Berlaymont at the eastern end of the Rue de la Loi, which stretches from the city centre to the Parc du Cinquantenaire. However, in the mid-1990s the building was closed for renovation to remove asbestos from the structure.

In 1967 the Community consisted of only six members. Its gradual expansion to 15 member countries, and the subsequent influx of their representatives, has increased the transferred to Brussels. The city thus became home to thousands of foreigners employed in the service of the European Community and NATO alone.

Brussels is the residence of some 165 ambassadors, and a country may be represented by no fewer than three missions. Ambassadors from some 120 countries are accredited to the royal court and most countries have diplomatic representation at the EU and NATO as well. Politicians and business people from every corner of the earth congregate in Brussels to present their interests to the European organisations. There are several hundred branches of worldwide trad-

cosmopolitan nature of the host city. Nations in both western and eastern Europe continue to apply for membership, which looks set to expand to include six more countries in the next accession due in 2002.

North Atlantic manoeuvres: In 1966, the French president Charles de Gaulle forced France's withdrawal from the North Atlantic Treaty Organization and expelled all NATO commands from the country. Consequently NATO moved its military headquarters to Belgium, to the vicinity of Mons; the administrative arm (the NATO Council, the Military Committee and the international staff) was ing organisations, European centres and an endless list of international company offices. The city is truly international on the hotel and restaurant scene, too, so every visitor is bound to feel at home.

Many European officials are conspicuous by the EUR numberplates on their cars. The diplomats and international officials receive privileges as well as expatriate allowances and tax advantages. This has an influence on the city's high prices and rents. Because of its bureaucracy, Brussels is ranked amongst the world's 10 most expensive cities. That said, and in spite of the flood of arrivals from all over the world, the city is one of the few in Europe where flats are still widely available at reasonable rents.

Virtually all nations can claim a community of some sort in Brussels. They each consist of an infrastructure of churches and schools. There are 21 international schools, including the European Schools for children of EU officials, and the schools for the German, French, Netherlands, Japanese, British and American communities – especially for the children of those families whose stay in Brussels is only temporary.

Guest workers form the biggest single body of foreign workers. In the past, they

In addition, Brussels has recently received a steady migration from the surrounding countryside, in particular following the closure of the coal mines and general decline in heavy industry in Wallonia. This flight from the land has resulted in a steady increase in urban unemployment.

On the other hand, the direct result of the city's rapid expansion was a corresponding flight from the city to the outskirts and the surrounding villages by old-established families. The outlying districts are much favoured by the members of the international working community. Since the 1960s, well over 100,000 people have moved out of

were generally Spaniards, many of whom worked in the coal mines; now, with rising living standards in Spain, they are more usually Maghrebians, Turks and Poles. African students, businessmen and dissidents from the states of Rwanda and Burundi (which were previously mandated territories under the control of the Belgian League of Nations) and Congo also form a significant racial minority in the city.

Left, a difficult choice: shopping at the Sunday "Exotic" Market at the South Station. **Above**, the city attracts visitors from all over the world.

the city. These population movements have completely altered the city's character.

Nostalgic note: Many of the city's old guard regret the passing of the lifestyle they enjoyed prior to 1958 and Brussels' transformation. The rapid development of the capital has destroyed much of the city's provincial nature. By and large, the citizens of Brussels accept the newcomers with characteristic nonchalance. However, coupled with high unemployment, this influx of wealthy expatriates and poor ethnic immigrants has no doubt caused resentment among certain sections of the city's indigenous population.

The citizens of Belgium speak either Walloon (French) or Flemish, a Netherlands dialect. However, as anyone trying to research the matter will quickly discover, the most recent figures on the percentage of the population belonging to each linguistic group are those dating from the Language Census of 1947.

Since then, the Flemish, finding themselves to be increasingly losing ground to the French speakers, have sought to prevent any formal tally lest it should highlight their demise. Even traditionally Flemish areas – for example, the city's scientific zone – have seen an influx of French-speaking residents and workers. Even casual observers may sense the deep feelings underlying the use of the two languages.

The Belgians do not make life any easier for the student of language who wishes to write down both the cultivated and colloquial forms of the language, not to mention standard and dialect forms. The very term "Flemish" is lacking in precision as a description of a language spoken for the past 1,000 years north of a linguistic boundary roughly running from Aachen to north of Lille. Flemish is actually a mixture of Flemish dialects and standard Dutch. Walloon, on the other hand is none other than French with a number of Walloon idiosyncrasies.

Flemish has never really developed an independent written language of its own. Instead, it uses standard Dutch, enriched by a number of Belgian characteristics. This form is also the spoken language used by the media, the Church and in schools, although both teachers and pupils revert to the dialect form after hours.

The long-standing quarrel between the two linguistic groups arose because of the chronological shift in the settlement of the territory of the *Belgae*. German peasants came from the North, whilst settlers from the Romance countries bordering the Moselle

and the Mediterranean made their homes primarily in the remote regions of the Ardennes, which remained undeveloped for many years.

No formal boundary was ever drawn between the two groups; their different lifestyles were adjuncts to their specifically Belgian political culture and mentality. Maybe they even needed to develop an eccentricity of this nature in order to assert their own individual character between the

powerful civilisations of the French on the one side and the Dutch on the other.

The relationship between the two languages was always a painful one; even today, it is tinged by an element of distrust. The Flemish are afraid of being swallowed up by French in its capacity as a world language; the Walloons look disparagingly upon Flemish – a language which sounds barbaric to their ears, and which has virtually no international application.

The linguistic battle has long been accompanied by mutual feelings of envy, particularly economically; nowadays, for example,

Left, a drum roll for the Walloons. **Above**, a Flemish farmer's wife confronts the police.

in view of the demise of the coal and steel industry, the Walloons in the South consider themselves at a disadvantage compared to the Flemish North, where Antwerp is the centre of a petrochemical boom. Maybe it is a particular strength of the Belgians to be able to survive despite this imbalance – an ability acquired during many centuries of foreign rule.

Historical evidence: The reasons why linguistic identity should play such an important role in Belgium can be traced to the historical development of the country. When the country was first formed within the boundaries of the present-day Benelux starkly with the more rural, overwhelmingly Catholic South. Not all Flemings became citizens of the hard-fought "Republic of the United Netherlands". The frontier remained some 50 km (31 miles) north of Antwerp; south of this border, what would later become Belgium started to develop.

Belgium was still far from independent, however, as it formed part of the Habsburg empire. The language which enjoyed the higher prestige – especially during the Age of Enlightenment – was still French. When, in 1794, post-revolutionary French troops began to conquer Belgium for France and a rigid centralised government as well as a

States under the Dukes of Burgundy, French – the language of the court – became the symbol of power and social success. However, at the same time, the flourishing cloth trade with England enabled the Flemish provinces of Flanders and Brabant to gain high economic status.

When, during the 16th century, the Netherlands (including present-day Belgium) revolted against the Spanish Habsburgs, a clear north-south division within the Dutch-speaking area was already evident. The predominantly urban North, devoutly Calvinist in the wake of the Reformation, contrasted compulsory "Religion of Reason" took over, the most impassioned resistance fighters were the peasants from Flanders. The Flemish legacy stood them in good stead against France on the battlefield.

At the Congress of Vienna in 1815 Belgium was annexed as part of the newly-created Kingdom of the Netherlands under William I, who introduced Dutch as the official written language. It transpired, however, that the Flemings had developed their own identity at last. Even they found the language forced upon them boorish – *boerentaal* – and regarded their new masters as heretics. The border established 50 km before Antwerp divided a population which had diverged linguistically and culturally. Catholic Flemings and French-speaking Liberals united in revolt against the rulers of the United Netherlands. In October 1830 a temporary government proclaimed the newly-formed state of Belgium. From this point onwards controlling the linguistic power struggle in the country became a delicate balancing act.

The Belgian Constitution of 1831, created in the prevailing spirit of liberalism, calls for a strict principle of neutrality regarding the linguistic education of the nation's children.

the language used by the man in the street. This was the situation when *The Lion of Flanders*, a novel by Hendrik Conscience (1812–83), was published in 1838. The book, still counted amongst the works of world literature, fired the imagination of the Flemings. From then on the Flemings began to demand the *taalvrijheid*, the right not to be forced to use French in their dealings with official bodies.

The urgency of these demands was underlined in a gruesome manner during the trial of two Flemings living in Wallonia. The men, Coecke and Goethals, were falsely convicted of murder in 1865 because they

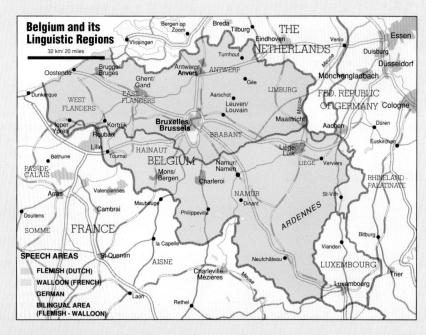

Belgium and its Linguistic Regions
32 km/ 20 miles

SPEECH AREAS
FLEMISH (DUTCH)
WALLOON (FRENCH)
GERMAN
BILINGUAL AREA
(FLEMISH - WALLOON)

School attendance was not made compulsory. This clause tended to work to the disadvantage of the Flemings. Their children were mostly instructed in the less well-equipped confessional schools while the more prosperous private schools introduced French as the teaching language.

French also became the language used in public administration, and continued to be regarded as the language of the refined classes. Flemish had the reputation of being

<u>Left</u>, clash of symbols: "Put that flag away, or I'll come and tear it down!"

were unable to follow the proceedings in French and were hence not in a position to defend themselves. In 1898 both languages were declared of equal official status. No boundaries were laid down to define the areas in which each should be considered predominant.

The divide widens: The language dispute has become even more acute during the 20th century. On two occasions, German troops invaded Belgian territory despite its declared neutrality. The ensuing occupations exacerbated the internal conflict between Flemings and Walloons. The majority of

Belgians remained anti-German, but one Flemish group, the "Activists", campaigned for an independent state as a German protectorate; during World War I, the group collaborated with the forces of occupation.

In 1917, two separate linguistic regions were determined within Belgium. Each had its own ministries in Brussels and Namur. Only a mass demonstration in Brussels on 11 February 1918 prevented total separation. After World War I, Flemish culture was widely despised as anti-Belgian. In external politics, Belgium moved closer to France.

During the 1920s the language dispute continued primarily within the walls of uni-

versities. The argument became particularly heated in Ghent. The justifiable demands for the creation of a separate Flemish institute of higher education, which were agreed to during World War I, were shelved after the war. There was frequent unrest among the Flemish speakers.

During the 1930s, the nationalist spectrum became polarised in accordance with the spirit of the times. Laws governing the use of language in administrative circles, and the insistence on the use of the local language as the official language in courts and classrooms, made Belgium a state with two linguistically homogeneous regions with equal rights. A strongly centralist principle continued to dominate; most leading officials in Brussels were either Walloons or non Flemish-speaking citizens. The validity of the French speakers' claims of "cultural superiority" was too obvious to be ignored.

World War II completely destroyed the status quo once more. This time there were collaborators not only amongst the Flemings (in fact, this time most Flemish associations resisted the German temptation). Walloon monarchists under the leadership of Leon Degrelle dreamed of Belgium belonging to a fascist corporate state. When the war was over, each language group ostracised the other in attempts to find a more appealing concept than peaceful coexistence.

Violent protest: Since July 1966 the governing principle has been one of strict monolinguality in predetermined regions (Brussels, which is bilingual, and a small number of linguistic enclaves enjoy special status). The Flemings were forthright in asserting their claims. They insisted, for example, that in the Flemish seaside resorts with an international clientele, French notices should appear beside those which are also translated into other foreign languages – as an indication that French, too, was "foreign". And they were not afraid to use violence: their repeated interruption of French church services and funerals during the 1960s resulted in a series of television films of furious, irreverent Flemings that shocked the world and shook the popularly perceived image of Belgian gentility.

Less controversial are the surprising statistics, which indicate that many schools in the Flemish-speaking regions offer French teaching of such a high standard that parents whose homes lie south of the language border send their children to them.

It is fair to say that the Flemings tend to speak better French than the Walloons speak Flemish, although the latter language has equal status. It is also clear that English is making rapid progress as a language of wider communication.

Left, signs everywhere are in two languages, which helps people find their way around (<u>right</u>).

To list all the important men and women associated with Brussels would fill an entire volume of *Who's Who:* the city is full of memorials to dukes, emperors and governors. The following account does not therefore pretend to mention all the politicians, soldiers, saints and artists that have lived in, died in or visited Brussels but it includes those that are remembered most affectionately by citizens.

A passing reference seems adequate in the case of Julius Caesar and all the other conquerors from the Dark Ages, for the history of Brussels proper begins in about AD 580 with St Gaugerich, also known as St Géry or St Goorik depending on which language you are using, who founded the city.

Other holy men and women associated with the city include St Michael and St Gudula (*see page 28*) and St Alène, daughter of the Lord of Dilbeek. Her baptism in the Church of St Denis in Forest so enraged her father that he beat her to death. According to legend, numerous miracles occurred at her grave as a consequence, whereupon her father converted to Christianity and Alène was canonised.

Later, the city was stage for many more quarrels concerning the one true faith. In 1921, Erasmus of Rotterdam, the famous scholar and humanist who preached tolerance during the great Wars of Religion, lived in the district of Anderlecht: the Erasmus House at Rue du Chapitre 31 has been converted into a museum in his honour.

Foreign blood: Over the course of Belgium's turbulent history the city lay in the power of a succession of rulers from many lands. Even the first king of Belgium, Leopold I, was not a native of the country, and when he ascended the throne in 1831 he travelled to Brussels from his home in London. His wife Louise was the daughter of

King Louis Philippe of France. Later members of the aristocracy also included a surprisingly high proportion of foreigners, including Elisabeth Gabriele Valerie Marie, the daughter of a Bavarian duke, who married King Albert I of Belgium in 1900 and came from Possenhofen near Munich; and Princess Astrid, who married King Leopold III in 1926 and was of Swedish extraction. Dona Fabiola de Mora y Aragon, who married the late King Baudouin, is a Spanish

noblewoman. King Albert's wife, Queen Paola, is of Italian origin.

Napoleon first visited Brussels in 1803. Twelve years later he was the reason for the arrival of another great soldier in the city, Arthur Wellesley, better known as the Duke of Wellington. Born in Dublin, Wellesley had risen to fame on the battlefields of the Iberian peninsula. He had hastened to the Belgian capital in order to join forces with the Prussians against Napoleon in the historic battle of Waterloo.

Another man who changed the world came to Brussels armed only with his sharp

Left, the struggle between enjoyment and piety depicted by Pieter Brueghel the Elder (1525-69). **Right**, *The Man in the Bowler Hat* by the Belgian Surrealist René Magritte (1898-1967).

wits. Just as Erasmus influenced the thinking of his age, so this newcomer would turn out to be one of the greatest philosophers of the capitalist era. His name was Karl Marx. Since 1843 Marx had lived in Paris, but in 1845, banished from the French capital at the instigation of the Prussian government, he moved to Belgium to live in exile with his wife and family.

Some of Marx's most important writings were produced in Brussels, including *The Poverty of Philosophy*. In collaboration with his friend and fellow-campaigner Friedrich Engels, this was followed by *The Holy Family* (not a religious work, as one might as-

sume from the title, but a criticism of Hegelian idealism), *The German Ideology* and finally *The Communist Manifesto*. Publication of the latter led to his expulsion from Belgium too; Marx subsequently moved via Paris to Cologne.

Europe's best sculptors and artists were employed to adorn Brussels. The achievements of the master masons and architects are preserved for posterity in the city's buildings. Brussels' most famous landmark is undoubtedly the Town Hall on the Grand' Place. The left wing and the lower section of the tower were built between 1401 and 1420

under the supervision of Jacob van Thiemen and Jan Bornay. Between 1449 and 1455 the tower was completed by Jan van Ruysbroeck. It soars to a height of 91 metres (291 ft) above the market place. From 1515, work continued on the King's House (opposite the Town Hall), also known as the Bread House and later the residence of royal officials. The mastermind behind the project was Anthonis II Kelderman, a member of the illustrious family of master builders.

The Grand' Place has been the setting for a number of historic incidents. Egmont and Horn, two counts who strove to win sovereignty for the Netherlands in the 16th century, died at the hand of the executioner on the Grand' Place in front of the Maison du Roi in 1568 – thereby gaining their place in the history books. The French Marshal de Villeroy found notoriety here when, in 1695, he and his troops bombarded the Lower City on behalf of King Louis XIV. The Grand' Place was almost completely destroyed during the attack.

Another Frenchmen, Barnabé Guimard, came to Brussels with more benign intentions. A master builder, he was responsible for the church of St James on the Coudenberg (whose construction began in 1776) and the Palace of the Council of Brabant (1778–83), which became the Parliament building.

The new age of the bourgeoisie demanded a new architecture different from that of the age of feudalism. Both contemporary and historic-style buildings stood side by side. The greenhouse in the Botanical Garden, constructed in 1826 by Tilman-Frans Suys, was a spectacular example of the new style. Together with Charles Vanderstraeten, the same architect created a neoclassical palais for the Prince of Orange between 1823 and 1829; today it is known as the Palais des Académies.

First-ever shopping mall: Another innovation popular in Europe at the time was the erection of covered shopping centres to serve the elegant wives of the continent's growing class of prosperous businessmen. The first such gallery was constructed in Brussels. The foundation stone was laid for Jean-Pierre Chuisensaer's Galeries Saint-Hubert in 1846.

The star architect of Brussels' bourgeoisie was undoubtedly Joseph Poelaert (1817–79). Together with Winand Janssens he designed the Church of St Catherine in Laeken in the neo-Gothic style which came to represent the Age of the Bourgeoisie; the same architect employed the style in the Palais de Justice, the largest monumental building of the 19th century. The terraced gardens around the Column of Congress were also his work, as was the rebuilding of the Théâtre Royal de la Monnaie.

At the behest of local citizens, Léon Suys designed the Stock Exchange in 1871 as a sort of temple of capitalism. One in the army

Hero of Art Nouveau: Horta (1861–1947) had studied in Ghent, Paris and Brussels. He was promoted to a professorial chair in 1912 and between 1927 and 1931 assumed the directorship of the Académie des Beaux Arts in Brussels. Together with van de Velde and Hankar, Horta is regarded as one of the leading exponents of Art Nouveau architecture in Belgium. He designed trend-setting apartment houses and hotels of stone and cast iron. One such building which has been maintained and restored to its original charm is the house of the cloth merchant Waucquez, since 1989 the home of the Comic Museum. Influenced by a trip to America,

of sculptors who came from Paris to adorn it with fine statues was Auguste Rodin.

The city's palaces were not built on the instructions of the ruling bourgeoisie alone. The working classes were gaining in influence and had a so-called People's House erected between 1897 and 1899. The trades unions commissioned their Maison du Peuple from an architect who sympathised with their political views – Victor Horta.

Left, a woodcut from *The Ages of Life* by Frans Masereel (1889–1972). **Above**, inside the Museum of Ancient Art.

Horta returned in his later buildings to a conventional neoclassical style; representative of this period are the Palais des Beaux Arts (1922–28) and the Gare Centrale (1936–41). A museum devoted to his life and work can be found in the Rue Américaine at number 23–25.

Another famous architect of the time was Henry Clemens van de Velde (1863–1957). A proponent of Art Nouveau, which was just beginning to make its mark, van de Velde had begun his career as an artist. In 1890 he turned his attention to architecture, becoming director of the Academy of Art in Weimar and opening a college of architecture in Brussels in 1926. Van de Velde was an open critic of the practice of imitating styles from the past. He campaigned for an approach in harmony with the purpose and materials of the building.

This approach was also endorsed by Auguste Perret (1874–1954), who was the first architect to make a point of using reinforced concrete. One of his pupils achieved even greater fame than he did; his name was Le Corbusier.

The Austrian architect Josef Hoffmann left his distinctive mark on the countenance of Brussels in the form of his Villa Stoclet. Rectangular forms predominate here, as in virtually all his buildings; as a result, he was nicknamed *Quadradl-Hoffmann* ("Hoffmann the Square").

A number of contemporary architects have produced noteworthy buildings, including André Waterkeyn, the architect of the Atomium, and De Westel, creator of the European Commission headquarters. From 1963 to 1969 De Westel followed an irregular cross-shaped ground plan in his design for the much-maligned Palais Berlaymont.

The great painters: Across the centuries, Brussels was always a forum of European trade. As trade flourished, the arts blossomed. It is therefore not surprising that panel painting was invented here. Painting was restricted to walls or books until, at the beginning of the 15th century, the brothers Jan and Hubert van Eyck developed the technique of painting pictures on wooden or canvas panels. This panel painting spread from Flanders to all the corners of the earth. The artists themselves were held in high esteem; they received commissions from home and abroad, and were elected official city painters.

Another of the city's official painters was Rogier van der Weyden (1400–64), a pupil of Robert Campin, the Master of Flémalle. Van der Weyden became the official artist of Brussels and influenced the work of Goes, Bouts and Memling. Hugo van der Goes (1400–82) became a master craftsman in Ghent. Dieric Bouts (1415–75) had great influence on early wood-cut book illustration and achieved fame as a portrait painter.

Hans Memling (1433–94), an immigrant, was an innovator in the Flemish school. His journeys along the Main and the Rhine took him to Cologne, where he probably learned his skills in the studio of Stefan Lochner. He completed his training under Rogier van der Weyden in Brussels and later became in many respects the personification of the spirit of Bruges.

An entire family also achieved artistic fame in Brussels: the Brueghels. Pieter Brueghel the Elder (1525/30–1569) – "Peasant" Brueghel – was the father of two sons who were both to become famous painters. Pieter Brueghel the Younger (*circa*

1564–1638) was known as "Hell" Brueghel because of the scenes of devils he liked to portray; his brother, Jan Brueghel the Elder (1568–1625) was nicknamed "Velvet" or "Flower" Brueghel. He became court painter to the Spanish governor and executed a number of works of art in collaboration with his friend Rubens; as Jan Brueghel's nickname indicates, he always painted the flower arrangements.

Peter Paul Rubens (1577–1640) was born in Siegen in Germany. An artist and freedom fighter, he was a remarkably self-confident individual who frequently served hostile sovereigns. In a great many respects, Rubens epitomises the baroque Age with its characteristic pendulum swings between universal reason and limitless exuberance. The herald of the power and glory of heaven on earth, Rubens became the court painter in Brussels in 1609.

This was a position also held by David Tennier the Younger (1610–90), the son and pupil of Tennier the Elder. Under the influence of Brouwer and Rubens, he banned all scenes of popular life from his canvases. His contemporary Lucas Fayd'herbe (1617–97) was a pupil of Rubens and worked as a sculptor and architect in Brussels.

virtues of republicanism in an antique setting, thereby spreading a revolutionary consciousness.

After the 1789 Revolution, David became a member of the National Convention, the Committee of Public Safety and the Popular Education Committee. When Robespierre was overthrown he fell from favour and spent two periods in prison.

However, Napoleon's rise to power revived his fortunes; he supported David and made him his "First Painter". David fled to Brussels in 1816 following the emperor's defeat; there he exerted a profound influence over the new generation of young artists, in

After this Golden Age had waned, many years elapsed before the oppressed Belgians once more managed to ascend the peaks of artistic creativity. The revival of Belgian painting was instigated by a revolutionary who sought asylum in Brussels: Jacques-Louis David (1748–1825). A leading representative of the Classical movement and a Jacobin, David liked to portray the civic

Left, part of a whole district had to be demolished to make way for the gigantic Palace of Justice, (built around 1900). **Above**, the splendid Galeries St Hubert, Europe's first shopping mall.

particular J.F. Navez. David's influence is evident in the works of Gustave Wappers, N. de Kayser, Louis Gallait, Edouard Bièfve and L. Leys; it extended to the work of Ferdinand Pauwels at the end of the 19th century.

Art in the Modern Age: Among the architectural successes of the 19th century was the Galeries Royales St-Hubert, designed by Jean-Paul Cluysenaer and completed in 1847. Equally famous was the artist Antoine J. Wiertz (1806–65), a forerunner of the symbolists and surrealists. His influence – his works depict cruelty and beauty – is honoured by a special museum in Brussels. Another trendsetter who pointed the way towards radically new artistic horizons was Guillaume Vogels (1836–96); he influenced Rops and Ensor and was one of the co-founders of the artistic association known as "XX" (Les Vingts). Félicien Rops (1833–96) achieved notoriety on account of his erotic fantasies.

Les Vingts itself played a notable role on the European art scene. It staged important exhibitions and invited famous artists from all over the world. Vincent van Gogh was a guest in Brussels for a short time between October 1880 and April 1881, when he studied art at the Academy.

Other artists in Belgium at this time were influenced by naturalism. Constantin Meunier (1831–1905) became famous for his sculpture of a man carrying a heavy load as well as his paintings of people at work. The works of Charles de Groux (1825–70) illustrate similar themes.

Other naturalist painters were Jan Stobbaerts (1839–1914), who rebelled against the doctrines of his established fellow-artists in Antwerp and moved to Brussels in 1885, and Léon Frédéric (1856–1940), the most popular Belgian painter during the 1920s, who painted mainly peasants and workers.

Alfred William Finch (1854–1930) studied with Ensor at the Brussels Academy and also belonged to Les Vingts. Another member was Theo van Rysselberghe (1862–1926), who studied in Brussels and became one of the leading Belgian Impressionists.

James Ensor (1860–1949), a virtual contemporary, is regarded as marking the beginning of the modern period. A friend of Khnopff and the protégé of Rops, Ensor remained a loner. His painting *Christ's Entry into Brussels* shocked public and critics alike. His expressive pictures remained largely unappreciated until the 1920s.

Another member of Les Vingts was Fernand Khnopff (1858–1921), a Symbolist without whose work Belgian imaginative painting would have been much poorer. Other representatives of the "Reality of Fantasy" are Degouve de Nunques (1867–1935) and Jean Delville (1867–1953), who studied and later taught in Brussels.

The most famous visionary of all was the Surrealist painter René Magritte (1898–1967). He trained in Brussels and later travelled to France, Britain and Germany, staying in Paris for three years between 1927 and 1930. When he returned to Brussels, he painted a number of murals for Belgian public buildings.

Another artist, Paul Delvaux (born 1897), destroyed all the paintings from his first creative period after witnessing the anatomical peepshow of the Spitzner Museum at the Brussels Fair. Naked bodies and skeletons peopled his works from that time on, and he became influenced by Magritte.

Also influenced by Magritte was Félix Labisse (born 1905) whose visionary paintings are characterised by nude figures often in iridescent shades of blue. Labisse was also influenced by Ensor and Delvaux.

Gaston Bogaert (born 1918) first came to Brussels as an actor. He then became an advertising designer for the Belgian airline Sabena. His first exhibition of paintings displayed in a Brussels gallery in 1965 place him as another member of the Brussels visionary school.

Contemporary art in Brussels does not consist only of the abstract, as the work of Pierre Alechinsky (born 1927), Marcel Broodthaers (1924–76) and John C.F. Delogne (born in Uccle in 1933) makes clear. And artistic contributions of another kind are supplied by the artists who have transformed the underground railway stations into a gallery of contemporary art.

Literature and music: Many men of letters also passed through Brussels across the years. Rousseau and Voltaire stayed in the Palais d'Egmont. Victor Hugo often paid visits to his friend Juliette Drouot, who lived in Brussels' Galeries des Princes. Colette and Cocteau were both members of the Royal Academy of French Language and Literature in Brussels.

Of the many Belgian writers, only a handful actually lived in their country's capital. Amongst them was the popular writer Charles Théodore Henri de Coster (1827–79), who lived in Brussels from childhood. His important prose epic *Tyll Ulenspeigel und Lamme Goedzak* made use of the Flemish narrative tradition, creating a national epic tale; de Coster also established the contemporary francophone literary tradition in Belgium.

Hermann Teirlinck, born in 1879, the year in which de Coster died, was another of the city's leading literary figures. A poet and playwright who is regarded as instigating the renaissance of the Flemish theatre, Teirlinck also taught languages at the royal court. He died in 1967; his house on the city outskirts at Uwenberg 13 has been transformed into a commemorative museum.

The writer Ernest André Jozef Claes (1885–1968) chose the peseudonym G. van

A professional violinist, Henri Vieux–temps (1820–81), occupied the professorial chair at the Brussels conservatory from 1871. The director of the Conservatoire was François Auguste Gevaert (1828–1908), a versatile composer, conductor, music scholar and patron of the music of Bach.

Another important supporter of the Bach renaissance in Brussels was Edgar Tinel (1854–1912), a composer of church music and organ works who became director of the Conservatoire in 1909.

A more modern composer was Paul Gilson (1865–1942), a member of the contemporary Flemish school.

Hasselt for the realist tales and novels for which he was to become famous.

The Queen Elisabeth of Belgium Music Competition, established in 1937, has provided the stepping stone to success for many of the country's musicians, including its very first winter, David Oistrakh.

Another violinist who was amongst the friends of Queen Elisabeth, a member of the Bavarian Wittelsbach dynasty, was the scientist Albert Einstein.

Above, James Ensor's *The Entry of Christ into Brussels* (1888) shocked both critics and public.

Marcel Poot (born 1901), a neoclassical composer and director of the Conservatoire, achieved international fame. So, too, did Henri Pousseur (born 1929); he studied in Brussels and Liège and composed electronic music in series.

Brussels has also made a name for itself on the popular music scene. The singer Dani Klein and the double-bass player Dirk Schoufs met in one of the city's bars. The band Vaya con Dios achieved fame well beyond the city boundaries, proving that in this sphere, too, Brussels talent can compete with the best.

THE COMIC MUSEUM

If you want a museum that absorbs children for hours and offers something for adults too, head for the Comic Museum, occupying the house at Rue des Sables 20/Zandstraat. Allow plenty of time for your visit (the museum is open to the public every day except Monday, from 10 a.m. until 6 p.m) and take your time over the hands-on exhibits; whoever completes first – you or the kids – can take advantage of the reading room, comfortably strewn with cushions and comics.

This treasure-chest of picture stories is a gem in itself, because the building in which it is housed is

Rémi) first introduced them to the newspaper-reading public in 1929. They are his most popular cartoon characters, followed by the twin detectives Thomson and Thompson, Captain Haddock and the absent-minded Professor Calculus. For 70 years their adventures have entranced the whole world in every imaginable language. The museum contains sketches, drawings, relief plates and many other items.

Incredible though it may seem, the lovely Horta-designed building was at one stage poised for demolition. The *Magazins Waucquet* had closed its doors in 1970 and the building was threatened by the same fate that befell many other buildings in the city centre, including the "House of the People", mentioned in every account of the city's

a prime example of Flemish Art Nouveau architecture. Known as the Magazins Waucquez, it was built in 1906 for a fabric merchant named Waucquez by the famous Belgian architect Victor Horta, who lived from 1861 to 1947 (*see preceding chapter, page 77*).

In those days, customers to the fabric shop entered through a fine portal and then mounted the sweeping staircase. Today these same stairs serve as the launching pad for the red-and-white checked rocket which Tintin and Snowy used to reach "Destination Moon" long before the Americans managed it.

Tintin – who outflanks even Manneken Pis in fame – and his faithful terrier are omnipresent in the museum. Their artist-creator Hergé (Georges

architecture. The capital of Europe needed more space to house its increasing numbers of politicians and businessmen. The demolition was short-sighted and ruthless. No account was taken of the loss to Brussels' cultural heritage.

However, Horta's Magazins Waucquez was saved from the same fate. Artists and architects managed to persuade the Belgian Minister of Housing and Construction that the house in the Rue des Sables should be saved and restored. The ingenious idea of turning it into a comic museum was widely supported by Brussels' citizens. The plan was to create a symbiosis between Art Nouveau and the "Ninth Art" – that of cartoon drawing. King Baudouin and Queen Fabiola added their support for the project; it was in their presence that the new museum was at long last inaugurated in the autumn of 1989.

The treasures of Belgian comic art were thus preserved for posterity. The indiscriminate and reckless sale of comic books, magazines, drawings and printing plates was stopped in its tracks. Previously, early printing plates of Hergé and Morris cartoons were sold to collectors abroad for about £10,000 each.

The museum is not just a home for Tintin and Snowy and their many fans, as a brief tour of the exhibition rooms indicates. It is entertaining and educational, a place for meeting friends from your past – whichever generation you belong to.

On the ground floor, to the right, lies the brasserie-restaurant, "Horta"; to the left, there is a cartoon films are made, including sketches and drawings at every stage of development.

Ascending the staircase, the visitor passes Tintin's rocket and arrives at the first floor. Here, the auditorium of the King Baudouin Foundation is reserved for special events.

Also on the first floor is the Museum of the Imagination, the place to meet all those old friends. In the room dedicated to the journal *Spirou* visitors find the cunning bellboy himself, and in the Vandersteen Room you will find Professor Barabas's time machine.

In the room housing the Jacques Martin collection you can experience a thunderstorm by night in ancient Rome, and in the Tillieux Room you will find Jeff Jordan's favourite saloon. Entering

bookshop named Slumberland after the Art Nouveau comic strip about Little Nemo. Also on this floor is a permanent exhibition commemorating the life and work of master architect Victor Horta, and two libraries – one of which is for leisurely reading while the other is reserved for more serious study.

On the mezzanine floor, the visitor enters the Saint-Roch Treasure House, where original manuscripts are preserved. Also here are a cinema, a video library, and an exhibition explaining how

Left, the *Adventures of Tintin* spread to outer space in *Destination Moon*, first published in 1953. Above, no turning back for Tintin, Snowy and crew.

Gaston's office in the Franquin room, it seems as if Marsupilami cannot be far away; and in the Hubinon Room you can stand on the aircraft carrier next to Buck Danny. In the Morris room you encounter the shadow which shoots faster than Lucky Luke.

That is only a sample of the experiences in store at the museum. In addition, prepare to meet Jacobs' Blake and Mortimer, Roba's Boule & Bill, and Peyo's Smurfs.

There seems no end to the range of comic figures created by Belgian artists. Quite apart from the established artists who have now become classics, there is a steady stream of new talent in the country. Belgium boasts more comic characters than anywhere else in the world.

Brussels' reputation as a city of faceless civil servants has some foundation in truth. If one thing symbolises the city better than the exquisite white pillow lace that adorned the rich and powerful in the 16th century, it's the ranks of rich and powerful bureaucrats – the army of ministers, diplomats and influential industrialists – that populate the city today.

The people inside Brussels' committee rooms and offices manipulate the fates of millions: the committees of the European Union determine everything from member states' environmental policy to workers' rights, and the North Atlantic Treaty Organization plays a major role in world security and defence. In addition, more than 1,000 other international associations and over 1,300 multinational industrial concerns have headquarters here.

Rise and fall: American companies were the first – during the 1960s – to discover the many advantages of Brussels' location. The city lies at the geographic heart of Western Europe and even then seemed set to become the focal point of the Western bloc. Furthermore, the city was attractive for its low wages, the tax advantages for foreigners, and an apparently inexhaustible supply of residential and office accommodation. One American concern after another set up branch offices in the secret capital of Europe.

Then, as the 1970s waned and the 1980s dawned, the unexpected happened. The flow of foreign investment capital from across the Atlantic suddenly dried up. Many American firms decided to leave the city; the fall of the dollar, the vastly inflated wage and social security costs and rapidly escalating housing prices had suddenly made Brussels an expensive place in which to work.

Today, however, Brussels is experiencing a recovery. As before, investors from America are well ahead of their competitors in Europe and the Far East. A recent survey showed that Brussels contained offices of 600 US concerns, and smaller numbers from

The alternative way of getting to the office.

France (350), the United Kingdom (160), Germany (147), Japan (128), Switzerland (115), Italy (84), Spain (60), Denmark (28), Canada (27) and Norway (12). A fairly recent development is the growing number of Swedish investors who, in anticipation of EU membership, poured large sums of money into the city, and who now operate 130 companies in the capital.

There are several reasons for this change in investment behaviour. In 1982 the Brussels government, alarmed at the departure of so many American firms and struggling with the reality of a general economic crisis, took pre-emptive action. As well as tightening sels have greatly increased during the 1980s and 90s, they are still very low compared with those in cities such as London, Paris, Berlin and Madrid.

In order to ensure that relatively inexpensive rents continue to attract foreign enterprises to Brussels, even more office space will be required. Construction of office blocks continues at an extraordinary pace and no-one in Brussels doubts that they will readily find occupants. Indeed, the European Union, all set for the next expansion of its membership in the early years of the 21st century, is guaranteed to absorb much of this additional space.

domestic spending, it offered foreign investors tax incentives on top of the benefits they already enjoyed. This policy has continued, and today foreign employees of international firms with a branch in Belgium, for example, need only declare 50 percent of their income for tax purposes, a useful incentive in a country with punitive personal income tax levels.

The progress towards European unity has also contributed to the improvement in Brussels' prosperity. Property prices are evidence that Brussels has been a popular investment choice. While office rents in Brus-

Brussels has also sought to strengthen its position as a financial centre, and now ranks fifth in Europe. There is a strong foreign presence; 65 foreign financial institutions have offices here. The Belgian Stock Exchange – founded in 1801 – is highly active.

Fair competition: Brussels has proved most successful as a centre for trade fairs and congresses. Three modern complexes in the heart of the town have made the Belgian capital the second-largest conference city in the world.

With a 75-hectare (185-acre) trade-fair site including 12 hectares (30 acres) covered

by buildings, Brussels is the leading trades fair centre in Europe. Throughout the year, businessmen and women flock in their thousands to participate in the 100 or so events, such as the Leather Goods Fair in January, the Euroba trades fair for bakers, chocolatiers and confectioners, the International Trade Fair in March, the car accessories fair Autotechnica in April, and the International Furniture Fair and Horesca – an international hotel fair – in November. The 1958 International World Exhibition provided much of the infrastructure for today's conference facilities. Its other legacy was one of Brussels' most famous landmarks – the Atomium.

around 100,000 of the foreigners living in Brussels are here to work at the international organisations and industrial headquarters. The remainder represent the guest worker and overseas population to be found in any large city.

In spite of the increase in the service industries sector, which now provides over 80% of the capital's jobs, Brussels is still the second industrial centre in the country after Antwerp. The range of products manufactured is as varied as the people who live here: lace and carpets, chocolate and beer, plastics and pharmaceuticals, computers and cars. Traditional items and high-technology goods all

The strong presence of political institutions, international associations and multinational companies has made Brussels into a cosmopolitan city. According to census figures, almost one-third of the Belgian capital's 1 million residents was born abroad. The European Union and NATO account for some 20,000 foreign diplomats and officials.

Many countries have three diplomatic representatives: one at the Belgian court, one at the EU and one at NATO. It is estimated that

Left, "Elvis Pompilio hats suit me best." **Above**, the trade fair site by night.

have their place. Excellent transport links guarantee efficient distribution of manufactured articles.

Brussels is an important European and worldwide transport hub in the centre of a well-developed air, rail and motorway network. In addition, the Willebroek Canal, constructed during the 16th century and widened at the beginning of the 20th, connects Brussels with Antwerp and Charleroi, forms a vital supply link and gives the city with direct access to the North Sea. The Port of Brussels handles some 14 million tons of traffic every year.

The largest industrial employer in Brussels is, surprisingly enough, not a Belgian concern. Volkswagen has its world headquarters in Wolfsburg, but in the factory in Forest – one of the 19 communities which make up the Brussels metropolitan area – workers make a significant contribution to the company's global output.

When Volkswagen set up in Brussels in 1948, it did not do so entirely of its own free will. The Belgians had far-sightedly decided to allow the import of automobiles only in the case of foreign manufacturers who already had an assembly plant operating in the country. Volkswagen profited handsomely

an excellent reputation all over the world. It exports to 36 countries and has 2,000 retail outlets. The company produces 21,000 tons of chocolate per year, one-quarter of the total Belgian market. Competition for exports among chocolate producers is intense as Belgian domestic consumption levels off, though at over 8 kilos per person a year, it is still some way above the European average of 5.4 kilos.

Another major manufacturer, Godiva, established in Brussels in 1926, acquired the royal seal of approval in 1968; as official court supplier, it continues to enjoy an advantage over its many competitors, but the

from this decision, and invested heavily in the expansion of its Brussels plant.

Of course, the citizens of Brussels have benefited from the arrangement, too; they have been able to claim the highest per capita vehicle production in Europe, despite the fact that they had no automobile company of their own. Each year, hundreds of thousands of cars from a variety of European manufacturers roll off the assembly lines in Brussels, as well as in Antwerp and Ghent.

Sweet sensation: Belgium is well known for its chocolate and the long-established Brussels confectionery firm of Neuhaus has

competition is healthy, for there are many excellent chocolate manufacturers. Today the company operates on a worldwide basis.

In addition to Volkswagen, another long-established foreign company in Brussels is the US technology firm IBM, which has had a presence in the Belgian capital since 1936. Many transnational corporations operate out of Brussels, such as Shell, Exxon Chemicals, Toyota, Mitsubishi Bank, ICI, 3M, Proctor & Gamble, Monsanto, Bayer, Ericsson and a host of other household names. They are attracted by the presence of the EU institutions, Brussels' geographic location, competitive property and labour costs, a multi-lingual population and a high quality of life for their employees.

Brussels promotes itself as a biotechnology centre, with the commune of Evere dubbed the Silicon Valley of Belgium. The country's beer-making tradition laid the foundations for today's biotech industry. The pharmaceuticals giant SmithKline Beecham employs 2,000 people in Rixensart, just south of Brussels. Their Hepatitus B vaccine was developed in collaboration with the Free University of Brussels.

Brussels can demonstrate a long tradition of innovative technology. Under William I,

metals based on the rich copper, cobalt and zinc deposits in the southern Belgian Congo. Although its activities once accounted for one-third of the national economy, it is now under French ownership, as is the Belgian steel industry.

Nowadays it is the task of the Brussels Regional Development Agency to persuade high-technology firms and other modern businesses to establish themselves in the area. Through a package of tax, investment and research incentives, they have succeeded in bringing forward-looking enterprises to the city and providing the citizens of Brussels with thousands of jobs. Foreign

who ruled the Netherlands and Belgium for a short while as the kingdom of the "United Netherlands", the "Société Générale de Belgique" was founded in Brussels in 1822. Together with the "Banque de Belgique", founded in 1835, this powerful holding company determined the country's economic development and was responsible for maintaining over many years Belgium's dominant position in the smelting of non-ferrous

Left, handmade Belgian chocolates. **Above**, the modern city of busy ringroads, high-rises and international companies.

investment is now vital to the economy in the wake of the decline of the country's traditional industries.

The Brussels business community was not unscathed by the recession of the early 1990s, but austerity measures by the Belgian government to bring the economy into line for European economic integration have paid off: Belgium was in the first wave of countries which joined the Euro on 1 January 1999. Projections for the economy are cautiously optimistic. Its position at the centre of Europe has ensured its survival and looks certain to guarantee its future.

BRUSSELS LACE

Brussels lace is famous the world over. Developed during the mid-19th century and initially used to adorn the shirt collars and cuffs of the nobility, Brussels lace was soon being used extensively. At one point it was fashionable to wear gowns made entirely of the precious fabric.

Brussels lace was particularly sought after at the royal courts in Paris and London. Queen Elizabeth I of England reputedly owned 3,000 lace dresses; it is said that Empress Eugénie more than 12 years of age. During the 17th century, 22,000 women and girls worked as lace makers; during the 19th century, the total reached around 50,000. In Brussels alone, the capital of lace production, the figure was some 10,000.

Brussels lace was unsurpassable as regards both the fineness of the thread and the beauty of the motifs. The capital's churches and museums are full of examples of the delicate work produced. A particularly fine specimen of the lace maker's art can be found in the Royal Museum of Art and History: a bedspread which Albert I and his wife Isabella

of France owned a lace gown which 600 women had toiled over for 10 months using a total of 90,000 bobbins.

By the second half of the 16th century, women throughout Belgium were engaged in the craft and lace was being exported to prosperous families all over Europe. At the end of the century there was scarcely a young girl, even in the most rural areas, who was not employed by the lace merchants.

The labour intensive industry created a number of unforeseen problems, namely a shortage of serving maids in the homes of the wealthy. Eventually a decree was passed prohibiting the manufacture of lace by girls of received as a present upon the occasion of Albert's elevation to Duke of Brabant.

Other masterpieces include the Virgin Mary's veil, on display in the church of Notre-Dame-du-Sablon, and a lace bedspread, carefully preserved in the Museum of Costumes and Lace, which belonged to Emperor Charles VI. The bedspread is decorated with the imperial eagle, symbolising the pomp and circumstance of monarchy.

The production of large covers and entire robes was only made possible when the technique of lace-making moved away from the use of a single continuous thread towards knotting. Until this point it had only been possible to produce small pieces of lace, the size of which was determined by the length of the thread wound on to the bobbin. The technique of joining together individual motifs to produce a single large piece revolutionised the industry. This method permitted the creation of large-scale items with highly imaginative patterns within a relatively short time.

Following this method of production many women produced the same motif time and time again. The creative aspect of the craft was thus gradually lost in a sort of mass production. Other workers were allotted the task of joining the individual pieces together.

lution lace-making in Belgium was in decline. The craft experienced a brief renaissance during the 19th century but was never able to regain its previous fashionableness or degree of skill.

Today, the craft attracts only a modest following in its country of origin. Very few women possess the requisite skills. Two schools, in Mons and Binche, train young women in what was once a world-famous art. Unfortunately, nowadays too few Belgian women want to learn the intricacies of lace-making to satisfy the rapidly increasing demands for hand-made lace. Much of that on

None of the lace makers ever became famous or rich. Their reward for their arduous work was determined by the lace merchants, few of whom were generous; the lace makers were often forced to work in badly-lit, damp cellars where the thread would be less likely to break.

Until well into the 18th century, Brussels lace remained a popular symbol of luxury for the rich. Inevitably, however, fashions changed and by the time of the French Revo-

Left, *The Lacemaker* **by Jan Vermeer van Delt (1665). Above, even expert lacemakers can't produce more than a few inches a day.**

sale in Brussels today was actually made in China. The Asian product is considerably cheaper but inferior in quality.

One of the largest lace merchants in Brussels is the Manufacture Belge de Dentelles at 6-8 Galerie de la Reine. A wide variety of antique and modern lace is on sale. Those who prefer simply to look at fine Belgian lace should visit the Museum of Costumes and Lace just behind the Town Hall at 6 Rue de la Violette. There is also an excellent lace collection in the Royal Museum of Art and History in the Parc du Cinquantenaire; the entrance can be reached through the park or via the Avenue des Nerviens.

Eddy Merckx, the legendary racing cyclist of the 1960s and '70s, is probably the only Belgian sportsman whose name is familiar to non-Belgians. At various stages in his career, Merckx won every major international cycling race, gaining the coveted Tour de France trophy no less than five times.

All in all, however, Brussels does not play an important role on the international sporting scene and Merckx is the only world-calibre athlete that the country can boast. Even so most Belgians enjoy participating in one or more sporting activities and support their national teams with enthusiasm.

Brussels sports fans are particularly well catered for, with a choice of six stadiums, three horse-racing tracks and several ice rinks. There are top-ranking football teams such as R.S.C. Anderlecht, and an internationally famous light athletics meeting (Ivo van Damme Memorial).

Since 1985 Brussels has been haunted by the tragedy of Heysel stadium. This was when hooligan supporters of the British national champions, Liverpool, staged a brutal riot during the European Cup Final against Juventus Turin. This terrible episode cost 39 Juventus fans' lives and resulted in British clubs being banned from European tournaments. The event had a profound effect on the city; it had little to do with the everyday sporting reality – active or passive – of the average Brussels man-in-the-street.

A nation on its bike: Cycling is without doubt the favourite national sport. It holds a place in the national soul comparable to that of baseball in America, cricket in England, bullfighting in Spain, or ice hockey in the Soviet Union and Canada. Cynics maintain that its popularity represents nothing more than escapism from the boredom of a Belgian Sunday. Either way, hardly a day goes by without a cycling race somewhere or other, and they are always supported by thousands of enthusiastic spectators; a clas-

sic cycling race from Liège to Bastogne and back, for instance, will be lined by throngs of spectators all along the route.

But it isn't just the cycling that people come to see. A rally is also a social event. Friends meet, drink a beer, marvel at the speed at which the cyclists race past, and enjoy listening to the results on the radio later on. In addition, cycling events are often accompanied by fairs and other attractions appealing to younger family members.

Speculation as to why this enthusiasm for cycling should have grown up in Belgium usually mentions the topography of the land. One ideal precondition is without doubt the flatness of the countryside. Except in the hilly eastern provinces, Belgium – like the Netherlands – makes the bicycle the most convenient and inexpensive mode of transport. Children organise impromptu races on the way to school, and farmers' wives use their ancient bone-shakers to reach the nearest village. When national heroes such as grocer's son Eddy Merckx make headline news in the international press, their success

Left and __above__, billiards is a popular pastime, as is cycling – here at the Zandpoortvest in Mechelen.

fires the enthusiasm of the aspiring youth. The popularity of the sport has little to do with the prospect of monetary gain; apart from the trophies, the prizes are not usually very significant. In a small country like Belgium, the few sportsmen who make it to the top become role models to a far greater extent than elsewhere.

The Belgians are a convivial people; they love their families and enjoy celebrating with friends. A Belgian who participates actively in some form of sport will naturally tend to belong to a club. For Flemings and Walloons alike the latter performs the role of a second family, a second home.

frequent events; many take place through the streets of towns, with all speed limits temporarily lifted (be warned: barriers to protect the spectators are seldom erected). Tens of thousands flock to see the race at Spa-Francorchamps, hoping to witness as many hazardous thrills as possible. Celebrations know no bounds when a compatriot wins, and heavy disappointment descends if a Belgian entry is eliminated early on in the race. However, competing is considered the most important thing.

Billiards: Brussels citizens with more limited sporting ability tend to retire to the city's bars to indulge in a quiet game of billiards, a

An example of this sociability can be found in the cycling club at Plombières, in the three-country triangle between Aachen, Maastricht and Liège. Although the lively club has had no active cycling members for years, it still continues to organise a "Grand Prix of Plombières" each autumn. The winner is usually from the Netherlands. A crate of beer is the prize for the fastest circuit, and the winner is rewarded with a trophy and a certificate.

Sport in Belgium has a great deal to do with spectacle. The louder and more colourful the event, the better. Motor races are

favourite evening pastime. The professional standards reached by some of these players are well demonstrated by the string of world championship titles which have been won by the nation's experts.

Apart from cycling, football and billiards, the other sports enjoying popularity in Belgium include tennis and golf – both as fashionable here as elsewhere on the continent. Cross-country skiing is practised in the winter in the hills of the Ardennes; and during the summer months, sailing and surfing are both popular pastimes on the English Channel coast between Knokke and De Panne.

Rugby is played predominantly in the French-speaking provinces, where it is a favourite spectator sport.

Top sportsmen have a difficult time in a small country. Belgium has produced few world-class athletes, although it has established a winning tradition in a number of disciplines. Gold medals or unexpected success produce a spirit of national euphoria. During the World Football Championships, if the Belgian team does well, cars full of triumphant fans cruise the streets tooting their horns; celebrations last until well into the small hours. Apart from that, however, things are quiet on the higher sporting plane.

century ago. The archers attempt to shoot down the containers; if they succeed in their aim, the cages shatter in mid-air; the rats fall to the ground and lie there stunned until their throats are slit. The local newspaper, *Het Nieuwsblad*, which always sponsors the event, maintains that this is a more humane death than poisoning.

Twice a week between 15 October and 1 May (on Tuesday and Saturday), a hunt takes place in the Vielsalm region. It is a full-blooded mounted chase in which a stag is pursued by hounds and horsemen to the bitter end. The hunt can last as long as 10 hours. The host of the event is Baron Eric

Rat catching: The combination of sports and spectacles has a long tradition in the country. Every August in the village of Zaffelare, near Ghent, an archery contest is held – a sporting event, but with the spirit of a funfair. The chief aspect of the contest is somewhat gruesome. The targets are not the normal ones used in archery, but cages full of rats which are suspended at a height of 27 metres (86 ft). The event marks a plague of rats that descended on the village over a

Jansen, whose guests for the occasion are drawn from the aristocracy and the highest echelons of industry. After the killing, the hunting party recovers at an exclusive champagne reception.

Public outcry at blood sports of this nature is vociferous in Belgian. Protest is also directed against a substantial number of birdcatchers, who are inclined to describe theselves as animal lovers and sportsmen. Each year in the late autumn and early winter, almost 1 million migratory birds are caught, ending up in the country's aviaries and cooking pots.

<u>Left</u>, Belgium is ideal for cycling. <u>Above</u>, the less energetic try their hand at minigolf.

The best way to get acquainted with Brussels is to put on your most comfortable shoes and walk. Start with the the Rue Royale in the Upper City, a route which leads past the parliament building and across the municipal park as far as the magnificent Place Royale in front of the Royal Museums of Fine Arts. The most imposing building in the entire city, the monumental Palais de Justice, can be approached via the Rue de la Régence or the Rue aux Laines. At its feet nestles the Marolles, an historic district where you will find, squeezed side by side, the chic, the original and the poor.

If you like wandering through colourful markets, collecting bric-a-brac, books, fake antiques or exotic spices, you will be pleased to discover that every day is market day in Brussels. Belgium's capital is a maze of shopping arcades where you will find genuine Brussels lace, French *haute couture* and precious jewels alongside postcards and souvenirs.

Brussels is also the place for gourmets. You can eat better here than almost anywhere else in the world. The best place to head for is the Ilôt Sacré, where the restaurants lie cheek by jowl. Try more than mussels and chips (a Brussels speciality); the variety of restaurants is as wide as the price range. Beer drinkers in particular are spoiled for choice, because some 400 kinds of ale are available. Not for nothing is the Petite Rue des Bouchers known as the "Stomach of Brussels".

The Lower City contains the city's most famous sites. Passing through a maze of little side streets, you will reach one of the loveliest city squares in Europe: the Grand' Place (Grote Markt), graced by baroque, Gothic and Renaissance architecture. Nearby you will find Manneken Pis, the best dressed statue in the world. His outfits – he has well over 300 – change according to the season.

Later on during your visit you may like to make an excursion from the Palais Royal in Laeken to the Parc du Cinquantenaire, or visit the Atomium on the Heysel plateau. You can round off your visit to Brussels with a trip to the university town of Leuven or the village of Waterloo, where Napoleon made his final stand.

Preceding pages: bowler hats are not just a preserve of the English; a Maypole celebration takes place in the city in August; Brussels contains a host of noble restaurants; modern art is displayed in a number of galleries. **Left,** taking in the sights.

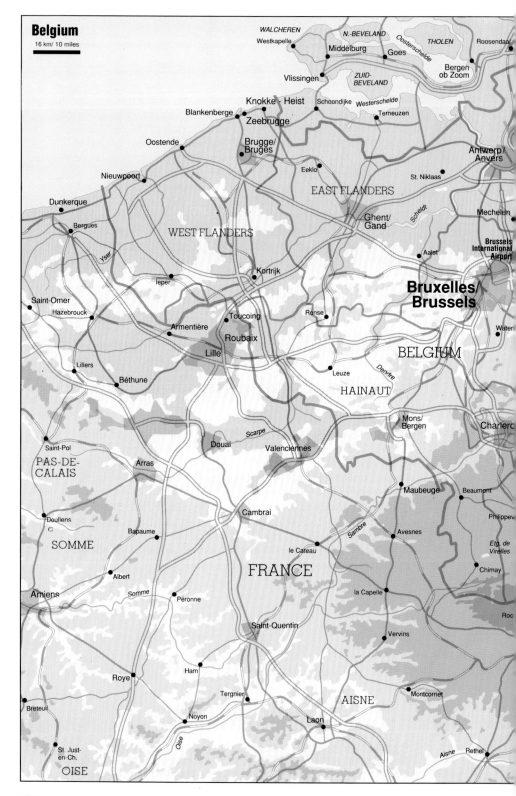

Belgium

16 km/ 10 miles

WALCHEREN
Westkapelle
N-BEVELAND
Middelburg
Goes
Oosterschelde
THOLEN
Roosendaal

Vlissingen
ZUID-BELAND
Bergen ob Zoom

Knokke - Heist
Blankenberge
Schoondijke
Westerschelde
Terneuzen

Zeebrugge

Oostende
Brugge/Bruges
Eeklo
St. Niklaas
Antwerp/Anvers

Nieuwpoort

EAST FLANDERS
Ghent/Gand
Scheldt
Mechelen

Dunkerque
Bergues
WEST FLANDERS
Brussels International Airport

Saint-Omer
Ieper
Kortrijk
Aalst

Hazebrouck
Toucoing
Ronse
Bruxelles/Brussels

Armentière
Roubaix
Water

Lillers
Lille
Leuze
Dendre
BELGIUM

Béthune
HAINAUT

Mons/Bergen
Charlerc

Saint-Pol
Scarpe
Douai
Valenciennes

PAS-DE-CALAIS
Arras
Maubeuge
Beaumont

Doullens
Cambrai
Sambre
Avesnes
Philippe

SOMME
Bapaume
le Cateau
Etg. de Virelles

Albert
Somme
Péronne
la Capelle
Chimay

Amiens
FRANCE
Roc

Saint-Quentin
Vervins

Ham
Roye
AISNE
Montcornet

Breteuil
Tergnier
Laon

St. Just-en-Ch.
Noyon
Oise
Aisne
Rethel

OISE

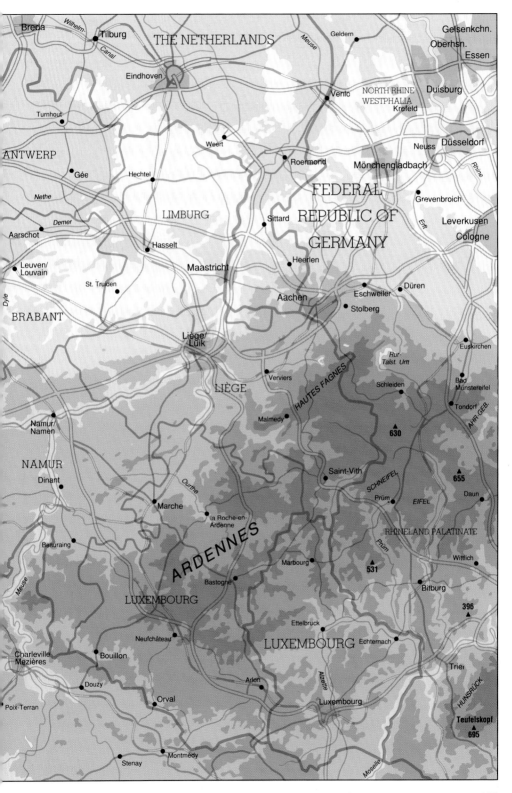

Greater Brussels

1600 m / 1,0 miles

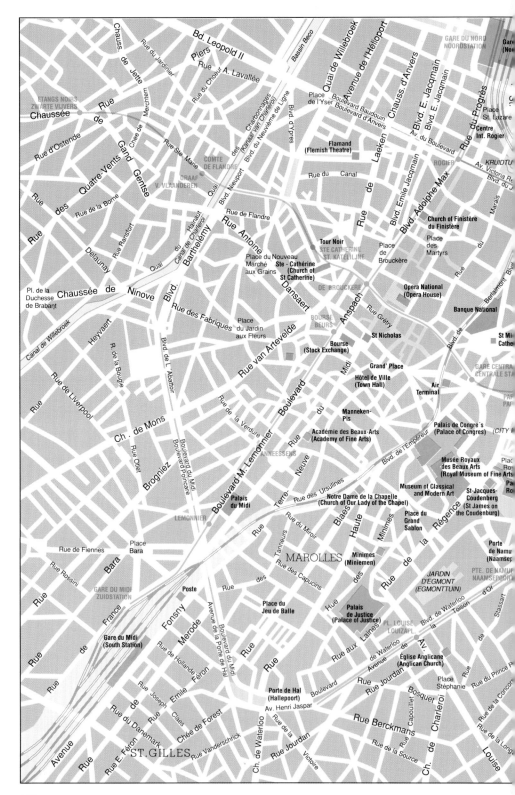

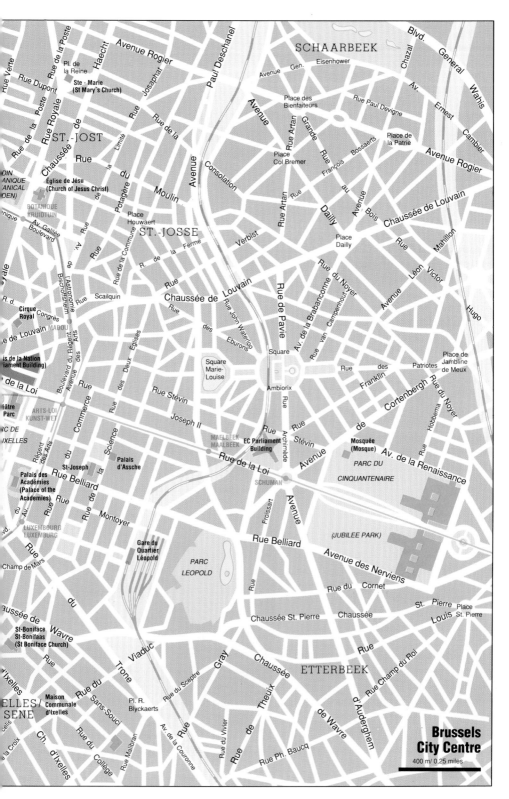

Brussels
City Centre

400 m/ 0.25 miles

The most attractive route through the Upper City starts at the junction of the Boulevard du Jardin Botanique/Kruidtuinlaan and the Rue Royale/Koninginstraat. Here, in times gone by, stood the city gate on the road leading from Brussels to Leuven.

Turning from the Boulevard du Jardin Botanique into the Rue Royale in the direction of the city centre, you will pass in front of the glass pavilions of the **Botanical Garden** (Jardin Botanique National de Belgique/Nationale Plantentuin van Belgie).

The park, which contains a fine collection of exotic flora, was completed in 1830. The large iron-framed greenhouse was constructed in 1826. In 1944, when the Botanical Garden outgrew its original site, it was transferred to the park of the Domaine Bouchot, on the northern side of the city. In 1984 the former glasshouses were converted and now house the French Community Cultural Centre, whose facilities include a library, cinema, theatre and a number of exhibition halls. There is also a terrace café overlooking the gardens and open-air concerts in summer.

One of the capital's oldest hotels is the Pullman Astoria. Built in 1909, it also stands on the Rue Royale.

Continuing in the direction of the Place Royale/Koningsplein, the visitor should skirt around the right-hand side of an old district, where almost all the houses in the area were destroyed and rebuilt with fine contemporary facades during the course of the 19th century. Most of the streets originally converged on open spaces, which later developed into squares; the focal point of such a square is usually a monument to a famous past citizen.

On the right, you will see the **Congress Column** (Colonne du Congrès/

Right, the domed Schaerbeek entrance to the Botanical Gardens, a cultural centre.

Kongreszuil). This was erected between 1850 and 1859 and designed by Joseph Poelaert, one of the country's most famous architects. The monument commemorates the founding of the Belgian state in 1830; important dates and the names of the men and women who were instrumental in the Revolution are inscribed in golden letters.

A statue of the first king of Belgium, Leopold I, of the house of Saxe-Coburg-Gotha, occupies pride of place at the top of the column; it was the work of the sculptor Guillaume Geefs. On the pedestal at the monarch's feet sit four female figures representing the fundamental civic rights which until 1830 had been denied: freedom of education, freedom of worship, freedom of the press and freedom of assembly.

At the base of the column, the eternal flame burns on the grave of an unknown soldier in remembrance of all those who died during the two world wars.

Taking Rue de la Ligne to the left of the Column, you arrive at the cathedral, which is dedicated to the city's twin patron saints, St Gudula and St Michael. Constructed between the 13th and 15th centuries, the cathedral is basically Gothic in style, although the chapels surrounding the main edifice were added during the 16th and 17th centuries. It possesses some particularly fine 16th and 17th-century stained-glass windows, including portraits of Charles V and Isabella of Portugal in the North transept and King Louis II of Hungary and his wife, Marie, Charles V's sister, in the South transept; both were modelled on sketches by the celebrated artist Barend van Orley. Also of note are the carved wooden pulpit by Henri Verbruggen illustrating the Last Judgment, and a number of paintings from the school of Rubens. (*See also the chapter on the Lower City, page 183*).

Returning to the Rue Royale via Place Ste-Gudule and the Rue des Colonies, turn into the Rue de la Loi/ Wetstraat. After a few paces is the **Parliament Building** (Palais de la Nation/

Trams still run in Brussels.

Paleis der Natie). The twin chambers of the representative bodies of the Belgian people, the House of Deputies and the Senate, meet here behind a neoclassical facade. The surrounding buildings house various ministries.

These *palazzi* were originally constructed for the Supreme Council of the Duchy of Brabant; at one stage, the courts of justice also sat here. The entire complex was rebuilt during the 1880s following a fire.

Royal connections: Lying opposite the Lower House is the **City Park** (Parc de Bruxelles/Park van Brussel), a model of geometricity. As long ago as the 14th century it served as the royal hunting grounds; the present formal layout dates from 1776 to 1780.

The **Royal Park Theatre** (Théâtre Royal du Parc/Koninklijk Parktheater) can also be reached via the Rue de la Loi. Opposite the Royal Palace, but still within the gardens, stands a bust of the legendary Russian Tsar, Peter the Great. According to the story he went out for a breath of fresh air in the palace grounds after a sumptuous banquet in the Old Castle, and didn't live to return. The bronze likeness marks the spot where his excesses finally got the better of him.

East of the Palace Square stands the **Palace of the Academies** (Palais des Académies/Academienpaleis). The building was originally planned as the residence of the Prince of Orange; it was completed in 1829 in the style of the Italian Renaissance.

Barely 50 years later, the *palazzo* became the headquarters of the Academy founded by the Empress Maria-Theresia. Today it houses the Academy of Sciences, the Academy of Literature and Fine Arts and the Academy of Medical Sciences.

The central path leads straight to the **King's Palace** (Palais du Roi/Paleis van de Koning). Although the Royal Family now resides in Laeken to the north of the city, the building houses the Royal Chancellery and a number of

audience rooms and offices. When the Royal standard flutters from the roof, it is an indication that the King is present on official business. Parts of the palace are open to the public from late July to early September.

In earlier times the site of the present palace was occupied by the Dukes of Brabant. The building was destroyed by fire during the cold winter of 1731. There was virtually no water available to extinguish the inferno because everything was frozen. An attempt was made to quench the flames with beer, but it was to no avail and the castle was burned to the ground. During the 19th century Leopold II had the castle rebuilt in the style of Louis XVI. Then, at the beginning of the 20th century, it was remodelled and extended once again.

At No 7 Place du Palais, behind the Royal Palace, is the **Museum of Dynasty** (Musée de la Dynastie), which is housed in the beautiful Hotel Bellevue, the former royal apartments, which alone are worth a visit. The museum contains a reverential history of the Belgian Royal Family from King Leopold I to the King Baudouin.

At the junction of Place du Palais and the Rue Royale, continuing northwards along for a short distance, the visitor will soon arrive at the **Palace of Fine Arts** (Palais des Beaux Arts/Paleis voor Schone Kunsten). Lying between the Rue Royale and the Rue Ravenstein/Ravensteinstraat, it contains a number of assembly halls for banquets, exhibitions and is Brussels' premier concert hall. The building was designed by Victor Horta and completed in 1928.

Double back and you find yourself on **Place Royale/Koningsplein**, built during the 18th century on the summit of the Coudenberg hill. Constructed in the style of Louis XVI, it still retains the elegant proportions which characterise many of the sections of the city rebuilt in the latter half of the 18th century under the orders of Charles of Lorraine. He governed Brussels from 1744 on behalf of Empress Maria-Theresa, under

In the Parc de Bruxelles: three men and a dog.

whose reign Brussels enjoyed a long period of prosperity and stability.

Of particular note are the classical facades of the houses lining the square. Behind a pillared portico with a flat gable recalling the entrance to a Roman temple is hidden the elegant **Chapel of St James on the Coudenberg**, the "Royal parish church", which dates from the 18th century, although there has been a place of worship on this site since the 12th century. Surveying the scene from the middle of the Place Royale is the statue of **Godfrey of Bouillon**, the famous crusader who with 20,000 soldiers joined the First Crusade in 1096 with the intention of recapturing Jerusalem from the Saracens. He was duly elected ruler of Jerusalem in 1099, but died after a reign of only a year.

Originally standing sentinel here was a statue of Charles of Lorraine, upon whose orders the square was constructed. When metal was in short supply during the French Revolution, the bronze statue was unceremoniously melted down.

From the opposite side of the Place Royale there is a fine view of the Lower City. On the horizon the slim tower of the Town Hall soars skywards above the Grand' Place. The foreground is dominated by ministry buildings, the National Bank, the Philips Tower and – to the far right – the massive St Michael's Cathedral, overlooking the Lower City.

Museums and modern art: Just off the Place Royale is the Old England building, a former department store. As from summer 2000 it will be the spacious new home of the **Instrument Museum** (Musée Instrumental), which will contain an outstanding collection of over 6,000 exhibits, many of them unique: bronze-age musical instruments, simple Indian flutes, a collection of handsome wind instruments, including the saxophone, patented in 1845 by Adolphe Sax, an inventor from Dinant in southern Belgium.

Relaxing opposite the Church of Notre-Dame-du-Sablon.

A few metres past the square lies the the **Royal Galleries of Art** (Musées Royaux des Beaux Arts de Belgique/ Koninklijke Musea voor Schone Kunsten van Belgie). Napoleon laid the foundations of the collection in 1801, with the aim of introducing beauty into the lives of the people, and it has been extended many times over the years. Since their complete restoration in 1984, the galleries have been considered to be amongst the most important collections in the world.

The **Museum of Ancient Art** contains works from the 15th, 16th, 17th and 18th centuries. Among the masterpieces displayed are paintings by Brueghel, Rubens, Jordaens, Tintoretto, Tiepolo, Bosch, Hals and Rembrandt.

The equally impressive **Museum of Modern Art** (Musée d'Art Moderne/ Museum voor Moderne Kunst) was completed in 1984, although it cannot actually be seen by passers-by since the galleries are contained in eight under-ground floors. It includes French and Belgian paintings and drawings and sculpture of the 19th and 20th centuries. Many of the artists whose works are to be seen here enjoy international fame, among them Stevens, de Baekeleer, Dubois, Khnopff, David, Coubet, Gauguin, Delacroix, Corot, Ensor, Delvaux, Dali and Magritte.

Turning right into the Rue du Musée/ Museumstraat, you come across the quiet and graceful square of the **Place du Musée**, dominated by the pleasingly proportioned facade of the former residence of Charles of Lorraine. A statue of him surveys the palace from a pedestal across the square.

Forming another part of this extensive complex is the **Royal Library of Albert I** (Albertinum) on Boulevard de l'Empereur. On view in the Albertinum are the private apartments of Charles of Lorraine, as well as woodcarving etchings in the **Prints Collection** (Chalcographie). The Albertinum was given its present form in the middle of **Affairs of the heart.**

the 20th century in memory of King Albert I, who died in 1934.

The library itself contains over five million volumes, including the reconstructed studies of Emile Verhaeren and Michael de Ghelderode. Within the library are several smaller museums. The **Museum of Books** (Musée du Livre et Cabinet des Donations, entrance on the Mont des Arts) illustrates the history of the book, from the 10th century to the present day, with valuable printed works and manuscripts, some of them gifts of prominent families. The **Audio-visual archive** is a collection mainly related to French and Belgian literature. Also worth visiting is the **Museum of Printing**, which includes typefaces, lithographic equipment, bookbinding and typesetting apparatus from the 18th to the 20th centuries.

The **Mont des Arts** is an extensive complex lying between the Place de l'Albertine/Albertinaplein and the Place Royale/Koningsplein. It was constructed during the 1950s in accordance with plans drawn up by a team of architects, Ghobert, Houvoux and Van Steenberghen.

Returning to the Place Royale, the tour continues along the Rue de la Régence/Regentschapstraat. After a short distance the visitor will reach the **Eglise du Sablon/Zavelkerk**, also known as the Eglise Notre-Dame-des-Victoires (the Church of our Lady of the Victories). It was erected and magnificently decorated by the archers of Brussels during the 15th and 16th centuries. Of particular interest are the stained-glass windows, chandelier, the murals in the choir and the carved wooden pulpit (1697) as well as the tomb of Count Lamoral and the Thurn & Tassis family chapel. The Eglise du Sablon is considered to be one of the finest examples of high Gothic architecture still standing.

The centre of the **Place du Grand Sablon** is dominated by the Fountain of Minerva, a present from the Earl of Aylesbury in recognition of the asylum

At the local greengrocer's.

granted to him by Brussels during his exile from England.

Surrounding the square are antique shops, street cafés where you can watch the world go by, and a number of excellent restaurants, including **L'Ecailler du Palais Royal** and **Castello Banfi**. The Sablon District as a whole is dominated by the antique trade, and there is a lively antiques market here on Saturday and Sunday mornings.

Returning to the Rue de la Régence, cross the street to reach the **Place du Petit Sablon/Kleine Zavel**. The small, well-tended park in the centre is a pleasant place to stop and rest your feet and is surrounded by attractive wrought-iron railings; it is distinguished by a set of 48 bronze statues, each representing an ancient guild or craftsmen's association. The first bears the features of Henry Beyaert, the master builder whose bust is also to be seen on the older Belgian 100-franc notes. Dominating the ensemble is a group of statues at the centre of the park; it depicts the two counts Egmont and Horn, the twin heroes who were beheaded in the Grand' Place during the uprising against the bloodthirsty Duke of Alva in the 16th century. The two noblemen are surrounded by famous humanists such as Dedenée, Mercator and Van Orley.

Forming the background to the square is the **Palais d'Egmont**, built during the 16th century and remodelled along classical lines during the 18th century. Among its famous residents were Louis XV and Voltaire. Today it is the home of the Foreign Ministry. It was here that Denmark, the United Kingdom and Ireland signed the Treaty of Accession to the European Community in 1972.

Symbol of power: Continue the tour either by returning to the Rue de la Régence or by taking the Rue aux Laines/Wolstraat, which passes in front of the Palais Egmont. Both streets lead to the magnificent **Palace of Justice** (Palais de Justice), whose enormous bulk dominates the whole district. A large section of the Marolles, one of Brussels' oldest *quartiers*, had to be demolished to make way for its construction. The hill on which the palais stands used to be the site where public hangings were carried out in the city.

The architect, Joseph Poelaert, was commissioned to design a monument to the Belgian constitution. In other words, it was intended that the building should be larger than any other sacred or military edifice in the city. In the end, his project developed into a complex of gigantic proportions which symbolised Belgium's rise to industrial and colonial power in the world.

The dome is 104 metres (333 ft) high; the total floor area comprises 25,000 sq. metres (30,000 sq. yards). The palais includes 27 audience chambers and 245 smaller rooms. Then there are numerous offices, and of course the prisoners' cells. The entrance hall alone measures 3,600 sq. metres (4,300 sq. yards). The Palais de Justice was constructed between 1866 and 1883; unfortunately its

The Porte de Hal, one of the old city gates.

creator did not live to see its completion, for he died in 1879. Poelaert chose to construct the palais in the eclectic manner, uniting virtually every architectural style into a synthesis of the arts.

However, in recent years, the behemoth has become more a symbol of miscarriages of justice. The paedophile and corruption scandals, in particular, have made the courts a natural focus for citizens' protests against the ineptitude of the judicial system.

At the feet of the Palais lies the **Marolles** district, the true heart of the city (described in greater detail in its own chapter). It was in the Marolles that the Brussels dialect *brusseleir* evolved: a hotchpotch of Flemish, French and Spanish with a liberal sprinkling of Hebrew and German expressions.

Taking one of the side streets onto Rue des Minimes and then Rue Haute, visit one of the loveliest churches in the city, the **Church of Our Lady of the Chapel** (Eglise Notre-Dame-de-la-Chapelle/Kapellekerk), which is situated on the corner of the Boulevard de L'Empereur/Keizerslaan.

The architecture demonstrates characteristics of various epochs: it was begun in the 12th century, but the main nave dates from the 15th century and the existing tower from the 18th century. Apart from a lovely wooden statue of St Margaret of Antioch dating from 1520 the church contains the tombs of Pieter Brueghel the Elder – whose black marble monument is surmounted by a copy of a Rubens original of Christ handing over the keys of heaven to St Peter – and Anneessens (the Anneessens Tower, a remnant of the old city wall, stands on the Rue de Rollebeek/Rollebeekstraat).

South of the Marolles is the **Porte de Hal/Hallepoort**, the remains of one of the seven gates of Brussels' second fortified wall surrounding the city, which roughly followed the route now taken by the modern boulevards du Pentagone. The original masonry is untouched apart from some alterations carried out during the 19th century.

The Belgians eat their chips either with mayonnaise or mussels.

THE MAROLLES

Standing on the terrace on the west side of the Palais de Justice and surveying the town from above, you may fail to spot the district closely stacked at your feet – the Marolles. To notice it, cast your eyes downwards and then look out towards the south. At the end of the 19th century a considerable section of the Marolles had to be demolished to make way for the massive Palais de Justice.

The district developed in the 17th century as a residential area for the craftsmen working on the palatial homes of the Upper City. It remained a thriving working-class district until the 1870s when, with the paving over of the Senne, the wealthier artisans moved out to the city's suburbs. From then on the district declined, eventually becoming a refuge for the poor and every new wave of immigrants in the city.

The continued survival of the Marolles and its inhabitants is due purely to their dogged determination to hold on to their district; they have taken up a common and yet highly individual fight against their wretched living conditions and intruders alike. The traditional appearance of the entire district is perpetually threatened by urban redevelopment and property speculation. An even more insidious enemy, however, is the deterioration of the fabric of the buildings, for the inhabitants have no funds available for essential repairs. Many of the historic buildings are crumbling; some are falling down.

The Marolles seem condemned to economic ruin because the forces of economics of the modern metropolis have deprived many of the small businesses and shops of their livelihoods.

The district has no clearly defined boundaries; it suffices to note that it lies beneath the Palais de Justice, from the Boulevard de Waterloo, the Porte de Hal, the Boulevard du Midi and the Avenue de Stalingrad as far as the Chapelle des Brigittines on the edge of the aristocratic Grand Sablon district. The principal through roads, running side by side from one end of the Marolles to the other, are the Rue Haute and the Rue Blaes.

The district's inhabitants, some 10,000 in all, lead lives largely independent of the outside world. The daily round and the passing of the seasons have retained their original significance here. Traditionally, the Marolles was a district through which one passed rather than a place where one stayed, and a clear boundary exists between life in the Marolles and the rest of the city, despite the periodic incursions of outsiders.

The original inhabitants are gradually dying or moving away and being replaced by a variety of newcomers. Maghrebis and other immigrants from Mediterranean countries make up half the present population. Most share one characteristic with the original residents: poverty.

However, as the members of the various action groups for the preservation of the Marolles are well aware, property developers have acquired ambitions in the area. The community of immigrants and indigenous Marolles residents has been joined by a high-earning, fashionable crowd, and independent traders and shop owners have jumped on the bandwagon with a succession of boutiques, jewellers, galleries and restaurants. As they penetrate ever deeper into the district they are gradually eroding its true countenance.

And yet, the drab little snack bars are still found on almost every street and for certain at every crossroads, hawking mussels, watery stews, soggy chips and thin draught beer. Also typical are the large, dilapidated tenement blocks containing council flats. One of the city's largest hospitals, the Saint-Pierre, also lies within the Marolles – as does the former fire brigade barracks at the Place du Jeu de Balle, where a series of businesses – mainly art galleries and antiquarian booksellers – have set up shop next to expensive modern houses.

Early each morning the cafés surrounding the Vieux Marché opposite the Fire Station attract their first customers; as many of these

flats of the prosperous Grand Sablon. Here, the contrasts are too marked for comfort.

In some corners, however, the visitor will notice successful attempts at restoration. The numerous action groups are attempting to breathe fresh life into the district and encourage the residents to renovate their homes. Public funds, however, are only available sporadically, the authorities often preferring to place their trust in property sharks and international building firms. For many years they allocated no money at all for the rebuilding of this socially deprived district, finding it easier and more lucrative to encourage

establishments are open until the small hours, some of them – logically enough – do not bother to close at all. They are typical of cafés of this type to be found all over the world: each has its own individual character and its own type of clientèle.

The outsider may well react with incomprehension or consternation at such evident despair, particularly in the La Samaritaine district lying cheek by jowl with art galleries, antique shops, gourmet restaurants and luxury

Left, hanging out the washing in the Marolles. **Above**, fortunate tenants live in the front courtyard; the poorest have to live in the back.

private investment by collaborating with builders and property dealers. Private investment, however, is not a realistic proposition in the Marolles, since the deprivation of its inhabitants is so severe that they are unable to finance any restoration work themselves.

The only real chance for the survival of the traditional countenance of the Marolles lies in the collective organisation of its residents, in negotiations with a clearly-defined third party, and in the abandoning by the municipal authorities of their paternalistic approach to the problems. It remains to be seen whether the individualists who live here will be able to adapt to a workable planning concept.

THE "OTHER" UPPER CITY: PLACE LOUISE

It would perhaps be inaccurate to say that there were two Upper Cities existing side by side in Brussels. On the other hand, the contrast between this upper city and the poor Marolles district or even the grand but more austere Rue Royale is marked.

The complex of streets in question extends from the Porte de Namur down to the Porte de Hal, radiating out from the Louise métro. The city side is demarcated by the **Boulevard Waterloo/ Waterloolaan**; opposite is the **Avenue de la Toison d'Or/Guldenvlieslaan**. Each side of the dual carriageway has its own name.

The boulevard and the Avenue Louise, together with some of the surrounding lanes and passageways, represent the most chic and exclusive district of Brussels, particularly for residential purposes; the main thoroughfares were built around the middle of the 19th century to link the city centre with the Bois de la Cambre.

Life in this upper city is top-notch, as visitors soon realise. The whole place exudes a sense of luxury: shops are chic, residences are discreetly expensive, and the clothes and accessories worn by their wealthy inhabitants are by famous fashion designers. The Boulevard and the Avenue are catwalks as much as thoroughfares.

The most exclusive section of this district is centred on the **Place Louise**, where even the underground station is smart. Alighting from the train, visitors are treated to a blast of jazzed-up classical music. Artistic mosaics, stained glass, enamelwork and a tapestry all contribute to the carefully-tailored ambience of the place.

(Such artistic touches aren't confined to the station on Place Louise: in an effort to individualise the underground stations contemporary artists were brought in to assist in the planning of a

From the Upper City, looking down on the Lower City.

number of the city's stations, including St-Guidon, Aumale, Jacques Brel, Gare de l'Ouest, Osseghem, Etangs Noirs, Comte de Flandre, Rogier, Botanique, Arts-Loi, Luxembourg, Porte de Namur, Anneessens, Bourse, Parc, Mérode, Thieffry, Pétillon, Hankar, Herrmann Debroux, Montgomery, Joséphine-Charlotte, Gribaumont, Roodebeek and Vandervelde.)

The impression of exclusivity hits everyone emerging from the Louise underground station. Walking along the Waterloo side of the boulevard towards the **Porte de Namur/Naamsepoort**, visitors pass art galleries and jeweller's shops in between the chic boutiques of international designers: Yves Saint Laurent, Givenchy, Armani and Jil Sander among them.

Shortly before the Boulevard Waterloo becomes the Boulevard du Régent/Regentlaan, it crosses the **Rue de Namur**, where you can find more boutiques and a couple of antique shops, as well as Pablo's, a lively TexMex restaurant, which has occasional live music

Beyond the Porte de Namur the surroundings becomes somewhat more drab. The area is dominated by European Commission offices, administrative headquarters, banks and insurance companies. Here, your best course of action is to turn round, cross the street, and stroll back along its other side, where the scene quickly becomes more attractive.

On this side the boulevard is known as the **Avenue de la Toison d'Or**. It is flanked by a number of extensive multi-storey shopping arcades. Some of them date originally from the 19th century. These elegant shopping malls reflected the new confidence of the increasingly powerful bourgeoisie of 19th-century Brussels. They were an exciting new concept in retail trade.

One such arcade, bearing the name of the boulevard itself – **Galeries de la Toison d'Or** – lies just a few steps away. The shopping gallery also links the avenue with the Chaussée d'Ixelles/

Elsense Steenweg. Beyond this, you reach another arcade of shops, the **Galerie d'Ixelles**. Leaving this at the Chaussée de Wavre/Waverse Steenweg, the visitor will soon arrive at yet another shopping paradise, the **Galerie de la Porte de Namur**.

The range of goods on offer in these arcades is impressive: perfumeries, fashion boutiques and department stores are interspersed with restaurants and cafés, as well as chocolate and confectionery shops, and a variety of other small boutiques selling items from every corner of the earth.

Continuing along the Avenue de la Toison d'Or towards the Place Louise, you will come across a short flight of steps leading up to the **Church of the Carmelites**. The building contains no ancient art to admire, but it is the setting for regular concerts of classical and church music played on a famous organ. The performances are frequently broadcast on Belgian radio or included in recordings.

Not far away is another gallery bearing the name of the square near which it stands: the **Espace Louise** – a modern version of the celebrated Galeries St-Hubert. This, together with the **Galeries de la Porte Louise** and the **Galeries Louise**, form a glittering labyrinth of stores, ranging from top designers to more affordable high street fashion. Eventually, you reach the Avenue Louise, a lively street with yet more shops selling luxury items.

If you choose to leave the arcade at the Place Stéphanie/Stefanieplein, you will have to retrace your steps for a short distance if you want to explore the **Rue Jourdan/Jourdanstraat**. This pedestrianised street is lined with a rapid succession of popular bars and restaurants, some of which remain open until the small hours of the morning.

As a complete contrast from Avenue Louise, you could venture into the *Matongué* quarter between Chaussée d'Ixelles and Chaussée de Wavre. This is a lively area mainly inhabited by Brussels' Zairean immigrants. The moment you cross the threshold, you are transported into a world of market stalls loaded with exotic food, loud music issuing from cafés and women in brightly coloured African dresses.

Great escapes: You do not have to be an energetic walker to enjoy a short detour to the Cistercian **Abbaye de la Cambre/Ter-Kamerenabdij**. It isn't very far from Avenue Louise and it is well worth exploring. To find it, go down the flight of steps behind Rue du Lac and through a little park as far as the Lakes of Ixelles/Elsene.

Follow the signposts to the right and you will soon reach the abbey, which lies in the middle of a park. The setting is idyllic: fish ponds shimmer amidst the tranquil lawns. The garden terraces, which are laid out on five different levels, attract large numbers of visitors, both locals and out-of-towners, at weekends. The abbey itself, which was founded in the 12th century, has endured numerous tribulations during its

Authentic originals in the Upper City.

long history. Many of the old buildings have recently been restored and today it houses a military academy and Brussels' College of Decorative Arts.

For many years the long, broad avenue leading away from the Place Stéphanie had a long strip of grass and trees in the middle; until 1957 its use was reserved exclusively for horse riding. Today, however, tram lines occupy the open space. The streets to the right and left of the Avenue Louise comprise one of the most expensive residential areas in Brussels today.

The end of Avenue Louise leads directly into the **Bois de Cambre/Ter-Kamerenbos**, Brussels's largest park. It is a large, undulating green space and a favourite destination for local residents – and their dogs. On Sundays in July and August. live music adds to the relaxed atmosphere.

Keener walkers might like to try another popular escape lying to the southeast of the city: the **Forest of Soignes**, which extends into **Tervuren Park**.

Formerly the preserve of charcoal burners and a hunting ground of Emperor Charles V, today the woods extend over 4,380 hectares (17 sq. miles) of hilly countryside and offers plenty of opportunities for walking and cycling. Nestling in one of its valleys are the ruins of the ancient **Abbey of Groenendael**.

Also of interest hereabouts is the **Royal Museum of Central Africa (Musée Royal de l'Afrique du Centre/Museum voor Midden-Afrika** in Tervuren, with displays portraying Belgium's colonial past. It has a wide range of exhibits on Africa's wildlife, environment, culture and historical development, with particular emphasis on the Congo (*see also page 211 of the chapter "Around Brussels"*).

Situated on the edge of the Forest of Soignes is the fairy-tale **Rixenart Castle**, dating from the 17th century. Built of red brick in the style of the Renaissance, it houses a valuable collection of historic furniture, Gobelin tapestries and wall hangings from Beauvais.

The wealthy reside in houses such as these.

THE MARKETS

If you can't find a particular item on the market stalls of Brussels, it probably doesn't exist at all, for you can buy virtually anything here. Brussels' markets are some of the best places to find authentic local colour; and every day of the week is market day somewhere in the city.

One of the most interesting of the city's various markets is the **Antiques Market** which takes place every weekend (Saturday 9am–3pm; Sunday 9am–1pm) on the Place du Grand Sablon; you may even be lucky enough to find a bargain here, though you will probably have to search for it amongst a good deal of junk, some of it overpriced junk. In the Antiques Market, as elsewhere, the line between art and kitsch is a thin one.

Visitors should be wary of paying the asking price without question. Bartering with the stall holders is expected and considered to be part of the fun. Your best tactic if something catches your eye is to take a stroll around the square whilst you consider your purchasing strategy and the maximum amount you want to pay. Whatever the price you finally agree to, you can be quite sure that it will be less than you would pay in any one of the numerous antique shops found in the area.

Any self-respecting town has a weekly market, but in terms of kaleidoscopic colour and sheer variety few can compare with the market at the Gare du Midi (South Station). It resembles nothing as much as a superb supermarket in the open air; known as the **Exotic Market**, it takes place every Sunday morning from 6am–1.30pm.

The range of goods on offer is almost overwhelming. You can buy clothes for every season of the year. Food of every kind is on sale here too, from live snails to chocolate gâteaux. In between are fragrant bundles of fresh herbs, mounds

of exotic fruits, nuts and spices, piles of pots and pans, pictures, leather goods and books. This is the place to buy olives and spices, fresh cheese and charcuterie. The noise can be deafening: CD and cassette traders turn the volume controls on their speakers to maximum while greengrocers and ironmongers attempt to draw attention to their wares. Cries in Flemish, French, Turkish and Arabic add to the babel of voices. As Jean Cocteau once maintained, "the city of Brussels is one big stage". The market is no exception.

Be sure also to explore the immediate vicinity of the market. The ever-expanding network of stalls has spilled beyond the spacious square itself and now extends into the surrounding side streets, where some of the best buys are to be found, particularly clothes, fabrics and electrical goods.

The city's other markets are decidedly more tranquil. One of these, the daily **Flower Market**, is held from 8am–6pm every day apart from Mondays,

_eft, a
jentleman of
3russels.
Right,
bargain-
hunting at
he Sablon
lea market.

including during the winter months, on the Grand' Place/Grote Markt. The stallholders sit patiently as they wait for interested customers. Their buckets, pots and vases are always full of magnificent blooms. The function of the large umbrellas, in the traditional local colours of red and green, is not merely to provide protection from sun and rain. When they are tipped sideways at a right-angle to the pavement it is a sign by the stallholders that business is bad on the Grand' Place.

On the weekend closest to 15 August every other year (2000, 2002), the blooms and blossoms are not for sale at all, but form part of a magnificent display. On these occasions the city's gardeners and florists spread a gorgeous carpet of flowers right across the square. The best view of the spectacle is from a window of one of the surrounding houses.

Another relatively peaceful market is the **Bird Market**, where only the birdsong disturbs the peace. Every Sunday from 7am to 2pm, breeders arrange their cages in front of the Grand' Place. The contents of these cages range from brightly-coloured songbirds to rather less ostentatious game.

A chorus of avian squawking forms the background music to trading here. High-pitched twitterings are accompanied by the sonorous quacking of ducks, interspersed by the clucking of hens and the cooing of doves. In addition to the stall selling birds, you will find other traders selling bird paraphernalia: seed, nuts, medicines, toys, gadgets and cages of every variety and size.

Not every visitor to the bird market comes with the intention of making a purchase. Many of the enthusiasts just turn up for a chat with the breeders or to discuss the merits of the latest bird seed for their pet canary or budgie. It is a place where experiences are exchanged and hobbies are nurtured.

Sunday best: Lovers of flea markets should try to catch the **Vieux Marché aux Puces** on the Place du Jeu de Balle/

Two of a kind.

Vossenplein. Here, in the heart of the old Marolles district, a small number of stalls can be found on any day of the week. The best day to visit, however, is on Sunday (7am–2pm), when the number often rises to 200. While you're there, take time to explore the rest of this interesting quarter, felt by some to be the very soul of Brussels, with its unusual shops and relaxed atmosphere.

Another Sunday market is to be found on the **Quai des Usines**, where between 7.30am and 1pm used cars are offered for sale at auction. There are some good bargains to be had among the old bangers, but go with someone who knows something about cars if you're seriously intending to buy. New and second-hand car dealers can also be found on the weekends from 6am–1pm in the **Rue Heyvaert** in Anderlecht, to the west of the city centre.

Another favourite Sunday morning stroll takes the visitor to the **Place de la Reine Astrid/Koningin Astridplein** in Jette, where there is a market for paintings, secondhand-books, toys and jewellery, as well as food stalls.

In addition to these regular markets, it is common to see clusters of stalls occupying the various squares dotted across the city. Some of these, however, vanish as quickly as they spring up, or disband without warning for weeks or even months at a time. When winter frosts set in, the number of people willing to man an open-air stall declines. Fair-weather traders don't bother to emerge again until Brussels is enjoying the first warm days of spring.

Fans of old books and newspapers should head for the **Tram Museum** in Woluwe St Pierre, where there is a market on the first Saturday of every month between 8am and 5pm.

There are two traditional **Christmas markets** in December in the city centre: one on the Grand' Place and the other on the Place du Grand Sablon. Both offer arts and crafts for sale, as well as hot food and drinks to warm up a cold afternoon.

A paradise for browsers.

SHOPPING AND NIGHTLIFE

After a sightseeing tour of some of the principal buildings and sites of Brussels, a stroll through the city's shops makes an invigorating change. A leisurely shopping trip will give you a further insight into the way of life and culture of the people of Brussels, whether you're souvenir-hunting for lace or handmade chocolates, or prefer to scour the city's antique shops in the hope of finding a more unusual gift or even a bargain to take home.

The metropolitan area includes a wide range of shopping districts. The heart of the city forms one vast shopping centre. Visitors can pass many happy hours perusing their wonderful shop window displays and even more spending money. Many shops offer arrangements for tax-free purchases provided that the goods supplied are for export only.

Where to shop: The main department stores are not quite on a par with equivalent establishments in other European cities. However, the entire length of **Rue Neuve/Niewstraat** is a pedestrian zone, and contains a colourful array of boutiques and specialist shops.

Brussels proudly claims to possess more shopping arcades than any other city in Europe. Among the best-loved are the long-established **Galeries Saint-Hubert**, whose elegant classical facade is decorated by columns and a central Renaissance-style motif proclaiming *Omnibus omnia* – "everything for everyone" – as well as modern shopping centres such as **City 2** on the Rue Neuve.

Apart from housing a large number of small units, the lower level of City 2 has plenty of cafés and bars where you can revive before resuming your expedition. A variety of fast food establishments ply their trade: from sandwich and juice bars, Italian pasta and icecream to hamburgers with typical Belgian chips. There's also a GB supermarket. The shops themselves sell mainly fashion and electrical goods. FNAC is good for CDs, concert tickets and books in several languages, and Inno is Belgium's premier department store.

The shopping centre's designers placed great emphasis on the visual appearance of the shopping complex. However, some decades later, although the shops are still well worth exploring, the dazzling new Espace Louise puts it in the shade.

Rather nobler in appearance are the Galeries Saint-Hubert: the **Galerie du Roi**, the **Galerie de la Reine** and the **Galerie des Princes**. The elegant glass roofs are supported by a steel-framed vault; the shopping galleries, dating from 1847, house mainly luxury boutiques. Here you will find everything the well-heeled Brussels citizen might need, from jewellery and leather to curtain fabric and books, but don't expect it to be cheap.

Emerging from the Galerie du Roi, just across the road to your right, you will see **La Mort Subite**, one of Brus-

A basement near the Grand' Place sells old engravings, maps and pictures.

sels's best-loved bars, and a fine place to soak up some atmosphere along with a glass or two of excellent Belgian beer.

While in Brussels, it's definitely worth sampling some of the capital's particular specialities. When it comes to making chocolates the Belgians are in a class of their own, and there are shops everywhere. Godiva and Neuhaus are the classiest; Leonidas are cheap and cheerful, but still taste pretty good. Other specialities are crystal, particularly Val St Lambert, pewter ware, and Villeroy & Boch china. Comic-strip fans should head for La Boutique Tintin on Rue de la Colline.

The Grand' Place is always full of tourists, and as a consequence the neighbouring side streets are riddled with souvenir shops. If you want to purchase some genuine Brussels lace you are advised to avoid the shops here and go to Galeries St Hubert and La Manufacture Belge de Dentelles. Also, ask the origin of the lace before you buy; some of the cheaper lace comes from Asia.

In accordance with the French tradition, most so-called cafés here are actually more like pubs, but coffee and cakes are not difficult to find if that's what you want. The city possesses excellent *pâtisseries*, for example Wittamer, and Le Pain Quotidien on the Grand Sablon and Rue Antoine Dansaert. Virtually every street corner has a stall selling the eternally popular waffles, which smell good but tend to glue your jaws together. Popular street food in winter includes hot snails and whelks, and chestnuts.

The galleries between the Grand' Place and the Boulevard Anspach, **Galerie Agora,** the **Galerie du Centre** and the **Galerie Saint-Honoré,** invite the visitor to browse at leisure. Every taste and budget here are catered for here: jeans, leather goods, fashion items and jewellery, souvenirs, and CDs, not to mention body-piercing and tattoos. It is tempting to take a breather from shopping in the galleries in the many little cafés, a number of which are fronted by

a terrace. Two traditional, brown cafés are recommended for a break: **Au Bon Vieux Temps** just outside the Galerie du Centre, and **A La Becasse** on Rue de Tabora.

The **Boulevard Anspach/Anspach-laan** in the neighbourhood of the Stock Exchange is a lively thoroughfare. Lining the section as far as the Place de Brouckère/De Brouckereplein is a succession of fashion boutiques, newsagents, chocolate shops and electrical stores. **Rue Antoine Dansaert** is the place for upmarket designer clothes.

Many cafés are to be found lining the avenues of the inner city in the vicinity of the opera house and the Stock Exchange, including **Le Cirio** and **Le Grand Café**. Definitely not to be missed is **Le Falstaff**, a bar as famous for the beauty of its interior as for the arrogance of its waiters. It is on Rue Henri Maus, and recently re-opened under new management.

The Grand' Place/Grote Markt is where art lovers tend to head first; but music lovers, too, will find plenty to interest them here. In the **Rue du Midi/Zuidstraat** there are numerous music shops. Apart from new and second-hand instruments, many hand-made, musicians can have a damaged instrument repaired. Artists and philatelists are catered for on this same street.

Top shops: The district housing the most attractive luxury boutiques and jeweller's shops lies in the Upper Town. Here, along the **Boulevard Waterloo/Waterloolaan** and in the **Avenue Louise/Louizalaan** between the **Place Louise/Louizaplein** and the **Porte de Namur** you will find branches of every well-known European designer. A number of talented Belgian couturiers, such as Olivier Strelli, have established a reputation beyond their own national boundaries.

The shopping arcades in the Upper Town are amongst the most elegant and expensive in the city. The are the **Galerie Espace Louise**, the **Galerie Louise** and the **Galeries de la Toison d'Or**.

Left, city shops. Right, Galeries Saint-Hubert.

Antique lovers should head for the district surrounding the **Place du Grand Sablon**. As well as the permanent shops surrounding the square, an antiques market is held here on Saturdays and Sundays. It's a lively and picturesque affair, the stalls set against the backdrop of the square's attractive historic facades. It's worth having a good rummage through the goods on sale. Rare stamps, weapons and crystalware are amongst the many items which can be found.

Unlike in some countries, in Belgium the word "antique" is not synonymous with "old junk". A distinction is made between antique dealers, interior decorators and secondhand furniture dealers. Antique dealers belong to a special organisation, the *Chambre des Antiquaires*. By virtue of their membership in the association, antique dealers guarantee the authenticity of the items they sell. It is customary for such dealers to place a large sign bearing the message "Chambre des Antiquaires" in their shop window.

The so-called "interior decorators" do not deal exclusively in antiques. They see themselves as merchants of period furniture, offering for purchase examples of every imaginable period. The secondhand furniture salesmen are really flea market traders. They attempt to sell anything and everything which looks as if it is old and well-used. Their shops and stalls can be found all over town, including on the Marché aux Puces, the flea market in the Marolles district.

Also worth a look on the Place du Grand Sablon is the **Sablon Shopping Garden**, Belgium's longest art gallery.

Since business hours for shops are not controlled by law, some shops open late into the evening, particularly in the city centre. On Fridays larger shops and supermarkets are open until 8 or 9pm; on the remaining weekdays they are open until 6 or 7 pm. In addition, some bakers, butchers and small retailers open their shops on Sunday mornings.

Brussels is the ideal place for those who enjoy strolling through markets. In

A welcome Belgian beer.

spite of all the chic boutiques, the citizens of Brussels love a bargain and you will come across clusters of stalls at almost every turn. The preceding chapter of this book deals with this aspect of the city's everyday life.

Time to boogie: In the city's nightlife, too, a clear distinction is drawn between the Upper and the Lower City. The differences are most obvious in the style and prices found in the various bars and discotheques. Whereas in the Lower City casual dress is the order of the day, a tie and jacket are essential prerequisites for an evening's entertainment in the smart hotels of the Upper City. Establishments in the Upper Town tend to be more expensive.

Brussels offers its visitors a wide choice of nocturnal entertainment: great restaurants, dancing and live music, plus a huge variety of bars, both traditional and trendy, open late into the night, as well as night clubs and discos. And Brussels' love of cafés has gone beyond the neighbourhood local, to generate an

aminated and cosmopolitan scene, often with music attached.

Encouraging scene: Although it may once have been the case that Brussels and nightlife are two mutually exclusive ideas, the reality is a good deal more enjoyable. While most *Bruxellois* are probably happiest when placing an order at their favourite restaurant, or settling in for the evening at their neighbourhood café, there is plenty of action going on elsewhere. And the scene is developing constantly, acquiring the sophistication worthy of the city's aspiration to be Europe's capital.

If you're in search of a night on the town, the following areas are full of bars and restaurants, and buzzing with life at night: Place du Châtelain, just off Avenue Louise, Rue Marché au Charbon and the area surrounding Place St-Géry.

The **Mirano Continental** on Chaussée de Louvain remains one of the smartest dance-venues in town, where the young and hip can admire each other — and themselves of course. Only hot-blooded Latin types need apply at **Cartagena**, in Rue Marché au Charbon, along with all those cool northerners whose blood could use a little heat.

Le Garage in Rue Dusquenoy has lately lost brownie points with the really chic crowd, but its near-Grand' Place location makes it a popular disco with tourists and locals alike.

Jazz is one of Brussels' passions. As well as the annual Belga and Brosella Jazz Festivals and the Jazz Rallye, there is a steady diet of good music throughout the year.

Jazz bars come and go, but there are several perennially popular venues which are a good bet for a night out. **Preservation Hall** in Rue de Londres remains a suitably smoky and crowded joint. The programme changes frequently but the quality remains high, and it occasionally features musicians from its namesake in New Orleans. **Sounds** is a well-established bar on Rue de la Tulipe, where the live music nor-

Adult entertainment at Chez Flo.

mally starts around 10pm. Both these venues are in the Upper City close to the Porte de Namur. The **Brussels Hilton** on Boulevard de Waterloo does a jazz brunch on Sunday, while **Travers** on Rue Traversière in St Josse features modern jazz.

Fans of Parisian-style cabaret could try **Black Bottom** in Rue du Lombard, whose compères, Jerry and Martigny, keep things moving in a languid sort of way. Transvestite cabaret is on offer at **Café Flo** on Rue au Beurre just off the Grand' Place.

Le Show Point in Place Stéphanie is also a cabaret, of sorts. It's a glitzy, platinum-card kind of place, with lots of scantily-clad dancing girls, and others waiting in an interested sort of way outside.

Food first: Brussels is a bastion of gastronomy, as shown in the chapter "Brussels à la Carte" (*see page 149*). Some of the best restaurants are in the neighbourhood of the **Grand' Place** and **Place Ste-Catherine** on the Quai au Bois à Brûler and Quai aux Briques. In general, the quality of the food on offer in the city's 1,800-plus restaurants is high. Belgian cuisine includes meat, fish and poultry dishes; typical examples are *waterzooi*, a delicate soup-cum-stew with fish or chicken, Brabant-style pheasant (with braised chicory) and beef stewed in Gueuze beer.

For wide-awake revellers, there are well over 100 restaurants offering a wide range of food late at night. Two typical Belgian restaurants serving good food in pleasing surroundings are **Cap de Nuit** on Vieille Halle-aux-Blés near the Grand' Place, and **La Grande Porte** on Rue Notre Seigneur, on the edge of the Marolles district.

And if you don't want a full meal when you emerge from a nightclub, head for a *friture* – a snack bar serving chips with everything, especially mussels, kebabs and sausages; every district has one and many stay open till dawn. Try the Rue des Bouchers and Rue de la Violette.

On tonight: the Big Kaai Bigband.

Anyone searching for famous sons and daughters of Brussels might well begin with a survey of the city's street names. Every other plaque and signpost that you come across on a tour of the town comemmorates a local celebrity.

A leisurely stroll through the city centre may well start from the Place de Brouckère. This square recalls **Charles de Brouckère**, one of the fathers of the Belgian constitution of 1831. He later became the Minister of the Interior and the Minister of Defence; in addition, he was one of the founders of the Free University of Brussels and the Bank of Belgium. De Brouckère's career was a long and varied one; at different points in his life it included university professor, a member of parliament, a city councillor and a magistrate. The reverential citizens of Brussels referred to him affectionately as the "Great Mayor".

Broad avenues fan out in all directions from the Place de Brouckère. The most famous thoroughfare in the entire city, the Boulevard Anspach, is named after **Jules Anspach**, who ruled Brussels in his capacity as mayor at the end of the last century. The city was in severe financial difficulties at the time; nonetheless Anspach was able to win the support of King Leopold I, a monarch known for his gargantuan building projects and ambitious plans for urban renovation.

Other names encountered here include those of Emile Jacqmain, Adolphe Max and Lemonnier. **Emile Jacqmain** was a member of the city education committee before World War I. Together with **Adolphe Max**, the mayor at the time, and the juror **Lemonnier**, he was arrested and deported by the Germans during the war. After their release in 1917 the three largest and finest avenues in the city were named after them.

Right, a welcoming face.

The decision by the city council of the time was virtually unanimous; Adolphe Max himself was the only councillor who abstained from the vote.

After the 1830 Revolution and the foundation of the Belgian State, the Stock Exchange underwent a period of rapid expansion. The **Bishoffsheim** family, wealthy bankers from Mainz, settled in the capital of the newly-created state and founded a private bank there. The youngest son of the family, Jonathan, was a juror, senator and director of the National Bank; he played a decisive role in the public life of the city. In addition to his many other good works, he founded several schools, including one for girls – quite a rarity at the time. The people of Brussels subsequently honoured their benefactor by naming a street after him.

Jean Brouchoven, Count of Bergeyck, is one of the city's less well known sons. Yet he played a not insignificant role in the everyday lives of the capital's inhabitants. At the end of the 17th century he was senior treasurer in the service of the governor Maximilian of Bavaria. He had the remarkable idea of introducing progressive taxation rates. In those days craftsmen and traders were liable to pay a fixed sum each year, regardless of whether a tradesman sold a single item or 100.

The idea that taxation should be linked to turnover was a radical innovation in those days. Naturally, Brouchoven's suggestion that tradespeople should be taxed according to this new principle was greeted with great enthusiasm by the governor. He was in severe financial difficulties at the time and could do with the extra cash it would raise.

Perhaps his enthusiasm wasn't shared by everyone in the country. The state took three centuries to decide to name one of the capital's street after the man responsible for boosting the public purse so effectively.

A question of identity: An account of the naming of the Rue Plétinckx is particularly interesting. According to one **Another masterpiece.**

explanation, the street was named after the worthy **Monsieur Plétinckx** who, just before the turn of the century, worked as the director of the "Amigo" – not the luxury hotel that bears that name today, but the drying-out cells in the Town Hall prison nearby, known mockingly among 19th-century Brussels citizens as the "Hotel Plétinckx".

Jean d'Osta, a Brussels folk historian, who supplied much valuable information on local personalities for this chapter and who knows Brussels as if it were his own backyard, hopes that a memorial may one day be raised in memory of M. Plétinckx (he was awarded the freedom of the city in his lifetime). He doubts, however, the veracity of this colourful explanation of the Rue Plétinckx's name and maintains less romantically that the street is named after a general who in 1830 crushed a popular revolt in the Lower City.

The first mayor of Brussels after the 1830 revolution was **Nicolas Rouppe**. The biography of this archetypal opportunist is truly remarkable. In 1786 he was a Doctor of Theology, he became a Jacobin during the French Revolution and in 1799 he was a *Commissaire du Directoire*. In 1830 he became mayor of Brussels for the first time. Even after the Revolution he was re-elected to this exalted position. In those days he was what is now known as a turncoat.

The overwhelming achievement of **Charles Buls** during his 20-year period as mayor of the city was to restore the city's market square, Grand' Place, to its former glory and magnificence. A sculpture of him with his little dog now stands on Place de l'Agora and a side street in the vicinity bears the name of this famous son of the city, who died in 1899.

In the same street, on the right-hand side of the Town Hall, stands a statue of another famous inhabitant, **Evrard 't Serclaes**. He freed the city from the tyranny of the Counts of Flanders in 1356. A local superstition claims that anyone who touches the statue's bronze

A portrait of the artist as an old man.

hand will receive good luck for a year. The tradition is a relatively new one. At one time the market traders had a monopoly on this source of good fortune, but during the past 50 years travel guides have notified a wider public about the statue's powers.

Nowadays hardly anyone would ever mention the names of the brothers **François** and **Jérôme Duquesnoy** were it not for the fact that the city owes one of them – which one is uncertain – the statue of the city's most famous "child" of all, **Manneken Pis**. Not far from the street named after the Duquesnoys lies the Rue de l'Etuve; it is here that the "Menneke", as he is known by local residents, has stood since 1469. (*Manneken* is the Dutch translation, and is therefore by no means popular with every resident.)

The full history of the capital's most famous son would occupy an entire book in itself. Menneke Pis has survived many trials and tribulations over the years: wars, kidnappings, wilful damage and all manner of official ceremonies. The little statue possesses over 300 outfits of clothing and folkloric costumes from all five continents; he has been mentioned in poems and songs. His story and its significance have been dissected by researchers and scientists, including sociologists and even sexologists. Traders in the vicinity of the statue are particularly fond of the Manneken – they make a fortune out of him.

For the people of Brussels the little statue is a symbol of their determination to resist repression. He is considered to embody all kinds of virtues, though not even his most ardent fans would claim he is in any way aristocratic. The citizens of Brussels see the little fellow ("*ketje*"), this son of the people, as cheeky, shameless, bold, fearless, cunning, inventive, mocking, rebellious and unbending. Above all, he has no compunction in showing his scorn for all oppressors, tyrants and despots.

The names of some less well-known but real Brussels heroes can be found in

Giant dolls in the August Meyboom procession.

the names of the 19th-century houses in the Marolles: Bals, Bruxe, Bullinckx, Canivet, Defuisseau, Gerard, Jacobs, Peters, Puttemans, Ronsmans, Van Capenberg. They were known in the district by names such as Dikke Louis, Madame Fanny, Fintje and Léon. **Brueghel** lived here for a period, too, at 130, Rue Haute. Only one side street in the Marolles was named after the celebrated Brussels artist.

A far less famous painter was a somewhat droll Brussels personality: **Joseph Stevens** who specialised in painting dogs. His memory is also preserved by a street name.

A more controversial figure was the local architect **Joseph Poelaert**, whose most monumental work, the Palais de Justice, is impossible to overlook. Many think of the 19th-century builder as a megalomaniac. The Palais de Justice was certainly a mammoth project.

Poleart made himself particularly unpopular with the local population of the Marolles because he built his "Palace of Justice" on the city's Execution Hill, scene of public hangings, which rises directly above the Marolles quarter. The people of the district, who even today see themselves as the "original inhabitants" of the city, considered Poelaert a tyrant who wanted to drive them out of their homes. To this day, the word "Architek" is sometimes used as a term of disparagement.

Illusions of grandeur: Madame **Albertine Fronsac**, who was better known to her many friends and admirers as "Titine", acquired a certain degree of fame in Brussels during the 1920s. She was a singer/actress who performed topical songs during the revues at the Alhambra, a venerably pompous theatre whose passing is still regretted by many local citizens. In 1959 she remained unshakeable in her conviction that the Place Albertine had been named after her. It had not, but the people in the cafés and brasseries around the "Monnaie" were quite happy to leave the ageing *chanteuse* to her illusions.

Below left, modelling jewellery. Below right, breather for a bandsman.

Another street at the heart of the city is named after **Auguste Orts**, a descendant of a famous old legal family in Brussels, who made his mark as university professor, member of parliament and juror.

Here the visitor will find traces of the most important theatre of the turn of the century, the "Olympia". It was the stage of the premiere of the most famous play in the Brussels folk repertory, *Le Mariage de Mademoiselle Beulemans* ("The Marriage of Miss Beulemans"). The work was translated into 10 languages and was performed by companies all over the world. The heroine's father, Mr Beulemans, is one of the most popular of Brussels folk heroes.

Those wanting to see living, breathing Brussels characters can meet **Paul van Kueken** in person in the Rue du Houblon. He is one of the multi-talented people characteristic of Old Brussels. He is a goldsmith, painter, humorist and chairman – or at least member – of various folk associations, including the

Organisation of Restaurateurs and Traders of the *Vismet* (Fishmarket). Nowadays, originals of the calibre of Van Kueken are a rarity.

The modern capital of today isn't very fertile ground for originality. Life moves too fast and, by and large, the citizens are too conservative, always keen to conform. For this reason, real individuals are seldom found outside the older districts.

The Toone family, the puppeteers who run the marionette theatre cum restaurant Toon VII, and Pol, local character and late lamented landlord of the old *Bierodrome*, represent a dying species, firm supporters of Brussels' traditions and festivals.One such is that of the *Riesen*, the giant-sized, massive folkloric dolls, with names such as Antje, Mieke, Jefke and Rooske, which every year on 9 August are carried in procession through the streets of the old town to where a giant maytree is planted.

Saintly rivals: The patron saint of all citizens of Brussels, great and humble, is St Michael. But, although it is his statue on the Town Hall that spreads protective wings over the city, his guardianship is not uncontested. St Gudula has some claim to the title; the capital's principal church, for instance, was always referred to by local residents as St Gudula's, even though it was actually dedicated to St Gudula and St Michael.

But the virginal Gudula, alas, did not have the support of the church authorities: on investigation, Cardinal Suenens discovered that the Vatican held no record of the canonisation of Gudula and peremptorily decided to dedicate the cathedral to St Michael alone. However, he had not reckoned on the local citizens' loyalty to their St Gudula. They felt no real affection for the warrior archangel Michael, always portrayed dressed in armour and brandishing his sword. They loved instead the gentle Lady Gudula, a native of Brabant who remained chaste her whole life long. Thus the cathedral remains what it always was: "St Gudula's".

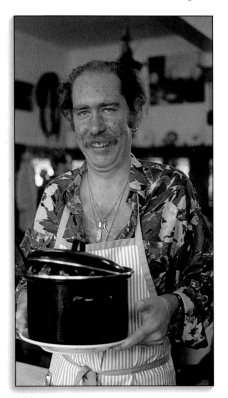

Left, mussels cooked with garlic and white wine, and eaten with chips, is a typical Brussels favourite. **Right**, roasted chestnuts are also popular.

BRUSSELS À LA CARTE

There are few cities on the continent which can claim a denser concentration of top restaurants than Brussels. Its only rival is Paris; and some connoisseurs would dispute even this. Gastronomic critics rate the restaurants in Brussels very highly; their standards of food and service are considered exceptional. Even the most discriminating food buffs can expect to have all their wishes fulfilled here.

Some gourmets maintain that the best chefs in France originally came from Belgium. It is certainly true that the country's cuisine, and in particular that of the capital itself, has a decidedly French accent.

International specialist gastronomic publications such as the *Guide Delta* provide the latest reviews of the Belgian capital's restaurant scene. In addition, a team of experienced restaurant critics produces an annual guide entitled *Restaurants Gourmet*, obtainable from the local tourist office (TIB) in the Town Hall on the Grand' Place/Grote Markt. It provides an excellent and up-to-date introduction to the best eating establishments in Brussels. The critics employ a fleur-de-lis rating system to guide readers in their choice. A maximum of five fleurs-de-lis is awarded to what they consider to be the most distinguished restaurants in Brussels.

In this city where culinary excellence is taken for granted it seems almost invidious to single out individual establishments for praise. The top restaurants in Brussels are world famous; and many of the gourmet places listed here are representative of other less famous establishments (*for further recommendations see also the index of restaurants in Travel Tips*).

Almost next door to each other in the vicinity of Koekelberg Basilika (Brussels, 1083) are a pair of celebrated restaurants bearing the names of their owner-chefs. **Bruneau**, owned by Jean-Pierre and Claire Bruneau (73–75 Avenue Broustin) is one of only a very few restaurants in the Brussels area to have been awarded the ultimate accolade – the coveted three Michelin stars. **Claude Dupont**, run by the man himself and his wife (46 Avenue Vital-Riethuisen), has two. The specialities on offer in both these restaurants vary according to season and reflect the chefs' daily visits to the local market: fresh game, fine poultry, vegetables and salads and herbs. Since neither restaurant is large, you are advised to reserve a table well in advance.

Dine in style: If you want divine style as well as superb cuisine head for **Comme Chez Soi** (23 Place Rouppe). Here Pierre Wynants, its owner-chef serves three-star nouvelle cuisine specialities in an exquisite dining room with a belle-époque atmosphere recalling the decorative style of Victor Horta, the famous Brussels architect of the 1920s and '30s.

Alternatively you might like to try **La Maison du Cygne** on the Grand' Place/Grote Markt lying at the very heart of the city. The entrance is discreetly tucked away in the Rue Charles Buls. It is a charming and elegant establishment and the perfect venue for a celebration dinner. The panelled interior is matched by original coffered ceilings, mellow woodwork, and walls hung with copies of Flemish masters. The cuisine combines French and Belgian influences. One impressed restaurant critic commented thus on a visit to the restaurant: "To sum up, we should rejoice that establishments like this one still exist here in Europe – not casual meeting places for the jet set but the focal points of a well-established tradition of *les plaisirs de la table*."

At **L'Ecailler du Palais Royal** (18, Rue Bodenbroeck), René Falk and Attilio Basso are renowned for their exquisite seafood delicacies: nowhere is the fish fresher or more skilfully prepared than here.

Preceding pages: lobster is a popular choice in Belgian seafood restaurants. **Left,** taking a break in the Falstaff.

Near the Bois de la Cambre stands the **Villa Lorraine** (28 Chaussée de la Hulpe), for many years a favourite gourmet rendezvous. The setting bordering the wooded park is splendid, particularly in summer. Among Freddy Vandecasserie's specialities are wild game in season and the incomparable *écrevisses Villa Lorraine*, fresh-water crayfish served with a sumptuous sauce of white wine and cream.

Many of the city's best seafood restaurants are concentrated around the Place Sainte Catherine. **La Belle Maraîchère** is an award-winning restaurant set in a gabled Flemish renaissance town house, whose specialities include *waterzooi de trois poissons,* a chunky fish stew made with three types of fish. **La Sirène d'Or** is one of Brussels' most renowned restaurants. The owner, Robert van Duüren, was once chef to the then Prince of Liège, now King Albert II. **Les Crustacés** on the Quai aux Briques is a shrine to the lobster, in all its forms.

Brussels' top hotels also offer *haute cuisine* created by distinguished chefs. **La Maison du Boeuf** at the Hilton Hotel on Boulevard Waterloo and the Radisson SAS's **Sea Grill** at 47 Rue du Fossé aux Loups are both renowned and luxurious restaurants.

The outskirts of Brussels are also blessed with a number of first-class restaurants, including **De Bijgaarden** (20 I. Van Beverenstraat) in Groot-Bijgaarden (7 km/4 miles northeast of the capital), **Le Trèfle à Quatre** overlooking the Lac de Genval (87 Avenue du Lac) and **Barbizon** in Jezus-Eik (95 Welriekendedreef).

Gastronomy on a budget: However, for those on a more modest budget, Brussels has a vast choice of cafés, bistros and bars. The area around the Grand' Place known as the **Ilot Sacré** is full of places serving good, affordable food. In some of the narrow alleyways hereabouts it seems as if every house has been converted into a restaurant of some kind. A typical example is Rue des

Waiting for hungry customers in the Ilôt Sacré.

Bouchers/Beenhouwersstraat where polished antique barrows and shelves piled high with fish and seafood are displayed in front of the restaurants to lure passers-by inside. When business is slack, waiters and chefs often come out and stand in front of their restaurants to drum up trade. Don't be shy of accepting their invitations. Such fare is typically Belgian and, due to the intense competition, reasonably priced.

The district as a whole is known as the city's "stomach". It is a fitting description, but you will find more than just places to eat. You will also find originality and a loving regard for centuries-old traditions. Of the many bistros in this area, a few are particularly worth trying: for *moules et frites* and the other Belgian favourite, steak and chips, you will not be disappointed at **Chez Léon**, a famous Brussels institution on Rue des Bouchers, or **Vincent**, round the corner on Rue des Dominicains. Slightly more sophisticated but still reasonably priced are **Scheltema** on Rue

des Dominicains and **Aux Armes de Bruxelles** on Rue des Bouchers. For fine French cuisine in a bistro setting, try **l'Ogenblik** in the elegant Galerie des Princes just up the road.

One of the most atmospheric places to eat in town is **Toone VII** (located at Impasse Schuddevelt 6, Petite Rue des Bouchers) – an old inn containing a puppet theatre, which is reached via a narrow passageway between two houses. The theatre (go up the rickety stairs) stages performances of classical plays such as *Hamlet* and *Faust*, interspersed by personal comments on the plot by Toone, a true Brussels character. His remarks – frequently profound, sometimes witty – lighten the tragic action on the stage. The puppet theatre/restaurant has been a feature of Brussels for several generations. Even foreign visitors who speak neither French nor the local dialect of the Belgian capital will find an evening here a delight.

The majority of bars and bistros do not provide quite such original enter-

tainment, but most of them offer a welcoming atmosphere. The décor, usually in rustic style and bearing the patina of age, radiates a relaxing ambience. The walls, stucco and beams are invariably brown with generations of tobacco smoke.

In such a setting the city's local specialities taste particularly good. Typical Brussels dishes are *poularde* (corn-fed chicken), chicory, usually stuffed or rolled in ham, and *waterzooi*, a delicious chicken or fish stew. A variety of national dishes feature meat cooked in beer, such as Flemish *carbonnade*. Asparagus and game are widely available in season. The wine offered to accompany them is usually French, but of course they all go down well with the national drink of Belgium: beer.

Like the French, the citizens of Brussels enjoy sitting at a table on the pavement in front of the restaurant or bar. Even in the sheltered, air-conditioned shopping galleries customers appear to have a marked preference for outside tables. Here you will usually find coffee and a selection of fattening cakes and pastries to choose from.

Elsewhere in the city, cafés-cum-pâtisseries tend to be thin on the ground. Hardly any are attached to an attractive café of the type common in Germany or Austria. However, there are some excellent cake shops, for example **Wittamer**, on the Place du Grand Sablon, is one of the continent's best, and the chain **Le Pain Quotidien** serves excellent cakes (and savoury food) all day long and has branches on the Sablon, on Rue Antoine Dansaert. Try also **Chaloupe d'Or** on the Grand' Place or the stylish café in the **Hôtel Métropole** on Boulevard Anspach.

Recipes to try at home: Finally, for those who would like to try their hand at some of the specialities offered in the city's 1,800 restaurants, here is a selection of recipes:

Brussels-style chicory: Chicory is served as a vegetable, a salad or stewed with potatoes and onions, seasoned

Left, a happy grocer. Right, Chocolatier Neuhaus draws the sweet-toothed.

with lemon and nutmeg. Experienced cooks recommend that when cooking chicory you should add half a lump of sugar in order to reduce the bitter taste. The vegetable will retain its attractive white colour if a few drops of lemon juice are added. **Brussels chicory with cheese and ham** (recipe below) is a particularly popular dish:

Ingredients: 1 kg chicory; one slice of cooked ham per plant; 50 g butter; 50 g flour; ½ litre liquid (chicory stock and milk); 100 g grated cheese; salt and pepper; breadcrumbs; a few knobs of extra butter.

Method: Wash the chicory thoroughly and boil it in lightly salted water; drain, reserving some of the stock. To make a sauce, melt the butter in a pan, and add the flour to make a roux. Cook for a few minutes, then gradually add the stock and milk. Thicken the sauce over the heat, then stir in the grated cheese and season with salt and pepper.

Wrap each chicory plant in a slice of ham; lay the rolls side by side in an ovenproof dish. Cover with the cheese sauce, sprinkle with breadcrumbs and dot with knobs of butter. Bake in a preheated oven until well browned.

Brussels sprouts: The classic way of preparing sprouts is to boil them in salted water and then toss them in butter or pork dripping. They are also delicious when puréed in a blender and seasoned with a little nutmeg.

Brussels-style mussels: This classic dish is surprisingly easy to make and is usually eaten with chips.

Ingredients: small piece of celeriac; one onion; a little finely-chopped parsley; approximately 1 kg mussels (clean them thoroughly in cold water and discard any which refuse to close when tapped); half a lemon.

Preparation: Finely chop the celeriac, onion and parsley. Fry gently in the butter in a covered pan for 10 minutes. Add the cleaned mussels, salt, pepper and the juice of half a lemon. Replace the lid and continue to cook gently for a further 10 minutes, until the mussels

Moules et frites **as served in Bij den Boer.**

have opened. Serve immediately with freshly-fried chips or French bread.

Brussels waffles: No meal is complete without a dessert and waffles are a perennially popular choice among the Belgians.

Ingredients: 1 kg flour; 250 g butter; 4 eggs; 50 g yeast; ½ litre water; ½ litre milk; ½ vanilla pod; 1 pinch salt.

Method: Warm the milk and water slightly. Melt the butter in a saucepan; add the egg yolks and, beating steadily, gradually mix in the warmed milk and water. Add the salt and the contents of the vanilla pod, and beat in the flour.

Dissolve the yeast in a little warm milk and stir into the dough. Allow to rise in a warm place away from draughts for 30 minutes. Shortly before the end of the rising period whisk the egg whites until they are white and fluffy. Fold into the risen dough. Bake the waffles one at a time in a preheated waffle iron. Serve hot with sugar, cream, ice-cream or jam.

To take home: Two other sweet specialities deserve a mention here: firstly, *pain à la grecque* – "Greek bread". It has no connection at all with Greece, but was invented over 500 years ago by a Belgian monk living in an abbey located next to a ditch. At first it was known simply as "Bread from the ditch" (in Flemish: *gracht*), but the French-speaking inhabitants gradually corrupted the name into "grecque". Sold in virtually every baker's shop and pâtisserie in Brussels, it often comes in heart-shaped loaves.

The second sweet speciality worth looking out for are *speculoos*, the Belgian equivalent of the German *spekulatius*, the popular spicy Christmas biscuits, but darker and available all the year round. At Christmas the *speculoos* are sold in the form of large figures in wooden moulds. These, however, are bought for decorative purposes rather than for eating A delicious variation on this type of biscuit, rectangular in shape and containing almonds, is **pain d'amandes** (almond bread). Bon appétit!/Smakelijk!

At Toone's you can enoy Belgian theatre as well as Belgian beer.

THE ANCIENT ART OF BREWING

A Latin inscription found on the gable of the "Maison des Brasseurs", the Brewers' House, overlooking Brussels' Grand' Place, translates as follows: "Thanks to St Arnold, the divine brew was created from the gifts of heaven and earth and human science."

The Benedictine monk commemorated by the inscription was responsible for spreading the art of brewing across most of Belgium. How a holy man acquired such expertise and felt it right to promulgate his discoveries has been the subject of much conjecture. It is said that Arnold was trying to find out why prosperous citizens and noblemen enjoyed a considerably higher life expectancy than the common people. After studying the matter, he attributed the reason to the fact that the better-off were able to quench their thirst with beer, whilst those whom fate had treated less kindly had no choice but to resort to water, which was often contaminated by harmful bacteria.

The barrels in his home abbey of St Peter at Oudenburg, near Ostend, were always filled to the brim. Father Arnold exhorted his flock to avoid water and to drink instead beer (in moderation). Arnold was canonised after his death, and has been the patron saint of brewers ever since.

For centuries the art of brewing beer remained in the hands of the religious communities. Their craft, which enabled them to develop a continuous succession of new processes and flavours, spread as far as the court of Spain.

Today, Belgium has no fewer than 115 breweries scattered across the country. The experiments of the god-fearing recluses were developed further, and today the country produces more than 400 different kinds of beer; their colours range from light golden through every shade of brown to a deep reddish hue.

One of the most unusual beers is the *Lambic*. This brew then forms the basis for a number of other beers: *Gueuze* (pronounced *gurz*, to rhyme with *stirs*), *Faro*, *Kriek* and *Framboise*. These are yeastless beers where the fermentation occurs spontaneously, set into motion by bacteria which enter the liquid from the air. It is claimed that the necessary microbes exist nowhere except in the atmosphere of the capital. In the Gueuze Museum (*Musée de la Gueuze*) the visitor can observe the brewers at work as they process the raw ingredients using methods developed by their ancestors. The museum is situated in the Rue Gheude/Gheudestraat; tel: 521 4928; open Monday-Friday 830am–5pm, Saturday 10am–5pm, or guided tours available by prior arrangement. The Musée de la Brasserie at 10 Grand-Place traces the history of the guild of brewers and their techniques. Tel: 511 4987; open daily 10am–5pm

A "young" beer must mature for three to six months and a "mature" one for two to three years. Fermentation takes place in both bottles and casks. The bottle method is used for so-called "Brussels Champagne". If cherries are added to the Lambic before the second fermentation, the resulting beer is known as *Kriek* (a Flemish word meaning cherry). *Framboise* results from the the addition of raspberries to the basic brew – 150 kg of fruit to 450 litres of beer.

Another variation is *Faro*, which is sweetened after fermentation with rock candy. Since beers of this type are subject to an uncontrolled fermentation, they may, like wine, taste different from one year to the next. Gueuze is only produced during cooler months; usually between October and April.

An interesting beer is brewed in West Flanders. The Rodenbach Brewery stores 10 million litres in oak barrels. Brewed from winter and summer barley, best quality hops, caramel and malt, a dark brown full-bodied beer is manufactured and subsequently filled into champagne bottles. It is known as *Dobbelen Bruinen*. The *Goudenband* was nominated by the beer pundit Michael Jackson as the best brown ale in the world.

Most of the 12 million hectolitres of beer which leave the filling plants of Belgian breweries every year are destined for the export market, which doubled in the years 1985–95.

Above, Brussels bars have more than 400 brands of Belgian beer to choose from.

THE GRAND' PLACE

The architectural climax of any sight-seeing tour of Brussels is undoubtedly the Grand' Place, the capital's market square where Gothic, Renaissance and baroque buildings are juxtaposed to such harmonious effect. It has been admired by visitors across the centuries, and attracted the attention of writers such as Victor Hugo and Jean Cocteau.

In French, the name for the market place is Grand' Place ("Great Square"); in Flemish it is known as the Grote Markt ("Great Market"). Facing each other across the square and occupying the two long sides are the Town Hall (Hôtel de Ville/Stadhuis) and the King's House (Maison du Roi). They are surrounded by baroque guildhalls with magnificent gables and sculptures.

The façades of most of the houses have been stained blackish-brown over the years, which actually contrasts well with the gilt ornamentation, figures, wrought iron and gables. The façades on the east side of the square and the Hôtel de Ville have undergone a lengthy period of cleaning and regilding to return them to their former glory.

As long ago as the 11th century, the market place – lying on a region of drained marshland – formed the focal point of Brussels. In those days, it consisted of nothing more than a handful of wattle and daub huts in which the peasants and craftsmen used to gather. From the 12th century the town experienced a period of economic expansion; at the beginning of the 15th century, work began on the construction of the Town Hall on the south side of the square. This period marked the summit of the city's significance and economic prosperity. Through its flourishing weaving indus-

Preceding pages: the "stern" of the "Horn of Plenty" guildhall, the house of the river boatmen. Left, flower market on the city's central Grand' Place.

try, Brussels had gained wealth and status; the new Town Hall was to be a symbol worthy of this newly acquired importance.

The Town Hall: With its high belltower, the Town Hall of Brussels is one of the finest Gothic buildings still standing today. Along with the church-like edifice on the main square in Bruges – also Gothic in style – it represents one of the most beautiful examples of Town Hall architecture in a country famous for its *hôtels de ville*. (The town halls in Leuwen and Ghent were completed during a later period and exhibit Renaissance features.)

Its left wing is ascribed to the master builder Jacob Van Thiemen and was completed in 1402. The right wing was added in 1444 by a craftsman whose name is unfortunately unknown to this day. The central tower, which is 96 metres (307 ft) high, was designed by Jan Van Ruysbroek. The lower rectangular section, incidentally, is not quite in the middle of the façade. According to legend, the builder threw himself from the top of the tower when he realised his mistake.

The base, which is four storeys high, is surmounted by an octagonal construction consisting of three storeys plus an openwork spire. This bears the massive gilt **Statue of St Michael**, one of the city's twin patron saints. The original was cast in bronze by Martin Van Rode, and survived of the fire of 1695, but was replaced by a copy during the latest restoration work. Visitors climbing the 400 steps to the top of the Town Hall tower will be rewarded by a spectacular view of the Grand' Place below and the entire city beyond.

The Great Fire of 1695 was an act of vengeance on the part of Louis XIV of France, who ordered Marshal de Villeroy to attack Brussels after the Belgians had fought against his armies in battle. On 13–14 April 1695 firebrands were shot on to the Grand' Place and its surroundings by cannons placed in front of the city walls. Most of the houses were

The guildhalls recall the wealth of their creators.

destroyed; a total of 4,000 buildings within the city were burned to the ground.

The local citizens refused to be disconcerted, however; four years afterwards, they were concentrating all their energies on the rebuilding of the Grand' Place, which was to be even more beautiful and magnificent than before.

Between 1708 and 1717, Cornelis Van Nerven built the section of the Town Hall between the Rue de l'Amigo/Vruntstraat and part of the Rue de la Tête d'Or/Guldenhoofstraat in the style of Louis XIV. It stands on the site of the second Weavers' Hall, which was built in 1353 and completely destroyed in the fire of 1695. It was reconstructed, and the Estates of Brabant used it up until the end of the Ancien Régime.

The façade of the Town Hall is decorated with numerous statues. These include several interesting specimens of 14th and 15th-century Brussels sculpture. Entering the courtyard, the visitor will notice two fountains. The one on the left, the work of Jan de Kinder (1714), represents the River Meuse; that on the right, created by Pierre-Denis Plumiers in 1715, symbolises the Scheldt.

Busts of all the mayors of Brussels since 1830 adorn the Grand Staircase inside, and its walls are decorated with paintings by Count Jacques Lalaing dating from 1893 which are known collectively as *The Glorification of Municipal Power*. The ceiling fresco is entitled *Castle Keep, Defended by All Powers of the Town against Plague, Famine and War*.

In times past it was usual for citizens to learn about the local byelaws by means of a formal proclamation from the balcony of the Town Hall. Another mural therefore depicts *To the Town and the World*, a municipal official reading a new regulation from the Town Hall tower. The main Council Chamber, today frequently referred to as the Gothic Hall, retains its original fittings from the days when it was once used for official ceremonies. It was here that the Dukes of Brabant took their oath of allegiance, swearing to uphold and defend the rights and privileges of the city.

The last such dedication took place in this hall on 21 September 1815. In the presence of the entire council of the States General, William I took the oath of loyalty as King of the Netherlands. Originally the chamber was decorated with several paintings by Rogier van der Weyden; these were unfortunately destroyed during the bombardment of the city in 1695.

Originally appointed in the neoclassical style, the Council Chamber was redesigned in the Gothic idiom in 1868. Tapestries adorning the walls depict the city's principal crafts and the guilds which practised them. The wall hangings were created between 1875 and 1881 in Mechelen, in the workshops of Bracquenié. Former presidents of the municipal council are represented as gilt bronze statues in front of the columns. The windows illustrate the coats of arms of noble families of Brussels.

The wedding chamber in the Town Hall has been completely restored. The large mural by Cardon depicts, in the middle, the City of Brussels, presiding over marriage. On the left stands the Law and on the right, Justice. The coats of arms of the old guilds can be seen on the ceiling, recalling the fact that the heads of the nine corporations would have met here in council. These corporations were formed in 1421 from the assembly of craftsmen's guilds.

These corporations met in council with the representatives of the municipal authorities to determine – amongst other things – the affairs of the town.

At the far end of the chamber is a row of wooden statues. They represent famous local citizens of the 14th, 15th and 16th centuries, among them the artist Rogier van der Weyden and Ludwig van Bodeghem, the architect of the "Bread House". The statues were carved by the Goyers brothers in Leuven.

Official guided tours include some of the offices of the mayor and jurors not normally on view to the public, and the so-called Brussels tapestries dating from the 16th, 17th and 18th centuries.

The King's House: The façade of the building opposite the Town Hall is divided into three sections: two magnificent rows of guildhalls flank the central "King's House" (*Maison du Roi*), which has had a long and chequered history. At the end of the 12th century this was the headquarters of the bakers of Brussels and hence was (and still is) known as the *Broodhuis* ("Bread House"). However, the bakers used it less and less frequently for the sale of their wares, and eventually abandoned it. In the 15th century it was renamed *'t Hertogenhuis* (The Duke's House), since the ducal assizes were held here.

In about 1512 the entire building had to be demolished because the clay foundations gave way. The most distinguished architects of the time were called in for the reconstruction: Antoon Keldermans, Ludwig van Bodeghem and Heinrich van Prede. The building

A detail of the house "L'Ermitage"

was again rechristened under Philip II, who had the royal assizes installed here. The new designation, *Pretorium Regium*, brought about the current name, "King's House", since it was here that legal verdicts were pronounced in the name of the King of Spain.

Archduchess Isabella had the King's House rebuilt in stone during the 17th century, dedicating it to the Virgin Mary, whose statue can still be seen today. During the Marshal de Villeroy's attack on the city the building was almost destroyed. It was not until 1768 that the authorities decided on its reconstruction, sadly ignoring the original style.

After changing hands several times, in 1860 the King's House was purchased by the municipal authorities. They had it demolished and reconstructed in accordance with the original plans under the supervision of the architect Victor Jamar, who also used old etchings in his search for authenticity. A stone tablet in the entrance hall records that the project took from 1873 to 1896

to complete, longer than the original building had done. The façade is of limestone and bluestone from Belgian quarries; the spire is of oak covered with slates. The weather vane bears a loaf of bread and a crown, reflecting the building's two names – the *Broodhuis* and the King's House.

In 1568 the celebrated Count Egmont and Count Horn, the two leaders of the revolt against the Catholic policies pursued by Philip II within the Spanish Netherlands, were held in the King's House before their execution on the Grand' Place. Lamoral Count of Egmont (1522–68), having distinguished himself in Charles V's military campaigns, subsequently became dissatisfied with Spanish rule.

Although his pleas for religious tolerance on behalf of the Protestants were to no avail, he remained loyal to the crown, refusing to side with Prince William I of Orange and suppressing Calvinist uprisings; nonetheless, after the arrival of the Duke of Alva in 1567 he was ar-

The place for lace.

rested and convicted of high treason. In memory of the rebellion, statues of the two folk heroes were erected and originally placed in front of the house; today they can be seen on the Place du Petit Sablon/Kleine Zavel.

In 1887 the City of Brussels transformed the King's House into the **City of Brussels Museum** (Musée de la Ville de Bruxelles). Also known as the "Brussels Community Museum", amongst its most important exhibits – apart from the collections illustrating various aspects of the city's development and a selection of typical local decorative arts – is a series of 26 paintings donated to the museum by an Englishman, John Waterloo Wilson. These include the *Allegory of the United Provinces* by N. Verkolie, *Still Life with Food* by Willem Glaesz Heda and the *Portrait of a Clergyman* which is attributed to the painter Josse van Clece.

Two 16th-century Brussels works of art also enrich the museum's collection: *The Wedding Procession* attributed to Pieter Brueghel the Elder and *The Legend of Notre Dame du Sablon*, probably the work of Barend van Orley.

Two unique works of art housed here are the 15th-century Saluces Altar-piece, and *The Marriage Proposal*, a tapestry depicting the story of Clovis, dating from the 18th century. One section displays Brussels ceramics from 1710 to 1845. The museum also contains the original sculptures from the Town Hall façade, renovated in 1840. The upper floor contains a Numismatic Collection, a Hall of Mirrors and a Lace Room.

The second floor of the museum houses – amongst other things – the 300 or so costumes of Manneken Pis (Garderobe de Manneke Pis/De Klerenuerzameling van Manneke Pis).

The guildhalls: Buildings which also suffered badly during Marshal de Villeroy's bombardment of the city in 1695 were the guildhalls. From the High Middle Ages until the middle of the 19th century, the guilds functioned as craftsmen's associations within the city.

Karl Marx once lived in "The Swan" house. Today the building houses a high-class restaurant.

Their houses surrounding the Grand' Place were originally built of wood.

After the destruction of the city, the prosperous craftsmen of Brussels wanted rebuilding to take place as quickly as possible and they commissioned the best architects of the day. A basic unity of style can be attributed to the fact that several of the new buildings were designed by Guillaume de Bruyn and Antoine Pasterona.

During the 17th century, most architects were members of a guild; they were by trade either stonemasons, carpenters, painters or sculptors. Their original profession naturally influenced the style of building they favoured.

The most important function of the guildhalls was for glorification of the guild concerned. Today, the name of each house recalls its former occupants.

The guildhalls were constructed in the Italian-Flemish baroque style. To the left of the Town Hall stands **L'Etoile** (The Star). This is the smallest of the guildhalls and one of the oldest build-ings still standing on the Grand' Place. During the 14th century it served as an office for the chief justice. In 1852 it was demolished to make way for a street-widening project, and reconstructed above an arcade in 1897.

Under the arcade stands a statue of Everard 't Serclaes, the Brussels folk hero. The figure's signs of wear are due to the custom of stroking its arm in passing in order to absorb some of the good luck it is supposed to endow. Everard 't Serclaes became famous for removing the flag which Louis de Maele, Count of Flanders, flew from the roof following his conquest of the Arch-duchy of Brabant in 1356. Everard was swiftly arrested and tortured by the Lord of Gaasbeek. A priest rescued him and brought him, badly wounded, to The Star, whereupon the local populace, outraged by the event, destroyed Gaasbeek Castle.

Next door to The Star stands **Le Cygne** (The Swan). Rebuilt by a private citizen in 1698, from 1720 the house was the

headquarters of the butchers' guild. Above the door is a carved swan with outspread wings; three statues above the second floor portray Abundance, Agriculture and Slaughter.

The house is famous above all as the setting where, along with Friedrich Engels, Karl Marx founded the "Workers' Association" and wrote the *Communist Party Manifesto*, shortly before being requested by the authorities to leave the country. The house later became the Belgian Workers' Party and finally the Belgian Socialist Party. Today, the *Maison du Cygne* is the premises of one of the city's top restaurants.

Also forming part of this row of guildhalls is the **L'Arbre d'Or** (The Golden Tree). It was once owned by the Brewers' Guild; they in turn had taken it over from the weavers. The statue of Maximilian II Immanuel of Bavaria, governor of the Netherlands at the time of the French bombardment, was replaced in 1752 by a gilt equestrian statue of Charles of Lorraine. Three bas-reliefs between the storeys depict different aspects of the art of brewing: the vintage, the transport of the beer, and the hop harvest. Today the building's cellars contain the **Museum of Brewing**, displaying an old brewery with a complete collection of tools and implements. Visitors also have an opportunity to sample different types of Belgian beer.

The next guildhall is **La Rose** (The Rose), which was owned during the 15th century by the Van der Rosen family. The unadorned façade is typical of the burghers' houses of the end of the 17th century.

The last house before the Rue des Chapeliers/Hoedemmakersstraat is the **Le Mont Thabor** (Mount Thabor). Originally a private house, it is known today as Aux Trois Couleurs (the Three Colours).

The upper short side of the Grand' Place is occupied by a row of houses known as the **Maison des Ducs de Brabant** (House of the Dukes of Brabant). It consists of a group of six houses with a common front. Their names are **La Fortune** (Wealth), Le **Moulin à Vent** (The Windmill), **Pot d'Etain** (The Pewter Jug), **La Colline** (The Hill) and **La Bourse** (The Stock Exchange); they were built in 1698 by the architect Guillaume de Bruyn.

Just as the King's House was never the residence of a monarch, so no dukes ever lived in the House of the Dukes of Brabant. The house was named for the busts of the dukes adorning the capitals of the Ionic columns along the façade.

Along the second long side of the square, past the corner of the Rue de la Colline/Heuvelstraat, stand three private houses dating from the 17th century. They are less elaborate in design than the rest of the houses surrounding the square. The first, **Le Cerf** (The Stag) is named after the emblem on the shield mounted above the door. Today this house is the home of a private club of the same name.

The next two houses, **Joseph** and **Anna**, share a common façade. They

A promising talent for the circus.

now contain a confectioner's shop where you can buy delicious traditional home-made chocolates.

Next door stands **L'Ange** (The Angel). The lower section of the façade is adorned with Ionic columns and the upper section with Corinthian columns.

La Taupe (The Mole) and **La Chaloupe d'Or** (the Golden Galleon) once belonged to the Guild of Tailors. They were rebuilt with a shared façade following their destruction in 1695. Again the architect was Guillaume de Bruyn. Here, too, the columns are Ionic below and Corinthian above.

The door is guarded by a bust of St Barbe, the patron saint of tailors. Atop the gable is a statue of St Boniface, a native of Brussels.

Le Pigeon (The Pigeon) was formerly the Artists' Guildhall. The classical façade has Doric columns at street level, Ionic on the first and Corinthian on the second floors. The French writer Victor Hugo lived here after being exiled by Napoleon III.

The last house before the King's House is **La Chambrette de l'Amman** (Official Rooms). The array of coats of arms on the façade has resulted in a second name, The Brabant Arms. It has a classical façade with three orders of columns.

The houses past the King's House – the **Helmet**, the **Peacock**, the **Little Fox**, the **Oak Tree**, **St Barbara** and the **Donkey** – reveal no specific classical elements. Today they house a number of restaurants.

The first house after the junction of the Rue au Beurre/Boterstraat, leading directly to the Stock Exchange, is the **King of Spain**. Since it was originally commissioned by the Bakers' Guild, the building is also known as the Bakers' Hall. The Bakers' Guild was one of the wealthiest corporations in the city. Their house, completed in 1697 in classical style, is thought to have been designed by the sculptor Jean Cosyn. A bust of Bishop Aubert, the patron of bakers, decorates the doorway. The in-

A haven for geraniums.

scription runs "Throughout his life, he was a saint remarkable for the compassion he showed to the poor."

Medallions depicting the Roman emperors Marcus Aurelius, Nerva, Decius and Trajan adorn the wall of the first floor. A bust of Charles II can be seen at second-storey level. On the balustrade above stand six statues of "Strength", "Grain", "Wind", "Fire", "Water" and "Prospects". An elegant golden figure standing on one leg can be seen atop an octagonal pedestal. The interior of the King of Spain is equally impressive, with some unusual touches, such as a stuffed horse, and sheeps' bladders which decorate the ceiling.

The next guildhall is known as **La Brouette** (The Wheelbarrow); it served as the meeting place of the city's tallow makers. The name of the architect of the Classical-style house is not known. The Corinthian columns on the third floor are roofed in by a gable, under which stands a statue of St Aegidius, the patron saint of tallow makers.

Le Sac (The Sack) is the guildhall of carpenters and coopers. The lower section of the building, which is Classical in style, escaped total destruction in 1695 and it was subsequently restored by a carpenter named Pastorana. Above the main entrance is the likeness of a man carrying a sack into which a second person is putting his hand.

The next house, **La Louve** (The She-wolf), was also only partly destroyed by the French attack. It was rebuilt in the Italo-Flemish style and subsequently acquired by the Guild of Archers. Several decorative elements on the façade at the height of the first floor allude to the art of archery. The balcony is decorated with cranks and quivers.

In front of each column on the second floor there is a statue, above which an inscription has been added. The house owes its name to the carved relief of the she-wolf with Romulus and Remus, the twin founders of Rome. The female statue on the far left is holding an open book; accompanied by an eagle, she

Dressed for an occasion.

represents Truth. The inscription reads "The pillar of the kingdom". The next figure is Falsehood. She is accompanied by a fox and is carrying a mask; her inscription reads "The nation's pitfalls". Then comes Peace, carrying a bundle and surrounded by doves, with the inscription "The salvation of mankind". The statue on the extreme right is Discord; since her inscription pronounces her to be "The ruin of the republic", she has wolves at her feet and carries a torch. Dominating all is a golden phoenix with outspread wings, bearing the inscription: "Charred, I returned more glorious through the efforts of the Guild of Sebastian".

Le Cornet (The Horn of Plenty) was the house of the river boatmen; the gable, adorned with a medallion depicting Charles II of Spain, has the form of the stern of a galleon. Beneath the gallery is a row of fish-like sea-gods. The house's original name was The Mountain. It was rechristened by the bargees in 1434. After it was destroyed in 1695 the house was rebuilt in the Italo-Flemish style by the carpenter Pastorana. He designed the gable in the form of the stern of a ship and adorned the façade with numerous items alluding to navigation.

The last house before the Rue de la Tête d'Or is **Le Renard** (The Fox). The architecture incorporates elements from several different styles. The fact that it originally belonged to the Haberdashers' Guild is clear from the subjects depicted on its façade: a stoneware merchant, a dyer's shop, a fabric shop and children preparing hides.

Five statues adorn the first floor: the central figure, personifying Justice, is blindfold, and bears a sword in one hand and scales in the other. The remaining statues symbolise Europe, Asia, Africa and America. At the height of the second floor stand four caryatids – Classical-style female figures in flowing robes which double as supporting pillars. A statue of St Nicholas, the patron saint of haberdashers, stands at the uppermost point of the façade.

Two men with a view.

THE LOWER CITY

The centre of Brussels is characterised by the striking contrast between the Upper and Lower City. In the former you will find much of the city's government and business infrastructure: the ministry offices, the parliament building, various official bodies and large insurance companies, for instance. The Flemish Old City, the so-called "Lower City" situated on the *Ilôt Sacré*, on the other hand, is one of the most lively districts in the capital, well known for its restaurants. The careful renovation and maintenance that has been lavished on the historic buildings of the area adds to its charm.

The Royal Decree of 1960 proclaimed that all rebuilding work should ensure that the historic facades of the buildings were retained. The city subsidises such projects with a 25 percent grant to help with the costs; this policy has worked to good effect in the Grand' Place, but came too late to save much of the lower city's architectural heritage.

Close to the Grand' Place is **Rue du Marché aux Herbes/Grasmarkt**, a narrow street housing a number of small shops and, at No. 63, is the Belgian Tourist Office. The excellent Brussels Tourist and Information Office (TIB) is in the Hôtel de Ville on the Grand' Place, where you can obtain a whole range of information on the city.

Since most of the sites people want to visit are found within a relatively compact area, you are recommended to explore the city on foot, starting from the Grand' Place.

Famous landmark: Southwest of the Town Hall, at the junction of the Rue de l'Etuve/Stoofstraat and the Rue du Chêne/Eikstraat, stands the city's landmark, the celebrated **Manneken Pis** – a

Preceding pages: Both Manneken Pis and Jeaneken Pis perform dutifully for tourists. **Right**, a lion guards the Victory Column.

bronze fountain in the shape of a naked boy. On 13 August 1619 Jérôme Duquesnoy the Elder (*circa* 1570–1641) was commissioned to produce the likeness. He was the head of a Brussels family of sculptors whose works were influenced by the style of Rubens (a contemporary) and whose son, François, was to achieve fame in Rome, working with Bernini on the famous baldachin in St Peter's, and in Naples, where his rendering of *putti* was greatly admired. The little bronze figure was to replace the statue on an earlier fountain.

It is one of the key landmarks in Brussels, not to mention a source of inspiration and income to the souvenir manufacturers. The imitations of the little fellow vie with each other in tastelessness. The figure's likeness has been modelled in every possible substance; some of the copies are even larger than the original.

Manneken Pis is revered as one of the oldest and most celebrated citizens of Brussels. Also known as Petit Julien (Little Julian), the statue was originally merely one of the numerous fountains which provided the city with water. At some point, however, Manneken Pis progressed from being just a public fountain to become a legendary figure, probably owing its popularity to the many stories surrounding its origins. Since no one knows for certain exactly where the statue came from, opinions vary as to which of the stories seems most likely. In any case, the little figure symbolises the local citizens' predilection for carping criticism, their cheekiness, courage and lack of respect – their so-called "ungovernable soul".

The best-known myth surrounding Manneken Pis's origins maintains that during the battle of Ransbeke the son of Duke Gottfried of Lorraine was suspended in his cradle from an oak tree to give the soldiers courage. At some stage in the fighting he got out of his cradle unaided and was discovered having a pee against the tree, thus demonstrating unswerving courage even as a child.

Chairs to look at...

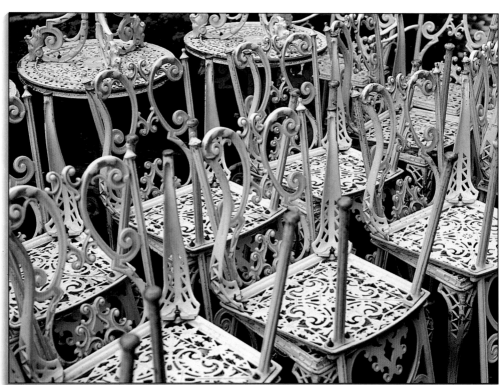

According to another legend, Manneken Pis is purported to have urinated on a bomb fuse, thus saving the Town Hall from terrorists who planned to destroy the building.

Yet another variation tells of the son of a Brussels nobleman who, at the age of five, cheekily left a procession in order to relieve himself. According to one version of this tale, a wicked witch put a spell on the child because he dared to wee against the wall of her house. She turned him to stone, thus condemming him to eternal urination. Such legends are legion.

The statue escaped damage during the bombardment of the city in 1695, but it was stolen on a number of occasions after this. In 1745 it was captured by the British; two years later the thieves were the French. But Manneken Pis was always recovered. By way of compensation for the French theft, Louis XV, who was in Brussels at the time, gave the statue a costume of precious gold brocade. The King had the culprits arrested and honoured Manneken Pis with the title "Knight of St Louis" to offer reparation for the lack of respect the French soldiers had shown the little statue.

In 1817 a newly released convict stole the statue, and when it was found it was in several pieces. These were used in the casting of the present bronze replica. On 6 December 1818 Manneken Pis was returned to its original site, where it can still be seen today.

On high days and holidays, the statue is dressed in costume. Many of its outfits reflect the various periods of history through which Manneken Pis has passed. On 6 April, for example, it wears the uniform of an American military policeman to recall the anniversary of the involvement of the United States in World War I. On 3 September every year Manneken Pis is dressed in the uniform of a sergeant of the Regiment of Welsh Guards to celebrate the liberation of Brussels in 1944; and on 15 September it is the turn of the uniform of

...and chairs to sit on.

a British Royal Air Force pilot – in remembrance of the Battle of Britain during World War II.

In all, the statue possesses 345 uniforms and medals, all of which are stored in the City of Brussels Museum on the Grand' Place (most of the time he doesn't wear anything at all). Manneken Pis is without doubt the most famous site in the whole of Brussels. The **Poechenellekelder** tavern opposite is worth a visit for its olde worlde charm and its collection of theatre marionettes.

Religion and capitalism: Leaving Manneken Pis and going down the Rue des Grands Carmes/Lievevrouwbroersstraat, the visitor soon arrives in front of **Notre-Dame-de-Bon-Secours/Onzelieve-Vrouw van Bijstand** (Our Lady of Succour). The church was built in 1664 by Jean Cortvriendt in the 17th-century Italian manner.

Another church in the vicinity, dating from virtually the same period, is **Notre-Dame-aux-Riches-Claires/Rijke Klarenkerk**, which has been rebuilt after a fire. It is the work of Luc Fayd'herbe (1617–1697), a pupil of Rubens known for his creation of colossal statues adorning church nave pillars. The ornate gables represent the typical Brussels interpretation of the Italian Renaissance.

Also near the Grand' Place, in the Rue Henri Maus/Henri Mausstraat, stands the Brussels **Stock Exchange** (la Bourse/de Beurs). This is the most important foreign exchange market in the country, before those of Antwerp, Ghent and Liège.

The Stock Exchange was founded on 8 July 1801, changing locations several times after its original foundation in the former Augustinian monastery. Once the city councillors became aware of the importance of such an institution, they decided to erect a more imposing building on the site left vacant by the demolition of the Récollets monastery, which had made way for the new boulevard crossing the city from north to south. Léon Suys, one of the capital's most

Hot snails on a cold day.

distinguished architects at the time, supervised the construction of the magnificent building between 1871 and 1873.

Built in handsome yellowish-beige stone, the massive exterior lends the Stock Exchange a fortress-like air. In particular, the broad staircase, over which two huge lions stand sentinel, lends the edifice a solid appearance. The rectangular facade is heavily ornamented and surmounted by a dome. The main entrance consists of a vast colonnade. Six Corinthian columns support a triangular tympanum decorated with a garland of fruits and flowers, above which sits a figure representing "Belgium".

Three magnificent portals lead to the inner halls of the Stock Exchange, which can be visited on weekdays between 11am and 2.30pm. Passing through an automatic double glass door, you will find yourself in an antechamber, from which you can observe the frenzied activity of the stockbrokers behind a glass wall; visitors wanting to penetrate the "inner sanctum" may only do so by prior arrangement and as part of a guided tour. The sombre main halls are decorated with pillars, ornaments, statues and galleries which call to mind a place of worship rather than one of the hubs of the Brussels financial scene.

The surrounding streets have been allowed to decline in familiar Brussels fashion. However, there are a couple of cafés to revive one's sinking spirits. **Le Fastaff** on Rue Henri Maus is a famous Art Nouveau affair due to re-open in autumn 1999 under new management. **Le Cirio** on Rue de la Bourse is a fin-de-siècle temple now somewhat fraying at the seams.

Before leaving the area, take a peek inside the little **Church of St Nicholas** (Eglise Saint-Nicolas/Sint-Niklaas-kerk). Dedicated to the patron saint of shopkeepers, the building has a colourful history reaching back to the earliest times of the city. It was originally constructed as a market church during the 11th and 12th centuries, and rebuilt in the Gothic style in the 14th and 15th centuries. Having suffered damage during the Wars of Religion which dominated the 16th century, as well as during the terrible bombardment of the city in 1695, the church was subsequently rebuilt apart from the tower, which was destroyed beyond repair.

The interior walls are lined with wood panelling and decorated with notable paintings. A Classical-style high altar, carved wooden confessionals and the pulpit date from the 18th century. The altar in the left aisle is adorned with a 15th-century Madonna. The pillar on the right-hand side of the choir supports a Spanish figure of Christ dating from the 16th century. A copper shrine in front of the pulpit recalls the martyrs of Gorcum, who were put to death in Brielle (near Rotterdam) in 1572 after suffering unspeakable torture at the hands of the Gueux. The painting of the *Virgin and Child Asleep* is attributed to the master Rubens.

Lunch-break.

Streetlife: Leading away from the Stock Exchange to left and right is the **Boulevard Anspach/Anspachlaan**, one of the city's busiest commercial thoroughfares. It is lined with businesses, shops and cafés, in front of which street musicians and traders with typical handcarts laden with mussels and snails ply their trade.

The avenue opens on to the spacious **Place de Brouckère/De Brouckère-plein**, where it meets the Boulevard Adolphe Max and the Boulevard Emile Jacqmain. The middle of the square used to be occupied by the **Anspach Monument**, a 20-metre (64-ft) high fountain in memory of Jules Anspach, mayor of Brussels between 1863 and 1879 and the prime mover behind the construction of the avenues.

The capital's main boulevards cross the entire length of the Old City from the North Station (Gare du Nord) to the South Station (Gare du Midi). Today the Anspach Monument stands on the **Fish market** between the Quai aux Briques/Bazsteenkaai and the Quai au Bois à Brûler/Brandhautkaai.

The glitter of the Place de Brouckère can best be observed at night, when the flickering of the neon signs and the street lamps bathe the entire area in a flood of light. Numerous cinemas, bars and cafés enliven the square.

Not far away is the **Place Sainte-Catherine/Sint-Katelijneplein**, at the centre of which stands the church of the same name. It was built in about 1850 by Joseph Poelaert in the eclectic style, a blend of Romanesque, Gothic and Renaissance elements. **St Catherine's** occupies the site of the original church, which was destroyed in 1850. The old tower, known as the Tour Ste-Catherine/Katelijnetoren, remains, and still serves as belfry.

Within the triple-naved church, a painting of St Catherine by G. de Crayer hangs above the altar in the right aisle. In the left aisle stands the **Black Madonna** (Vierge Noire), dating from the 14th-15th century. The statue was origi-

"Fasten bayonets!"

nally carved from a light-coloured stone, but over the years it has become almost completely blackened.

Behind the church you will come across remains of the first city wall, dating from the 12th century: the **Black Tower** (Tour Noire/Zwarte Toren). The Place Ste-Catherine has a daily market, where you can find street traders, their portable barrows laden with ready-to-eat delicacies such as oysters, mussels, snails and pickled herring.

Within easy reach of the square is the Rue du Cyprès/Cipresstraat, which leads to the **Church of St John the Baptist in the Beguine Convent** (St-Jean-Baptiste-au-Béguinage/Begijnhofkerk van Sint-Jan). The basilica, originally Gothic in style, was rebuilt during the 17th century and became one of the masterpieces of Belgian rococo architecture. Inside, the technique by which the baroque features were superimposed upon the original Gothic structure can still clearly be seen. The entablature, surmounting a line of arches, is particu-

larly harmonious as it rests on a row of winged angels' heads. The Beguine community itself, which totalled 1,200 members in its heyday, was dissolved during the 19th century.

The well-known **Petite Rue des Bouchers/Kleene Beenhouversstraat** ("Little Butchers' Street") crosses the city centre on its way from the Stock Exchange to the Galeries Saint-Hubert and the Galeries Royales. The street, which is closed to traffic, is also known as the "Stomach of Brussels", as it is lined with good but cheap restaurants. Street musicians serenade potential guests; in summer there are stands selling snacks of fish and seafood.

A fun place to dine: In a narrow cul-de-sac leading off the Petite Rue des Bouchers lies the **Museum Toone**, one of the most famous marionette theatres in the world. The theatre first came to public notice in 1830 under Toone I, who invented the "Woltje", the Little Walloon, who is seen as the epitome of the typical Brussels street urchin and

who has become an irreplaceable member of the cast. Dressed in a checked jacket and with his cap set at a jaunty angle, he acts as the narrator and speaks all the parts.

In 1911 a grim fate befell Toone III; he was discovered hanging dead between his puppets. Under José Géal, the seventh generation of the Toone dynasty, the marionette theatre experienced a new upsurge. In the 1960s he purchased an old house in the Impasse Schuddeveld and turned it into a puppet theatre and frestaurant. An antique pianola dominates the entrance; if you put a five-franc piece into the slot, it will tinkle old-fashioned songs. The tables and benches, together with the Gothic fireplace, give the restaurant a homely atmosphere. The traditional marionette theatre with a total of 50 seats is located up the stairs.

Even today, the plays are performed in the local dialect, which originally evolved in the Marolles, the historic district at the heart of the old city. Here the Walloon and Flemish workers came together, creating a strange patois. Though based on the French language, it also includes a mixture of Flemish words and Spanish expressions adopted from the soldiers of the Duke of Alva. The dialect is used for every performance in the Toone theatre repertoire of 500 plays. (This shouldn't put you off; a knowledge of the dialect isn't a prerequisite for enjoying performances.)

Shopping in style: From the end of the bustling Petite Rue des Bouchers, it is only a stone's throw to the Royal **Galeries Saint-Hubert**, divided into the **Galerie du Roi**, the **Galerie de la Reine**, and the **Galerie des Princes**, with a total length of 2,133 metres (6,998 ft). They were designed in 1845 by the Brussels architect Jean-Pierre Cluysenaer, then only 26 years old. Once again, many stories are associated with its founding. A barber, for instance, is reputed to have slit his throat rather than consent to abandon his property to make way for the project.

King Leopold I laid the foundation stone on 6 May 1846. One year later, on 20 June 1847, the official opening took place. They were the first covered shopping galleries in Europe and symbolised Belgium's new prosperity and confidence as an independent nation.

The shopping arcade is lined with noble and elegant boutiques and has four entrances – on Rue des Bouchers, Rue du Marché aux Herbes/Grasmarkt, Rue de l'Ecuyer/Schildknaapstraat and Rue des Dominicains/Predikherenstraat.

Leaving by the northern exit of the Galerie du Roi, the visitor can cross the Rue de l'Ecuyer and reach the Place de la Monnaie/Muntplein, the focal point of which is the **Théâtre Royal de la Monnaie/Muntschouwburg**, the Brussels Opera House.

Belgium's first musical stage was elevated to the rank of National Opera (Opéra National) in 1963. The name of the square, and that of the theatre, are derived from the building which origi-

Waiting for customers.

nally stood on this site – the Hôtel de la Monnaie (the National Mint), which was constructed here during the 15th century and which minted the coins for the Duchy of Brabant.

After the original building was demolished in 1531, a spacious square was laid out here. Jean-Paul Bombarda, the Governor-General of the Netherlands, had the first theatre – with seating for an audience of 1,200 – built on the site in 1698. During its early years it enjoyed only modest success.

Then the architect Damesne was commissioned to undertake a complete rebuilding programme. He planned a new edifice in the neoclassical style, surrounded by a roofed-in arcade. A triangular tympanum surmounted eight Ionic columns and was decorated with a bas-relief depicting the *Harmony of Human Passions*. The new building was opened in May 1819.

On 31 January 1855 a fire destroyed extensive sections of Damesne's building; restoration work was completed by Poelaert within the space of just one year. The pillars and the bas-relief had escaped damage; the auditorium was considerably extended during the rebuilding. After its official opening by King Leopold I, the restored theatre was reserved exclusively for performances of opera and ballet.

Call to arms: Brussels opera house was the scene of one of the most important historic events in the city. Here, on the night of 25 August 1830, the Revolution which was to lead to the country's independence was triggered.

The opera *Masianello* (also known as *La Muette de Portici*), by Daniel François Esprit Auber and based on the Neapolitan Revolution of 1647, had been scheduled to be performed at the Opera some time previously. However, following unrest in the city, the authorities had felt it wise to postpone its run.

The première was finally held on 25 August before a packed house. Its effect on the audience was electrifying. As the opera progressed they became increas-

Extremely hard to resist.

ingly disturbed and when, in Act IV, the call to arms rang out, it could not be contained. With patriotic cries on their lips they streamed out of the auditorium towards the houses occupied by Dutch families, and then to the municipal park. The Revolution had begun.

The Théâtre de la Monnaie was not only the starting point for the Revolution, but also the setting for a succession of glittering premières. Many operas have received their first performance in the French language here. The Brussels Opera rates among the best opera houses in Europe.

One man's name is inextricably linked with this success: Maurice Huisman, who took over the direction of the Opera House in 1960 and who breathed new life into the theatrical world.

Furthermore, for many years the Brussels Opera House was the headquarters of the Twentieth-Century Ballet under Maurice Béjart. Whilst most French-speaking Belgian actors move to Paris in search of success in their profession, Maurice Béjart left the South of France for Brussels, feeling that it offered him greater artistic freedom. His principal contribution to the contemporary ballet scene was the infusion of a much more masculine approach to dancing. This contrasted starkly with the classical tradition, which was dominated by the feminine style.

Looking rather out-of-place opposite the magnificent old Opera House is the contemporary **Centre Monnaie**, housing numerous shops, assorted snack bars and one of the largest post offices in Brussels. Until 1965 the site was occupied by the 19th-century Hôtel des Postes, the main post office, which was demolished to make way for the Centre Monnaie as part of the complete remodelling of the district between the Place de Brouckère and the Place de la Monnaie.

Another popular shopping street, the **Rue Neuve**/Nieuwstraat, leads off the Place de la Monnaie. It is a bustling pedestrian area packed with stores, bou-

Golden Mannekens for the grown-ups…

182

tiques and the shopping complex, **City 2**. Tucked away amongst these modern palaces of Mammon is the baroque **Finistère Church/Finistera-kerk**, built in 1708 and worth visiting for its elaborate interior decorations.

By taking a side street off the Rue Neuve the visitor will arrive at the **Place des Martyrs/Martelaarsplein**, which was formerly known as the Place Saint-Michel. Its symmetrical layout was devised by the architect Fisco in 1755. In the middle of the spacious square stands a monument by G. Geefs recalling the 450 heroes of the Revolution of 1830 who died fighting the Dutch. The crypt, in which these victims of the war of liberation were laid to rest, was consecrated on 4 October 1830 in the presence of government officials, the army and numerous Belgian patriots. The statue, *Belgia*, symbolises the newly-founded state.

To the cathedral: The area surrounding the Place des Martyrs is characterised by a number of houses which have been undergoing lengthy renovation. Wooden shutters before the windows and holes in the roof seem incongruous only 20 paces away from the lively, popular shops of the Rue Neuve.

St Michael's Cathedral rises majestically on the hillside between the Upper and Lower City. It is an important example of the Brussels Gothic style. Previously occupying the site was the Carolingian baptistry dedicated to the Archangel Michael. After the relics of St Gudula were placed here in 1047 the two saints came to be regarded as the joint patrons of the church.

Although work was begun on the present cathedral at the beginning of the 13th century, it was not completed until the end of the 15th. The building thus exhibits a number of different architectural styles. The early 13th-century Romano-Gothic elements blend harmoniously with the ornamental style of the final flowering of Late Gothic during the 16th century. The dimensions are impressive: the main body of the cathe-

...and Manneken lollies for the kids.

dral, 108 metres (345 ft) long by 50 metres (160 ft) wide, is flanked by twin 69-metre (220-ft) towers. These dominate the entire exterior and never fail to impress visitors.

A staircase erected in 1861 leads to the triple doors of the cathedral. The nave impresses above all by its clarity of form, characterised by 12 round columns and ribbed vaulting. The pillars of the nave are formed by life-sized statues of the 12 apostles dating from the baroque era. They were carved by Jérôme Duquesnoy the Younger (Paul, Bartholomew, Thomas and Matthew), Luc Fayd'herbe (Simon), Jan van Milder (Philip and Andrew) and Tobias de Lelis (Peter and John).

A typically Belgian baroque wooden pulpit, carved in 1699 by Henri F. Verbruggen, portrays the banishment of Adam and Eve from Paradise. In 1937, excavations between the pulpit and the organ loft revealed the remains of foundations of a 12th-century Romanesque vestibule.

Situated to the left and the right of the high altar are three monumental tombs: two are dedicated to Duke Johann of Brabant and his wife, Margaret of York, who died in 1312 and 1322 respectively. The third is in memory of Archduke Ernst of Austria, who died in 1595; the brother of Emperor Rudolf II, he was also the Governor-General of the Netherlands.

The choir stalls originally stood in the Benedictine Abbey of Forest. The monastery was destroyed by fire in 1764 and closed completely in 1789.

Of particular note are the tapestries dating from the 17th century. They were woven by **Van der Borght**, who appears to have drawn his inspiration from Rubens. They depict various scenes from the legend of the Miracle of the Sacrament. According to the story, in 1370 a group of Brussels Jews stole the Holy Sacrament and desecrated it with their fists in their synagogue. It is claimed that at this the Holy Christian Sacrament began to bleed, a phenomenon

Shades of autumn.

which was taken as proof of the guilt of the protagonists, who were all despatched to be burned at the stake.

Although there is no documentary proof of the truth of this story, the theme was chosen as the subject of religious works of art on numerous occasions across the centuries. Nowadays the magnificent wall hangings are only displayed in the cathedral on special occasions (usually mid-July to mid-August).

The stained-glass windows above the High Altar represent important characters from European history: from left to right can be seen Maximilian of Burgundy, Philip the Handsome and Joanna of Castile, Charles V and his brother Ferdinand, Philip II with his first wife, Mary of Portugal, Duke Philibert of Savoy and Margaret of Austria.

The remarkable windows in the north and south transepts were designed by Barend van Orley in about 1300. The first shows Emperor Charles V and his wife, Isabella of Portugal, standing in front of the shrine containing the Holy Sacrament; also depicted are their patrons, Charlemagne and St Elizabeth. The window was commissioned by Charles V himself.

The second window portrays Louis II of Hungary and his wife, Mary of Hungary; they are kneeling in front of the Holy Trinity, accompanied by their patrons St Louis and Our Lady. Mary of Hungary, the sister of Charles V and Regent of the Netherlands, donated the stained-glass picture.

Other stained-glass windows in the aisles date from the second half of the 19th century. They were executed by J.-B. Craponnier after drawings by Charles de Groux and they portray episodes from the legend of the Miracle of the Sacrament.

The first two windows in the south aisle are gifts of the two Belgian monarchs, Leopold I and Leopold II, in memory of their royal consorts Louise-Marie and Marie Henriette. Also portrayed are the coats of arms of the ruling family of Saxe-Coburg and Orleans, as well as those of the Kingdom of Belgium and the House of Habsburg.

In the ambulatory there is a statue of the Virgin Mary by Artus Quellinus the Elder dating from 1645.

The **Chapel of the Miracle of the Holy Sacrament** often serves as the setting for chamber concerts, especially in August. The stained glass was a gift of Charles V and his family. Here, too, are scenes from the legend as well as portraits of the donors. The three left-hand windows were created by Barend van Orley; the sixth was the work of J.-B. Craponnier.

Behind the 19th-century alabaster altar lie the tombs of Albert, a Governor General, and his wife Isabella, who died in 1621 and 1633 respectively. Their portraits hang on the wall nearby; the paintings are copies of works by Peter Paul Rubens.

Behind the choir lies the **Chapel of St Mary Magdalene**, built in 1282 and remodelled in the baroque style in 1675. It contains a 16th-century statue of the Virgin with Child, thought to be the work of Konrad Meyt. The Italian alabaster altar stood originally in the Abbey of La Cambre, which was destroyed during World War I by German troops.

The Gothic-style **Chapel of Our Lady of Redemption** lies to the right of the choir. The 17th-century sketches for the stained-glass windows are attributed to van Thulden, a pupil of Rubens. They depict scenes from the life of the Virgin Mary, together with donors and their patron saints.

The Cathedral, dedicated to St Michael and St Gudula, the twin patron saints of Brussels, is the city's principal place of worship. For centuries it has been the setting for the country's great official ceremonies. In 1960 it was also the stage for the marriage of King Baudouin of Belgium and the Spanish Countess Fabiola Fernanda de Mora y Aragon. In 1962 the cathedral was officially named "St Michael's Cathedral" when it became the seat of the Archbishop of Mechelen.

CHATEAU ROYAL TO THE PALAIS CINQANTENAIRE

When the black, red and gold-striped flag is fluttering from the roof of the palace at Laeken, it is a sign to the citizens of Belgium that the royal couple is in residence.

The **Royal Palace** lies not in the centre of Brussels, but in the outlying district of Laeken, to the north. It was built by Montoyer in the late 18th century and rebuilt in the style of Louis XVI during the reign of Leopold II.

Since it still serves as the private residence of the sovereign and his family, the palace is not open to the general public. The building stands on the site of a former knight's castle which was purchased by the Governors General Marie-Christine and Albert of Saxe-Teck. It was here that Napoleon Bonaparte signed the declaration of war against Russia in 1812.

Exotic plants: The famous **Royal Greenhouses (Koninklijk Domein van Laeken**) occupy part of the palace gardens and contain an intriguing collection of plants. The series of 11 interlinked greenhouses were erected on the orders of Leopold II, who took a considerable interest in architecture. The architect he chose for the project was Balat, whose ideas on the subject were revolutionary for the time.

Azaleas, geraniums and exotic plants bloom in colourful profusion. King Albert and Queen Paola often receive their guests in the glasshouses, in particular in the adjoining winter garden. Once a year in spring the greenhouses are opened to the public for two weeks (*see next chapter, page 197*).

The **Fountain of Neptune**, near the glasshouses, is a replica of the 16th-century original designed by Flemish sculptor Jean de Bologne. The original fountain is in Italy, where it adorns the Piazza del Nettuno in Bologna.

The **Chinese Pavilion** and the **Japanese Tower** lend the park an oriental air. King Leopold II commissioned them in the early 1900s, as part of a whimsical plan to fill the gardens of his residence with exotic architecture, which was much in vogue at the time. Both structures were designed by Parisian architext Alexandre Marcel, who had the panels of the Pavilion constructed in China and transported to Belgium to be assembled. It now contains a priceless collection of beautiful oriental porcelain from the 17th to 19th centuries. The richly decorated Tower is a monument-museum housing exhibitions illustrating different facets of Japanese culture.

The **Port of Brussels** extends right into the park at Laeken. It stretches from the Avenue du Port/Havenlaan to the Allée Verte/Groendreef. As early as 1434, the city had received from Duke Philip the Good the right to canalise the Senne, since the river was in grave danger of silting up. In 1477 a better solution was found to the problem: Mary of

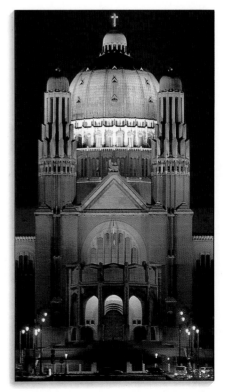

Burgundy gave permission for the construction of a lateral canal alongside the Senne, to link up with the Rupel near Willebroek. During the following years three harbour basins were added in Brussels itself.

Between 1829 and 1836, the Willebroek Canal was deepened and after further work, plans were developed in 1902 for the construction of a sea canal. The outbreak of World War I delayed the execution of the scheme; the new channel was finally opened in 1922 to sea-going vessels with a draught of less than 5.8 metres (18ft 6in). Today, the Port of Brussels has a direct link with the open sea; it also connects the capital with the industrial region of South Belgium via the Charleroi Canal. The city's waterways are used exclusively for the transport of goods.

The **Church of Our Lady of Laeken** stands at the junction of the Avenue de la Reine and the Avenue du Parc Royal. It was built by Poelaert in the neo-Gothic style on the orders of the first Queen of the Belgians, Louise-Marie. The sarcophagi of the country's deceased sovereigns lie in its crypt.

Also of interest in the church is a famous statue of the Virgin dating from the 13th century, and the early Gothic choir. A number of famous Belgian citizens are buried here, including the playwright Michel de Ghelderode, the architects Poelaert, Balat and Suys, and the violinist Charles de Bériot and his wife, who achieved fame under the name "La Malibran".

The tombs and chapels are decorated with numerous works of art, the most famous and impressive of which is undoubtedly the statue *The Thinker* by Auguste Rodin. The church is only open during services.

Home of the EU: Also within easy reach of the city centre is the **European Quarter**. In 1958, when Brussels was chosen as the administrative headquarters of the European Community, the various offices of the different departments were initially housed in buildings scattered

Europe in miniature under a giant atom.

across the entire city. One building for all officials was designed by the architect de Westel and constructed between 1963 and 1969 .

Known as the **Palais Berlaymont**, the headquarters of the European Commission lies on Rond-Point Schuman at the eastern end of the Rue de la Loi, which runs from the city centre to the Parc du Cinquantenaire. The officials moved in in 1967, when the then European Community consisted of only six countries. The highly conspicuous (some might say hideous) Palais Berlaymont, shaped like a four-pointed star, is currently closed while large quantities of asbestos are removed from the structure. The Commission has in any case outgrown its former home, now there are 15 member states, and its officials are once again dispersed throughout the city. Yet more office space will need to be found for the next round of countries (Cyprus, Czech Republic, Estonia, Hungary and Slovenia) waiting in the wings to join the EU in 2002. The main Com-

mission building is currently at 45 Avenue d'Auderghem, while the Council of Ministers sits in the massive Justus Lipsius building on Rue de la Loi, opposite the Berlaymont.

Near the European Union Headquarters lies the **Parc du Cinquantenaire**. It covers an area of 37 hectares (90 acres) and, as the name indicates, was created in 1880 as part of the celebrations marking the 50th anniversary of Belgian independence. Situated at the beginning of the Avenue de Tervuren, the park contains one of the largest museum complexes in Europe, and is a popular spot for jogging, sunbathing and walking the dog.

Around the periphery stand eight female statues symbolising the nine Belgian provinces. (The twin provinces of Flanders are represented by a single statue.) A **Triumphal Arch**, 60 metres wide (192 ft) and 45 metres high (144 ft) is visible from a distance. The openings in the colonnades on each side are 10 metres (32 ft) wide. The structure was

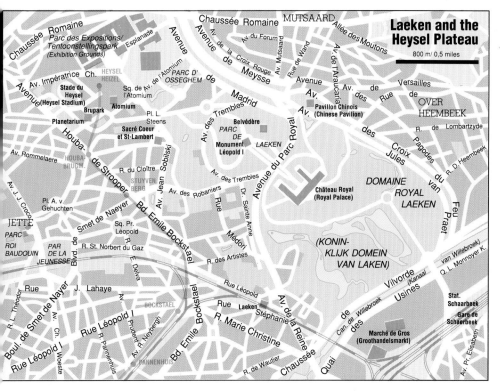

designed by Charles Girault. The four-horse chariot on top of the main arch is the work of Belgian sculptor Thomas Vincotto; it portrays a victorious Belgium, confidently facing the future.

The Cinquantenaire building is surrounded by lawns; one wing houses the Royal Museum of the Army and Military History, and the Royal Museum of Art and History.

The **Royal Museum of the Army and Military History** displays weapons, equipment and war posters from the last three centuries of Belgian history. Exhibits include sabres and cannon from the Brabant Revolution, as well as weapons used in both world wars. A separate section contains items tracing the history of the air force, including a display of some 100 aircraft dating from the early years of military flight (the *Nieuport*, a French aeroplane in use during World War I) to the British "classics" of World War II (the *Spitfire* and the *Hurricane*). The museum also includes a comprehensive library containing some 70,000 volumes on the history and technology of war, as well as documents and maps.

The **Museum of Art and History** is worth visiting for a grand overview of the diversity of world civilisations, from classical antiquity to the present day.

The collections housed here was assembled in 1880. The present department of antiquity displays Egyptian, Greek and Roman items as well as exhibits from the Near and Middle East.

The highlights of the museum are the famous 5th-century Apamea Mosaic from the Syrian town destroyed by the Persians in 612, and a bronze of the Roman emperor Septimius Severus. There are also sections where the visitor can investigate Belgian folk art and national archaeology. There are displays of handicrafts and interiors. Especially worth seeing are the sections covering a wide range of decorative arts, including Art Nouveau, and a large department devoted to non-European civilisations. Of particular interest here is the 13th-

Fountains at the old port.

century Civa Nataraja bronze from India, and a collection of painted Tibetan banners.

Classic cars: A further attraction within the Parc du Cinquantenaire is **Autoworld**, an impressive collection of vintage cars, within the Palais Mondial. The visitor can trace the development of the motor car from 1896 until the 1970s. Apart from the permanent displays, the automobile museum regularly holds special exhibitions. Its array of 450 top models from 12 different countries makes Autoworld the finest museum of its kind in the world. Apart from a large number of Belgian vehicles (for example, Rise, FN, Fondu, Hermes, Imperia, Miesse, Nagant and Minerva), the pride of the museum is the extensive display of veteran cars – many of them still in working order – from the **Ghislain Mahy Collection**.

Visitors wishing to move to a higher plane – metaphorically speaking – should include a tour of the **Air and Space Museum**, also within the borders of the Parc du Cinquantenaire. The exhibition provides a summary of man's attempts to conquer the skies from their earliest beginnings until the present day.

Outer space: To the north of Brussels, above the Parc du Cinquantenaire, is **Heysel**, another popular green area in the city. This was the site for the 1935 World Exhibition. The enormous halls were subsequently modernised, and are now in permanent use for the trade fairs, exhibitions and international congresses which are vital to the city's economy. The area also contains the **Bruparck** entertainment complex which includes Mini-Europe, the Océade water funpark and an IMAX cinema, Kinepolis.

The park is dominated by the massive **Atomium**, 102 metres (326 ft) high and visible from much of the city (*see chapter on The Atomium, page 201*). This model of an iron molecule, magnified 165 billion times, was designed by André Waterkeyn and constructed for the 1958 World Exhibition to symbolise the potential of Belgian industry.

THE GLASS CITY

The Royal Domain lies in the outlying district of Laeken, to the north of Brussels. This royal estate both complements and outshines the royal family's official city palace. The Belgian royal family are not noted city-lovers and infinitely prefer to live in the secluded country setting of Laeken. The magnificent botanical gardens and greenhouses, which rival the English equivalent in Kew, have earned the domain the title of "glass city". As a colonial power, Belgium revelled in the profusion of exotic plants shipped in from the Congo. Apart from the leafy estate itself, Laeken's appeal lies in the exotic oriental constructions and theatrical hot-houses that are sure to enliven any visit.

The royal domain revolves around the **Palais Royal** (Royal Palace), concealed behind railings on the Parc Royal. Although the palace is not open to the public, the domain is dotted with curious monuments and memorials. The Domain of Laeken was created by Marie-Christine and Albert of Saxe-Teck, the rulers imposed on the country by Emperor Joseph II of Austria. It is claimed that Albert himself, a keen amateur architect, drew up the initial sketches for the palace and its extensive gardens. At the end of the 18th century, Laeken was considered to be one of the loveliest estates in Europe. Not that Austria had long to enjoy its new possessions. In 1794, France annexed Belgium and the Austrians left, escaping with their prestigious art collection. This later formed the basis of the famous Albertina collection of paintings and drawings in Vienna, named after its founder, the Archduke Albert.

The Royal Palace was built by Montoyer during the second half of the 18th century but was remodelled in Louis XVI style under Leopold II. The occupying French forces planned to turn it into a public hospital. However, in 1804, Napoleon Bonaparte rescued the palace from total ruin, and used it as his residence until his defeat at Waterloo in 1815. It was here, in 1812, that Napoleon signed the declaration of war against Russia. William I of Orange-Nassau, the King of the Netherlands, became the next owner but only had a brief period to revel in the splendours of his stately home. A few years later, in 1830, the country gained its independence, and Laeken became the residence of Leopold I, the first King of Belgium, and uncle of the British Queen Victoria.

Leopold II, the second King of Belgium (1835–1909), was responsible for the creation of the fine park at Tervuren. However, his impact on Laeken was equally great. The king extended the palace and had magnificent avenues built from the domain to the capital. The park was embellishd by two oriental follies, a Chinese Pavilion and a Japanese Pagoda. The king's plans to expand the Domain of Laeken foundered on his death in 1909, with further development halted by the outbreak of World War I. However, Leopold's greatest achievement at Laeken was the creation of the so-called "glass city".

The Royal Greenhouses: The crowning glory was the construction of the Serres Royales, the Royal Greenhouses. This remarkable complex has remained virtually intact since its completion in 1875. Leopold II's predecessors had toyed with more modest schemes. A Chinese tower with adjoining orangery had been built by the ruling Austrian archdukes. Napoleon, too, had entertained grandiose plans for exotic hot-houses, but these came to nothing after his separation from the Empress Josephine. The orangery as it stands today was built under William I of the Netherlands. Leopold I also had a number of lesser greenhouses erected to supply the palace with orchids and pineapples.

But nothing was on the scale planned by Leopold II, inspired by his love of grandiose projects and the luxuriant vegetation of the Belgian Congo.

The Royal Greenhouses, one of the best-preserved complexes in Europe, are attributed to Alphonse Balat, one of the most prominent architects of the 19th century, and the young Victor Horta. In Leopold's day, the techniques required to build metal-framed glass buildings had reached new heights of sophistication. This permitted the construction of fairy-tale palaces which combined the romantic cult of the exotic with a longing for nature, exemplified by the sinuous forms of the Art Nouveau style. The resulting greenhouses present an architectural treasure that comprises a huge central dome, topped by an ironwork crown and flanked by a secondary chamber, cupolas, turrets and vaulted tunnels of glass.

For the principal extension of the Domain of Laeken, Leopold engaged the French architect Girault, famous for his buildings for the World Exhibition in Paris. He was responsible for the spectacular "theatre" hothouse.

The interlinked greenhouses allow the visitor to stroll from one end to the other, covering a distance of one kilometre. At its heart, a palm-tree complex meets a series of winter gardens, linked by an airy gallery. The palm-houses include a playful succession of passages and galleries abounding in startling perspectives. The winter gardens, however, are designed according to strictly formal lines: a row of large hot-houses is laid out along a central axis, with the *pièce de résistance* a vast dome-shaped hot-house.

The plants inside are rare and precious, perfectly in tune with the architecture. Leopold II particularly loved palms, which now curve majestically into the centre of the dome. These were joined by fuchsias and figs, geraniums, azaleas and begonias as well as tropical plants and camellias, the king's favourite flowers. Many species are of historical importance: most of the 44 species of orange tree are over 200 years old.

Bananas and myriad varieties of palms grow between wall ferns, overshadowed by broad palmyra palms. Ferns and orchids flourish beside camellias which are almost 200 years old, and which formed part of the hot-houses' original Victorian planting. Today, they constitute the most valuable collection of their kind in the world.

It was Leopold II's wish that the greenhouses should be open to the public once a year; and this tradition has been honoured ever since. Each year, in late April and early May, when thousands of flowers bloom in rainbow colours, the royal greenhouses open their doors. A night tour of the greenhouses is often the highlight of a visit to Brussels. The spectacle only lasts a week or so but draws thousands of local citizens who revel in the heady atmosphere of lush palms and exotic blooms. Visitors drift dreamily amidst the steamy fragrances of camellias and orchids, admiring the illuminated patterns of ferns and fuchsias.

Orchids and ferns in the Diana hothouse.

THE ATOMIUM

The **Atomium**, a gigantic model of an iron molecule, can be seen from many districts of the city. It dominates the Heysel Plateau lying to the north of Brussels (Boulevard du Centenaire/Eeuwfeestlaan); access is easiest via the motorway ring (exit 7 bis) or Métro.

Combined effort: This monument, built for the 1958 World Exhibition, was originally designed to symbolise in concrete form the potential of Belgian industry. The decision to build the Atomium resulted from a cooperation agreement between the Belgium metal industry and the Commissioner General responsible for the overall planning of the World Exhibition. In November 1954 André Waterkeyn, a professional engineer and director of the Association of Metal-Working Industries, developed the plans for the unusual structure.

It was his idea to represent the concept of the atom, which forms the basis of all sciences concerned with investigating the constitution of matter. His ambition was to portray the processes which take place in the microcosm in monumental fashion.

With the opening date of the exhibition imposing a strict deadline, it proved possible to construct the Atomium within a period of only four years. It became a huge success among the population. And after the Exhibition, the City of Brussels made a formal request that its new landmark should not be dismantled.

André Waterkeyn had chosen to represent an iron molecule, at a magnification of 165 billion times, as a symbol of the metal industry. In crystal chemistry, it is customary for the structure of crystals to be represented by spheres, whose central point indicates the central position of the atom within the network of crystals. The forces linking the atoms are represented by rods joining the spheres with each other.

The Atomium is based on this fundamental concept of a metal crystal. It consists of nine large spheres, represented in the basic constellation of a symmetrical three-dimensional system; each of the spheres is linked to the others by pipes measuring 3 metres (10 ft) in diameter.

All told, the Atomium is 102 metres (326 ft) high; each of the nine spheres or balls has a diameter of 18 metres (58 ft). Six of them can be visited by the public, who are transported from one sphere to the next by escalators – some of the longest in Europe at 35 metres (112 ft) and housed in the diagonal connecting pipes. The lift linking the bottom sphere with the top one is the fastest in Europe (it travels 5 metres/16 ft per second), enabling the visitor to ascend in only 23 seconds.

From the topmost sphere there is a spectacular view of the entire surrounding area. In the foreground are the buildings of the exhibition centre in the **Parc du Centenaire**, and an amusement park. This is the **Bruparck**, where a "**Mini Europe**" contains 300 of the continent's best-known monuments, built on a scale of 1:25 – which makes Big Ben 4 metres (13ft 2in) tall. The park also has an IMAX cinema, with a total of 14 auditoriums, a tropical swimming pool and the Heysel Sports Stadium. There is a permanent exhibition concerned with human genetics and a restaurant, Adrienne, in the top sphere.

Night lights: The Atomium is a prominent landmark in Brussels, mainly because of its size, but also because of its gleaming aluminium coating. At night the nine spheres are illuminated by a succession of circular light fittings positioned about 1.5 metres (3ft 3in) apart. The lamps are switched on alternately by means of revolving switches, thus giving the impression that points of light are revolving around the spheres.

The illumination was designed to illustrate the revolution of electrons around the centre of each atom of an iron molecule.

Left, impossible to miss: the Atomium.

SET TO BE CAPITAL OF EUROPE

By a convenient quirk of history, Brussels became the capital of Europe. As such, the city is charged with enshrining the European dream (as well as ensuring the protection of the Iberian lynx, French camembert, Belgian chocolate and the great British crisp). The Brussels bureaucrats are the archetypal European bogeymen, residents of a city famous for its faceless image. Behind the mask is a surreal world, more Magritte than Kafka, in which doubting Eurocrats and diplomats are inevitably beguiled. Bland bureaucracy is transformed into an expatriate playground of garden suburbs and gourmet lifestyles.

Brussels remains an anomaly, a French-speaking island in a Flemish-speaking region. Nearly one-third of the city's population is foreign, mainly European. Apart from being the capital of the European Union, Brussels is the headquarters of NATO and home to over 50 inter-governmental agencies, as well as countless trade associations and many international companies. The Brussels region is prosperous, and in terms of GDP per head, is the third wealthiest in the European Union.

Eurocrats and fat cats: As a capital transformed by institutional wealth, Brussels is a city of corporate lawyers and thrusting lobbyists, Europhiles and Eurosceptics, international agencies and multinationals. The Commission's role as European chief competition watchdog means that lawyers and lobbyists come to study or manipulate the Brussels political machine.

For business and bureaucracy, the lure of this city is great. With such a prestigious international role, numerous foreign companies have chosen to base their European operations here, from IBM and ICI to Bayer and Mitsubishi – Brussels has more office space per head than any other European capital. Sweet-

eners such as tax breaks and prime property locations ensure that Brussels finds favour with the multinationals. The capital prides itself in particular on offering a multilingual, cosmopolitan, highly-skilled labour force and excellent living conditions for foreign inhabitants.

Visually, the European district is something of a disappointment: Quartier Léopold, the city's most fashionable quarter in the 1850s, has disappeared under a dispiriting urban wasteland. As journalist Neil Buckley says, "Visitors to Brussels often expect to see an elegant European Union quarter, Europe's equivalent of Washington DC. They find instead a soulless administrative district where drab office blocks have replaced the 19th-century town houses, dotted with cranes and building sites and criss-crossed by six-lane highways."

The Council of Ministers (Métro Schuman) is a sprawling, low-slung building which opened in 1995. Nick-named the Kremlin, this peach-coloured fortress is already too small, designed for 12 EU members rather than 15. Facing it is Berlaymont, the former, and future, seat of the European Commission, the executive body. Nearby is the European Parliament, Espace Leopold (Métro Maalbeek), a glittering blue-green affair resembling a covered city.

The Commission is a curious constitutional hybrid, part executive body, part policy innovator and proposer of laws. As the European Union's civil service, it is a powerful employer, with 15,000 permanent staff, including a vast number of translators and interpreters. The Commission is only reluctantly practising what it preaches: publicly, it advocates flexible labour forces while privately protecting its own civil servants. These *fonctionnaires* enjoy generous perks and jobs for life. However, the concept of performance-related pay was raised in 1998, much to the horror of the personnel unions and to the delight of the Belgian public. EU civil servants are far better paid than their counterparts in the Belgian ministries. As well as avoid-

Left, welcome to Europe: the Palais Berlaymont.

ing punitive Belgian taxes, they can claim an expatriation bonus, child benefit and school subsidies.

Political farce: After the star-shaped 1960s eyesore Berlaymont was found to be contaminated by asbestos in 1991, the Commission's 3000 staff were evacuated to sites all over the city. During the move, over £140 million (US$230 million) of property mysteriously vanished, from cars to computers and carpets. The Eurocrats were outraged at the implication that their flats were furnished with purloined public property. As a French official retorted, "Have you seen the colour of the textiles? And everything is numbered, even the bland Euro-carpets." After ridding itself of asbestos, Berlaymont is due to re-open by the year 2000. In the meantime, it has become a bizarre landmark in its own right, wrapped in white plastic like a Cristo art work.

The new European Parliament is the latest symbol of European unity, set in Espace Leopold, the heart of the Euro-district. It is dubbed Caprice des Dieux, the folly of the gods, after the French cheese whose shape it echoes. The Parliament is paralleled by an equally grandiose European assembly to be unveiled in Strasbourg in 1999. The existence of two follies aims to assuage Gallic pride, and to prevent the French city from being sidelined by Brussels. Given the duplication of parliaments, on average, MEPs spend only two days a week in Brussels. However, as a talking shop and temple to self-aggrandisement, the Parliament has few equals.

Upon completion, this glass and steel behemoth became the biggest building project in Europe. Opened by King Albert II in 1998, the building cost $1.66 billion, and has vast annual running costs. The 626-member body will oversee the new European Central Bank.

At the inauguration of Parliament, French MEPs protested that the Spanish president could not address the King of the Belgians in English. English was

Europe's public servants are entitled to a special number plate.

originally chosen in order not to inflame the linguistic sensitivities of French and Flemish speakers. However, in a typical Belgian compromise to soothe ruffled feathers, the President gave the speech in four languages – and confirmed that the inauguration plaque on the Parliament wall was in Latin, the only uncontentious lingua franca.

Rampant bureaucracy: Eurosceptics wishing to find fault with Brussels need look no further than this folly: during sessions, there are often more multilingual interpreters than delegates needing translation. Likewise, the hemicycle, the huge debating chamber, holds 1,000 delegates but is used for only two weeks a year.

For members of the modern Euro-state, there is little need to visit the outside world. Apart from restaurants and sports facilities, there are 15 conference chambers, countless briefing rooms, and offices with bedrooms and bathrooms. Although the main corridors are as wide as motorways, a Dutch MEP has been forbidden from riding his bicycle through the building.

After two months, the giant glass monolith required repairs: Belgian birds, attracted to the luxuriant palm trees growing in the atrium, failed to notice the glass ceiling as they hurtled into the corridors of power. This is an apposite image for the Belgian attitude to the European institutions: an exotic honey-pot from which most native residents feel excluded. Belgian citizens often sense that "the capital of Europe" has little to do with their lives. There are great disparities in wealth between the corps of diplomats and Eurocrats and the average *Bruxellois*.

For the privileged Eurocrats, the comfort and convenience of life in Brussels transforms Europhobes into Europhiles. In time, civil servants at the Commission and NATO are accused of "going native" by their compatriots at home. "Going native" in Brussels tends to embrace pro-European views and gourmet cuisine in equal measure.

Show solidarity.

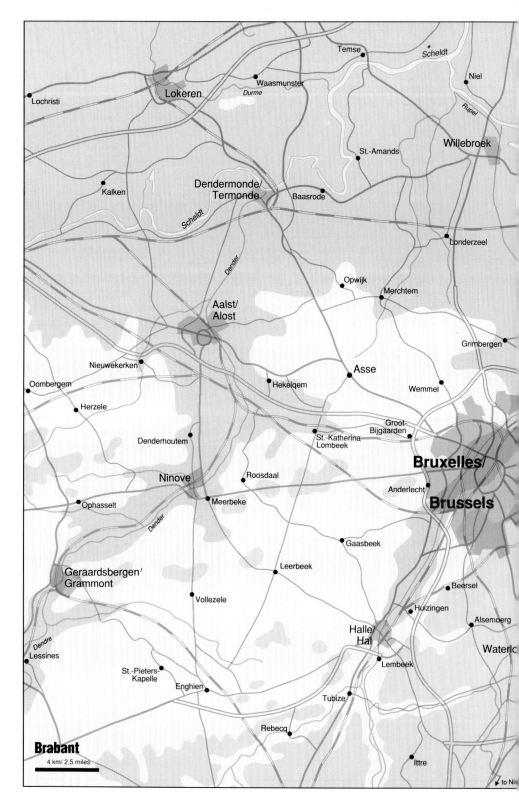

Temse

Scheldt

Niel

Waasmunster

Durme

Rupel

Lochristi

Lokeren

Willebroek

St.-Amands

Kalken

Dendermonde/
Termonde

Baasrode

Londerzeel

Scheldt

Opwijk

Dender

Merchtem

Aalst/
Alost

Grimbergen

Nieuwekerken

Asse

Oombergem

Hekelgem

Wemmel

Herzele

Groot-
Bijgaarden

Denderhoutem

St.-Katherina-
Lombeek

Bruxelles/

Ninove

Roosdaal

Anderlecht

Brussels

Ophasselt

Meerbeke

Dender

Gaasbeek

Geraardsbergen/
Grammont

Leerbeek

Beersel

Vollezele

Huizingen

Alsemberg

Dendre

Halle/
Hal

Waterlo

Lessines

St.-Pieters-
Kapelle

Lembeek

Enghien

Tubize

Ittre

Rebecq

Brabant

4 km/ 2,5 miles

to Niv

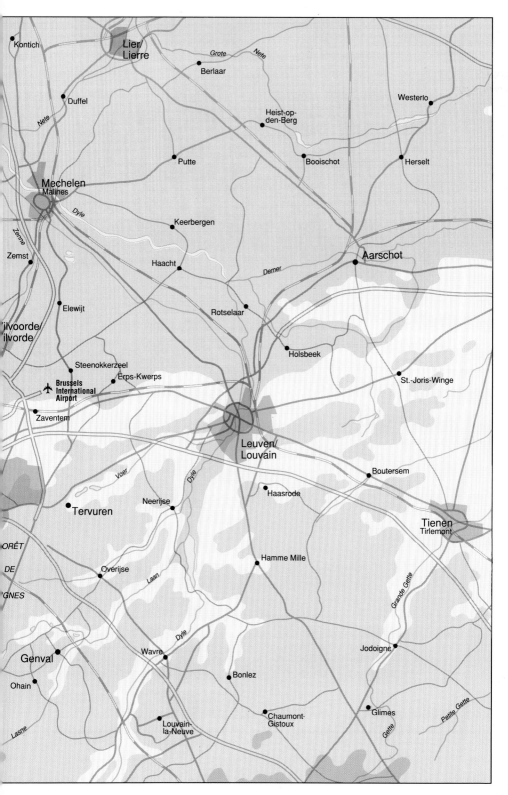

Kontich

Lier/
Lierre

Grote   Nete

Berlaar

Duffel

Westerlo

Heist-op-
den-Berg

Nete

Booischot

Herselt

Putte

Mechelen
Malines

Dyle

Keerbergen

Aarschot

Zenne

Demer

Zemst

Haacht

Elewijt

Rotselaar

ilvoorde/
ilvorde

Holsbeek

Steenokkerzeel

Erps-Kwerps

St.-Joris-Winge

Brussels
International
Airport

Zaventem

Leuven/
Louvain

Voer

Boutersem

Neerijse

Haasrode

Tervuren

Tienen
Tirlemont

ORÊT

DE

Hamme Mille

GNES

Overijse

Laan

Grande Gette

Dyle

Wavre

Genval

Jodoigne

Ohain

Bonlez

Lasne

Louvain-
la-Neuve

Chaumont-
Gistoux

Glimes

Petite Gette

Gette

AROUND BRUSSELS

As even the shortest journey through the immediate environs of Brussels will take the traveller through both Flemish and French-speaking areas, a degree of flexibility is required for any exploration of the area around the capital.

The historic little town of **Tervuren** lies only a stone's throw to the southeast of Brussels. It can be reached by taking the Avenue de Tervuren/Tervurenlaan, a boulevard constructed by King Leopold II.

During the 17th and 18th centuries **Tervuren Park**, with an area of more than 200 hectares (500 acres), was the setting for many a glittering court ball. Even today, its manicured lawns, lakes, flowerbeds and ancient trees make it a favourite destination for excursions from the capital. Originally serving as a hunting lodge, the palace was rebuilt by Albert and Isabella at the beginning of the 17th century as a princely residence. It was demolished in 1781 upon the instructions of Emperor Joseph II; only **St Hubert's Chapel**, built in 1617, and the **Palace Stables**, dating from the 18th century, are still standing. Near the chapel you can rent boats for sailing on one of the larger lakes.

Encounter with Africa: Today Tervuren is principally famous as the home of the **Royal Museum of Central Africa** (Musée Royal de l'Afrique Centrale/ Koninklijk Museum voor Midden-Afrika). It lies on the edge of the spacious gardens, above the terraces. The core of the exhibition was provided by Leopold II's Congo Collection, displayed in a palatial neo-classical colonial villa designed in part by Henry van der Velde. The original collection grew so quickly that Leopold II commissioned the present building, a dignified edifice

Preceding pages: Leuven Town Hall is a masterpiece of Brabant Gothic. **Left,** you can get to Tervuren by tram.

in the style of Louis XVI, from the French architect Charles Girault. The museum's entrance is on the Steenweg op Leuven. On the opposite side of the road, a massive stone elephant points the way.

Inside, exhibits include Central African ivory carvings, dancers' masks, weapons, everyday tools, cult objects and sculptures . Focal point of the main gallery is an exhibition evoking everyday life in the area, emphasising the common elements found in all the local cultures. Another section covers the customs and traditions specific to the individual regions.

The most popular attraction in the museum is a huge pirogue – a boat carved from a single tree trunk – housed in the right wing. The zoological, geological, mineralogical and botanical sections provide a wealth of information about this region of the Dark Continent. Some sections of the building are devoted to displays of beetles, insects, snakes and birds. Children of all ages love the dioramas displaying stuffed crocodiles, antelopes, water buffaloes, rhinoceroses, zebras, lions, giraffes and elephants set in mock-ups of their natural habitats. They'll have to be tolerant of crowds, however: the museum attracts 250,000 visitors each year.

After visiting the museum and the surrounding park, it's worth wandering round the town of Tervuren. The historic centre contains some fine examples of 18th and 19th-century townhouses, in particular those in the **Kasteelstraat**. The famous Art Nouveau architect Henry van der Velde lived in **Het Nieuwe Huis** (Albertlaan 3), built according to his own designs.

Capuchin monastery: If you are in need of a respite from museums and historic buildings, take a woodland stroll in the **Kapuzinenbos.** Leopold II had a little footpath laid between Tervuren and Jesus-Eik; it's a lovely route, skirting the domain of a former Capuchin monastery. An **Arboretum** was planted here in 1902, harbouring a collection of trees

The Royal Museum of Central Africa in Tervuren.

from the temperate zones as well as a number of more exotic specimens. Grouped in sections according to their geographical origins – Europe, China and Japan – the main collection covers some 35 hectares (86 acres), whilst species from America extend across a further 65 hectares (160 acres).

Medieval charm: The university town of **Leuven** (Louvain) lies some 25 km (16 miles) from Tervuren. Built on a succession of attractive terraces, the town has a pleasing aspect; its university, the oldest in the low countries, adds to its medieval character.

Leuven was founded as a trading settlement on the site of a fortress occupied by the Vikings, destroyed and later rebuilt by Count Lambert I during the 11th century. Thanks to its strategic position at the upstream navigable limit of the River Dyle and commanding the route linking the Rhine Valley region with the sea, it grew rapidly in importance and in the 12th century received its charter.

During the 12th and 13th centuries, its weaving industry made Leuven one of the most important cloth manufacturing centres in Europe. Until the end of the 13th century it was the seat of the Counts of Leuven; in 1190 they were created Dukes of Brabant. The monasteries and churches still bear witness to their tremendous wealth.

In 1378 the guildsmen and peasants revolted against the ruling aristocracy, and one of the nobles was killed by the mob as he attempted to flee. After reprisals at the hand of the Duke of Luxembourg, many weavers emigrated to England where the textile industries were beginning to thrive; the town itself, robbed of its raison d'être, ceded its dominant position to Brussels.

The brewing tradition established during the 18th century has been maintained until the present day, providing an interesting contrast to the remnants of medieval splendour.

The most famous sites in the town of Leuven are grouped round the market

Colonial days recalled in the museum's fine hallway.

place: the **Town Hall** (Stadhuis) and the 15th-century **Church of St Peter**. The Town Hall was built by Mathieu de Layens between 1448 and 1463 for the ruling Duke of Burgundy, Philip the Good. The three-storey building has 10 pointed-arched windows per floor and six exquisitely carved octagonal turrets, making it a masterpiece of Brabant Gothic architecture. The niches in the façade house statues of famous local personalities, and also illustrate in relief themes in the Old and New Testaments. These reliefs were carved between 1852 and 1872. The façade suffered damage from lightning in 1890, but was subsequently restored to its original form.

Picture of justice: Within the Town Hall itself, visitors may tour the jury room, once furnished by paintings by Dieric Bouts, a famous artist who was a powerful influence on German 15th-century painting, who for a time lived and in 1475 died in Leuven.

Two of the works that used to grace the building are based on a legend of Gottfried of Viterbo, and were designed to serve as a model of fair judgement for the magistrates. One painting depicts the Emperor Otto, who ordered the execution of a nobleman because he was reputed to be in love with the empress. The second painting depicts the widow of the dead man proving by setting fire to herself that her husband was the victim of a calumny on the part of the empress. Upon hearing of her suicide, Otto is supposed to have had his wife burned at the stake (in fact, the historical Otto was never married). Dieric Bouts' pictures are now in the Museum of Ancient Art in Brussels.

Directly opposite the Town Hall stands the late Gothic **Church of St Peter** (St-Pieterskerk). The cruciform basilica with ambulatory and chapels was never finished because the foundations proved too unstable.

The exuberantly baroque pulpit, dating from 1742, is adorned with reliefs depicting Peter's denial and the conversion of St Norbert. Three arches com-

The roof of Leuven's 15th-century Town Hall.

pleted in 1488 separate the choir from the nave. The church's most valuable treasures are two paintings by Dieric Bouts. The triptych illustrating the *Martyrdom of St Erasmus* is also of note.

The tabernacle is 12 metres (38 ft) high and contains the *Altar of the Last Supper*, in which the Apostles are shown gathered round a table, listening to the words of Christ. The figure of the latter is somewhat larger than those of the onlookers and is the only one looking out of the picture.

The **University** of Leuven has a venerable tradition. The "Studium Generale Louvaniense" was founded on 9 December 1425 by Pope Martin V at the request of Duke Jean IV of Brabant. The 12 teachers were summoned from Cologne and Paris.

Pope Adrian VI, Erasmus of Rotterdam and Justus Lipsius, who founded the discipline of classical and antiquarian studies, were all famous scholars with close links to the University of Leuven. The University printers produced the first Latin edition of Thomas More's *Utopia* (1516).

When the German troops invaded during World War I the entire archives, consisting of over 300,000 books, went up in flames. In May 1940 the new university library – a gift of the United States, and containing 1,000,000 books – was also destroyed.

For many years the University of Leuven was at the centre of the bitter feud between the Flemings and the Walloons. The problem was resolved in 1962, when the Catholic university, founded in 1425, was divided into two sections: a Flemish section (Katholieke Universität Leuven) and its French-speaking counterpart: (Université Catholique de Louvain).

When the language boundaries were decided by law, the French-speaking citizens of Leuven should theoretically have left the town. In 1969, however, **Louvain-la-Neuve** was built instead – "New Leuven". The division of the university into two halves was conducted

in an equally bureaucratic manner. The books in the university library were shared out between the two universities by allotting those with an even catalogue number to the one, and the odd numbers to the other.

Everyday life in Louvain-la-Neuve is dominated by the university. As in Cambridge, the institution forms an essential part of urban life. With the preferences of residents foremost in mind, the town planner, Raymond Lemaire, set about designing an attractive, open place in which to live. Since the diameter from one side to the other is only about 2 km, it is perfectly feasible to commute between residential, study and leisure centres on foot. The town centre proper contains banks, shops, offices and the station, which forms part of the direct line from Luxembourg and Namur to Brussels.

The **Park Abbey** lies a short distance outside the town; it was founded in 1129 by Premonstratensian monks from Laon. The character of the present building complex is dominated by the reconstruction work carried out between 1719 and 1730.

Tropical climes: In **Wavre**, some 25 km (16 miles) from Brussels, lies Walibi, the largest amusement park in Belgium. On admission, the visitor is transported into a fantasy world. Its tropical swimming pool draws the biggest crowds.

One of the most popular attractions in the entire province of Brabant – visited by around one million tourists from all over the world every year – is the battlefield of **Waterloo**, situated some 18 km (11 miles) from the capital. It was here that in June 1815 Napoleon suffered a crushing defeat at the hands of the united forces of Prussia and England. It led to his enforced abdication for the second time (*see the chapter The Battle of Waterloo, page 39*).

The best view of the site on which the fighting took place can be gained from the famous "Lion's Hill", the *Butte du Lion*. The visitor must first climb the 226 steps to the top of the artificial

A view from Leuven Town Hall.

mound. This was created in 1825 on the spot where the Prince of Orange was wounded whilst commanding an army of Dutch-Belgian troops. The hill takes its name from the cast-iron statue of a lion with its right forepaw placed symbolically on a globe. The statue, 4.5 metres (14 ft) long, 1.5 metres (5 ft) high and weighing 28,000 kg, was erected on a stone pedestal on the mound (soil scraped from the actual battlefield where thousands fell). At the foot of the hill there's a museum devoted to the battle.

The Belle Alliance, the inn in which Napoleon established his quarters, and the lodgings taken over by the Duke of Wellington are still standing. The village church dates from 1855; the numerous inscriptions on its walls recall the fallen multitudes.

Walking country: The region to the south of Brussels is ideal territory for taking extensive country walks. Nestling at the heart of this magnificent landscape lies the town of **Nivelles**, some 35 km (22 miles) from the capital. The town's history is closely linked to that of the **Abbey of St Gertrude**.

Founded in the 7th century, it is the oldest monastery in Belgium. According to legend, following the death of the Frankish ruler Pepin the Elder, his widow Itta retired with their daughter Gertrude to a villa on the hillside overlooking the Thines valley. After the death of her mother and after a declining marriage to Dagobert I, Gertrude founded the monastery, at the instigation of Amand, Bishop of Maastricht. She immediately set about ordering books from Rome and summoned monks from Ireland.

Nowadays, the abbey church is regarded as one of the finest Romanesque sacred buildings in Belgium. The present-day buildings were constructed in various phases from the 11th century onwards.

The porch is flanked by two small towers, the "Tour Madame" and the "Tour de Jean de Nivelles". Several explanations attempt to account for the name of the former, including the theory

Every festival is attended by a brass band.

that it derives from the fact that the abbess had to pass the tower on her way to the Collegiate Church. Others say that the name refers to the long list of abbesses who were in charge of the abbey from its founding in 645 until its secularisation in 1797.

The Tour de Jean de Nivelles contains a copper statue which has become a symbol of the town and which was donated by the Duke of Burgundy, Charles the Bold.

Sadly, after a fire in the church in 1940 only a handful of figures and fragments of architecture survived. There are a number of features worth seeing, however. Various reliefs depicting incidents in the life of Samson adorn the North Door, including a scene in which he is wreathed in garlands of flowers and fighting the lions; another in which Delilah is cutting his hair; and one in which he is blinded by the Philistines.

The South Portal of the church contains a statue of the Archangel Michael with outspread wings. The church consists of a main nave and two aisles, separated from each other by square and cruciform pillars.

The silver reliquary, containing the remains of St Gertrude, was crafted between 1272 and 1298 by Jacquemont de Nivelles and Colard de Duai, in accordance with a design by Jacques d'Anchin. Each year, on the Sunday following the Feast of St Michael, the bones of St Gertrude are carried in procession along a 12-km (7-mile) route through the town and its immediate surroundings, a tradition which has been observed since the 12th century.

The village of Nivelles grew up around the abbey and developed into one of the country's most famous weaving towns. It prospered until well into the 17th century, but fell into economic eclipse after the Weavers' Uprising and subsequent emigration.

To the east of Nivelles, the visitor will soon arrive at the ruins of the **Cistercian Abbey of Villers-la-Ville**, founded in 1146 by St Bernard of Clairvaux (1090–

Left, St Gertrude's monastery, Nivelles. Right, the madonna at Halle.

1153). Under his guidance the order blossomed and became known as the Order of St Bernard.

The monastery was completely self-sufficient. The monks worked on the land, and the order's estates were soon extensive. During the Netherlands Wars of Independence against the Spanish, some sections of the building complex were destroyed. It was subsequently rebuilt, only to be dissolved under Austrian rule and finally destroyed once more by the French in 1794.

During the 19th century the ruins were sold piecemeal by a private investor. It was not until the 20th century that any interest was shown in the restoration of what remained of the buildings and sculptures, which by this time were in danger of total decay. Today all that is left are Romanesque sections of the earliest buildings and the pointed arches of the abbey church.

Flemish Brabant: Further to the West, 15 km (9 miles) south of Brussels, lies the pilgrimage town of **Halle**. The **Ba-**silica of Our Lady**, formerly known as the Church of St Martin, contains a number of notable treasures. The building itself is a fine example of Brabant Gothic dating from the 14th century. The tower recalls the fortified towers of many Belgian town halls and weavers' halls. Inside is an extensive collection of sculptures tracing the development of Belgian sculpture across the centuries.

Of particular note are the statue of the Madonna and Child by the West door and the series of Apostles in the choir above the arches. Above the high altar is a wooden statue of Our Lady; carved during the Middle Ages and thought by some to possess miraculous powers. Processions of pilgrims visit the statue of Our Lady at Whitsun and at the beginning of September each year.

In the **Chapelle de Trezgnies** stands an exquisite alabaster altar by Jehan Mone. A Renaissance work dating from 1522, it is adorned with carved reliefs depicting the seven sacraments and various miniature statues. A marble memo-

Windmill scene on a country road.

rial in the chapel recalls the Dauphin Joachim, a son of Louis XI of France, who died in 1420.

In nearby **Huizingen**, the extensive park covering an area of 91 hectares (225 acres) provides an excellent place for recreation. The magnificent gardens display over 1,200 species of flowers and plants.

From here it is worth making a short detour to the medieval moated castle of **Beersel**, which lies on the wooded green belt surrounding the city of Brussels. The castle has three 14th-century towers soaring high above the moat. The entire building was restored in 1920.

Southwest of the capital, straddling both sides of the Charleroi Canal, is **Anderlecht**, a community forming part of the Greater Brussels Metropolitan Area. It is famous for its Gothic **Church of St Peter**, dating from the 15th century and boasting a belfry and magnificent frescoes.

In 1521 the famous humanist Erasmus of Rotterdam lived in Anderlecht for five months. The revolutionary philologist and critic vehemently attacked the malpractices of the Church, attempting at the same time to influence public opinion on the matter.

In memory of his stay in the little town, the house in which he lodged has been transformed into a museum. **Erasmus House**, once the property of Pierre Wichman, a canon and friend of Erasmus, occupies the east side of the square dedicated to Jan Dillen. The rooms, which are adorned with several valuable paintings, give a good idea of the original furnishings of the period. Erasmus's study still contains many of his possessions: his desk, his armchair, and even his inkwell and books. A reliquary holds his death mask and his private seal. The paintings in the house are ascribed to the artists Quentin Metsys, Albrecht Dürer and Hans Holbein.

The North: Beyond Brussels, near Antwerp, at the confluence of the Greater and Lesser Nete, lies **Lier** (Lierre). This **The Astronomical clock in Lier.**

town's main claim to fame lies in two famous sons: **Felix Timmermans** (1886–1947), the writer, and **Louis Zimmer**, the inventor of the astronomical clock.

Timmermans is one of the most significant Belgian folklore writers and painters. In his novels and stories he created a colourful, sometimes rather idealised picture, of life in Brabant – characterised by gentle humour and naive piety. Timmermans described Lier in many of his books and considered it to be the loveliest town in the country. His principal works include *Pallieter*, *The Child Jesus in Flanders*, and *The Gentle Hours of the Virgin Symforosa, the Beguin*.

The **Timmermans-Opsomer House** serves as a memorial to both Timmermans and the portraitist Baron Opsomer (1878–1967), who was also a native of the town.

Part of the ancient fortifications, the **Zimmer Tower**, still remain. The **Astronomical Clock** and the **Planetarium**

were both the work of the clockmaker Louis Zimmer.

The clock itself is 4.5 metres (14 ft) high and represents the life's work of the master clockmaker. It was built into the tower in 1930 as a present to the town. Although only 13 dials are visible from outside, within the tower itself are a further 57 dials showing the time in every part of the world as well as numerous astronomical phenomena, including the phases of the moon and the course of the stars.

In the centre of the town lies the **Grote Markt**. Its principal building miraculously escaped damage during the German occupation of 1914. The **Town Hall** was built in 1740 in the rococo style, with no less than 3,600 windowpanes. Linked to the building is a Gothic belfry dating from 1369. In Lier, too, you can view a number of paintings by famous Dutch and Belgian masters. The **Museum Wuyts van Campen en Baron Caroly** houses works by Rubens, Teniers, Pieter Brueghel and van Dyck as well as contemporary works.

Near the market square is the late Gothic **Church of St Gummarus**, dating from the 15th and 16th centuries. The building has some fine stained-glass windows in the choir, depicting Emperor Maximilian of Habsburg and his wife, Mary of Burgundy. The window entitled *The Coronation of the Virgin* in the southern aisle recalls the style of Rogier van der Weyden. The triple-arched choir screen was executed in 1536 in accordance with the designs of F. Mynsheeren and J. Wischavens from Mechelen; it represents the evangelists and the fathers of the church.

Other interesting features include the baroque shrine of St Gummarus, by Dieric Somers, dating from 1682 and containing the relics of the town's patron saint, and the tower, which is 80 metres (256 ft) high and contains a carillon of 48 bells.

Maximilian's son, Philip the Handsome, and the Infanta of Spain, Joanna, the sultry daughter of Ferdinand of Aragon and Isabella of Castile, married in this church in 1496. It was an event of great historical significance, for it marked the beginning of the influence of Spain in the Southern Netherlands.

When Philip died in 1506 after only a year on the Spanish throne, and poor Joanna was deemed insane and kept in confinement by her father (hence her nickname Joanna the Mad), their son Charles only had to wait for his grandfather to die before succeeding as king of Spain. And thanks to the wheeling and dealing of his grandfather, when Maximilian finally passed away in 1519, at the age of 61, Charles was also crowned Holy Roman Emperor of German Nations.

The **Beguine Convent** in Lier was founded in the 13th century and is the best-preserved in Belgium. Passing through the entrance the visitor arrives in front of the convent church, an example of Flemish Renaissance architecture dating from the 17th century.

Whichever direction you choose to take, it is easy to escape the bustle of the capital. North, south, east or west - the province of Brabant is a treasure chest of unexpected pleasures. Idyllic little towns, fairy-tale castles and handsome churches all bear witness to the country's colourful history.

Spiritual centre: The town of **Mechelen**, 15 km (9 miles) south of Lier, is also within the province of Antwerp. The Dyle (Dijle), a tributary of the Scheldt, splits into two before the gates of the town.

Mechelen's origins lie far back in history; excavations of pile dwellings have revealed that a small village existed here as long ago as Celtic times. An abbey was founded in 756 by St Rombout; but no further settlement developed until the 11th century.

The town experienced its Golden Age between 1507 and 1530 under Margaret of Austria, regent for the future Emperor Charles V. After her successor, Maria of Hungary, decided to transfer

Procession of Our Lady in picturesque Mechelen.

her place of residence from Mechelen to Brussels, the town became an archbishopric in 1556, with a primate whose authority extended across the entire Netherlands.

Ring out the bells: The town is dominated by the 97-metre (310-ft) tower of the **Church of St Rombout**, named after the local saint who had founded the first abbey here during the 8th century. The church itself dates primarily from the 14th–15th centuries. The tower, whose construction was begun in 1452, was originally intended to reach a height of 168 metres (538 ft). However, in 1578 William of Orange had the stones reserved for its completion carried away for use in the building of the fortress of Willemstad on the Holandsch Diep.

Two **carillons** with 49 bells hang in the belfry. The ancient art of campanology was revived in the 20th century in Mechelen by Jef Denijn. He established the only school of campanology in the world here. Carillon concerts take place on Monday evenings in summer.

The interior of the Church of St Rombout is baroque in style; the use of black, white and red marble indicate the town's former prosperity. A richly decorated choir blends with the three Gothic naves. The baroque high altar, in the shape of a Renaissance arch, is the work of the local sculptor Luc Fayd'herbe. Above the arch stands the statue of St Rombout. Equally famous is the painting *The Crucifixion* by van Dyck. Twin tombs recall two famous princes of the church: Cardinal Granvelle, the first bishop of Mechelen, and Cardinal Mercier, who died in 1926, and in whose memory a funeral chapel of black marble was erected. Cardinal Mercier was the revered spiritual leader of the Belgian Resistance movement during World War I.

Today, Mechelen is a thriving industrial town in which agriculture nevertheless continues to play a significant role. It is still one of the country's leading spiritual centres.

One of the most important secular buildings of the town is the **Town Hall** on the **Grote Markt**. The latter is the setting for the courthouse as well as a number of Renaissance and baroque buildings. Forming part of the Town Hall complex – which today houses the municipal art collections – is the Weavers' Hall, which was modelled on the one in Bruges.

The **City Courts** were built between 1507 and 1529, which means they are some of the oldest Renaissance-style buildings in the country. They were originally built by Rombout Keldermans as a palace for Margaret of Austria, but later became the residence of Cardinal Granvelle. The Grand Diet convened here from 1616 until 1794. Also of note is **St John's Church**, dating from the 15th century and housing the famous altarpiece *The Adoration of the Magi* by Pieter Paul Rubens.

Mechelen was once surrounded by no fewer than 12 gateways, of which only one – the twin-towered *Brusselpoort* (Brussels Gate) – remains today.

Funfair in the Grote Markt, Mechelen.

INSIGHT GUIDES

TRaveL TIPS

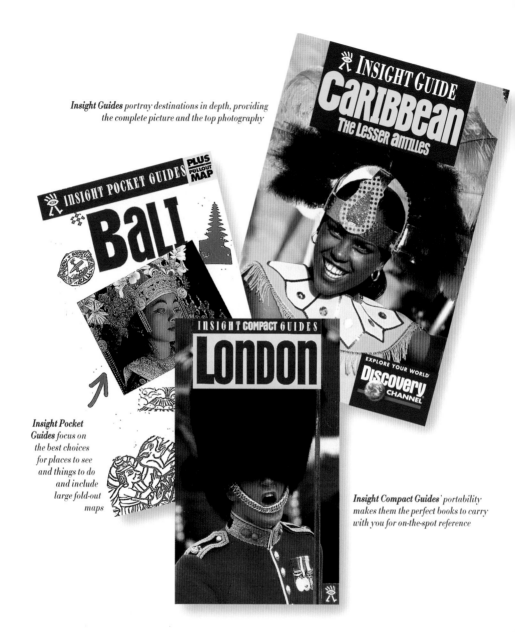

Insight Guides *portray destinations in depth, providing the complete picture and the top photography*

Insight Pocket
Guides *focus on
the best choices
for places to see
and things to do
and include
large fold-out
maps*

Insight Compact Guides' *portability
makes them the perfect books to carry
with you for on-the-spot reference*

Three types of guide for all types of travel

INSIGHT GUIDES Different people need different kinds of information.
Some want *background information* to help them
prepare for the trip. Others seek *personal recommendations* from someone who
knows the destination well. And others look for *compactly presented data* for on-
the-spot reference. With three carefully designed series, Insight Guides offer
readers the perfect choice. Insight Guides will turn your visit into an experience.

The world's largest collection of visual travel guides

CONTENTS

Getting Acquainted

Area: 30,510 sq. km/11,784 sq. miles
Highest mountain: Botrange (694 metres/2,272 ft)
Principal Rivers: Scheldt, Meuse and Sambre
Population: Belgium: approximately 10 million; Brussels: 970,500
Languages: Flemish (Dutch dialect) and Walloon (French)
Religion: Roman Catholic
Time Zone: GMT + 1 hour
Currency: Belgian franc (BF)/Euro
Weights & Measures: Metric
Electricity: AC 220 volts.
National Anthem: *La Brabançonne*
International dialling code: 00 32
City code: 02

Geography

Brussels is situated upon several hills along the Senne, a small tributary of the Scheldt River. In the 19th century, the river was completely built over within the centre of the city. The city centre lies at about 15 metres (50 ft) above sea level and the Forest and Duden Parks at about 100 metres (335 ft). Corresponding to its hilly character, Brussels falls naturally into two parts: the Upper and Lower Cities, the latter of which includes the old part of the town.

The Government

In accordance with the constitution of 7 February 1831, Belgium is a constitutional monarchy which is passed down through the House of Saxe-Coburg. The legislative branch is composed of the senate and house of parliament, and members of both are elected every four years. The head of state is the monarch. The executive duties of the government are carried out by the prime minister and his cabinet.

The constitution was reformed in 1970–71 to guarantee autonomy to the country's Dutch, French and German cultural groups.

Brussels is the capital city of the Belgian kingdom and of the province known as Brabant. Situated only a few kilometres north of the "language border" between Flanders (in the North) and French-speaking Belgium (in the South), it is officially bilingual. However, you'll find that in everyday discourse French is by far the most common language used throughout Brussels.

Greater Brussels, the "Agglomération Bruxelloise", is composed of 19 different districts (*communes*). Each district used to be a separate suburb; over time they have grown and expanded to create a single, urban area.

Aside from the old part of the city, the districts in Brussels are Anderlecht, Auderghem, Berchem-Sainte-Agathe, Etterbeek, Evere, Forest, Ganshoren, Ixelles, Jette, Koekelberg, Molenbeek-Saint-Jean, Saint-Gilles, Saint-Josse-ten-Noode, Schaerbeek, Uccle, Watermael-Boitsfort, Woluwe-Saint-Lambert and Woluwe-Saint-Pierre.

The Economy

The economy of Belgium as a whole is in a reasonably healthy state, after emerging from the austerity measures of the mid-1990s to join the first wave of countries to adopt the Euro on 1 January 1999. The economy is dominated by industry, which contributed 68% of GDP in 1998, followed by services at 30% and agriculture at 2%.

The economy of the city of Brussels depends on three main factors: the presence of the EU and NATO, conferences and industry.

Brussels is the headquarters of NATO and the seat of the European Union and its institutions: the European Commission, Council of Ministers and European Parliament.

Climate

Belgium enjoys a temperate maritime climate with relatively cool summers and mild winters. In the summer, the average temperature is about 16°C (60°F), in the winter about 3°C (37°F).

Strictly speaking, this is only a provisional state of affairs, awaiting a final decision by the member states on a permanent home for the EU, the sticking point being that Belgium, France and Luxembourg all wish to retain their slice of the cake. This compromise gives rise to the 'gravy train' where Members of the European Parliament and officials travel between Brussels, Luxembourg and Strasbourg, pocketing their generous expenses as they go.

The presence of the EU in Brussels stimulates the local economy in many ways, creating thousands of jobs not only in the institutions themselves, but also in lobbying and pressure groups, property and construction, entertainment and restaurants. It has also drawn to Brussels some 1,100 international organisations – a world record

The city is also an important international finance centre, where thousands of multinational enterprises maintain their headquarters.

Brussels has extensive conference facilities throughout the city, making it the second most important congress city in Europe.

The textile industry has traditionally played an important role in Brussels. Nowadays, metal, electrical, pharmaceutical and chemical concerns are more important. Brussels produces 20% of the country's exports and contributes 15% of Belgium's GDP.

People

Belgium derives its name from the Belgae, the first recorded inhabitants, probably Celts. It was conquered by Julius Caesar and ruled in turn by Rome, the Franks, Burgundy, Spain, Austria and France. In 1815 Belgium was made part of the Netherlands and in 1830 it became an independent consitutional monarchy. Today, Belgium has a population of just over 10 million, of whom around one million live in Brussels.

The Flemings of northern Belgium (about 60 percent of the population) speak Dutch, while French is the language of the Walloons in the south (40 percent). A German-speaking minority lives in eastern Belgium. This language difference has been an ongoing source of acrimony and, while prosperity has shifted between the regions over the years, the French-speakers have traditionally represented the aristocracy and the Flemings the bourgeoisie. In 1989, parliament took steps to ease the tension by transferring power from central government to three regions, Wallonia, Flanders and Brussels-Capital, but the language divide still influences daily working life, education, politics and culture.

Nearly one-third of the population of Brussels are foreigners. All the member states of the EU have substantial communities, and there are also many Moroccans, Turks, Zaireans and economic migrants from central and eastern Europe.

Planning the Trip

What to Wear

The people of Brussels generally dress smartly but conservatively. Visitors wanting to make it past the doormen of upmarket bars, especially in the Upper City, should take care to wear smart clothes. But in most places you won't feel at all uncomfortable or conspicuous in everyday, casual attire. Bring comfortable shoes for walking on the cobbles and don't forget a raincoat and/or umbrella as Brussels can be woefully wet and windy at any time of year.

Entry Regulations

VISAS & PASSPORTS

All visitors entering Belgium from countries which are members of the European Union or from Switzerland require a valid personal identity card or passport. Visitors from the United States, Australia, New Zealand, Japan and most other developed countries need only a valid passport; no visa is required. Children under the age of 16 must be in possession of a child's identity card/passport if their names have not been entered in one of their parents' cards.

Travellers bringing in cats or dogs are required to have an official certificate issued by a vet stating that their pet has been vaccinated against rabies. This vaccination must have taken place at least 30 days prior to arrival and be no more than one year old (in the case of cats, six months).

CUSTOMS

There is no limit to the amount of foreign currency that can be brought in or taken out of Belgium. Items for everyday use and those frequently transported by tourists, such as cameras and sporting equipment, may be brought into the country duty-free.

EU citizens: Visitors over 17 from European Union nations are not subject to restrictions on goods and conumable items for personal use.

Non-EU citizens: Citizens from non-EU nations are permitted to bring the following items into Belgium duty-free: 200 cigarettes or 50 cigars or 250g tobacco; 2 litres still wine; 1 litre spirits or 2 litres sparkling or fortified wine; 50g perfume and 0.25 litres toilet water.

The Euro

On 1 January 1999, Belgium adopted the Euro, which is now interchangeable with the Belgian franc and locked at the rate of 1 Euro = BF40.3399. There are now no official cross rates between the Belgian franc and the currencies of other Euro countries: conversion is via the Euro only. Most businesses now display prices in both Belgian francs and Euros.

Money Matters

The national currency is the Belgian franc (BF). There are 100, 200, 500, 1,000, 2,000, 5,000 and 10,000 franc notes and 1, 5, 20 and 50 franc coins in circulation.

Belgian notes and coins are interchangeable with those of Luxembourg.

BUREAUX DE CHANGE

There are many exchange offices in the city centre, most of them open daily for longer hours than the banks. Those located in the large railway stations offer competitive rates and are open daily including public holidays at the following times:

Gare du Nord: 7am–9.30pm
Gare Centrale: 7am–9pm
Gare du Midi: 6.45am–10pm

There is an automatic change machine on the Grand' Place which is open 24 hours.

Eurocheques can be exchanged for a maximum of 7,000 Belgian Francs per cheque.

CREDIT CARDS

International credit cards are accepted by most businesses throughout the city. If you lose your card, the numbers to contact in Belgium are:

American Express 676 2111
Diner's 206 9800
Eurocard, MasterCard, Visa 070-344 344

If you should lose your Eurocheque card, report the loss at once to your bank.

Getting There

BY AIR

Brussels' international airport, Zaventem, is 14 km (8 miles) northeast of the city centre. General information is available by telephoning 723 2345 (24 hour service), or on the internet: www.brusselsairport.be. International air services information is provided by the national carrier, Sabena (tel: 511 9030 or 753 2111). As the seat of the European Union, Brussels is well served by international airlines. By air, it is an hour from Paris, London, Amsterdam and Frankfurt. Sabena has particularly good links with Africa. From the US, American Airlines flies direct to Brussels from Chicago every day. United Airlines has a daily flight between Washington and Brussels. Airline offices in Brussels:

Aer Lingus, 98 Rue du Trône, tel: 548 9848 or at the airport: 753 2000.
American Airlines, 98 Rue du Trône, tel: 508 77 00.
British Airways, 98 Rue du Trône, tel: 548 2122/33.
Lufthansa, at the airport, tel: 745 4455.
Sabena, 2 Avenue E. Mounier, tel: 723 2323 (bookings and reconfirmations);0900 00747 (flight information); 723 6011

(luggage recovery, head office and general services); 723 3111 (airport).
Swissair, Sabena House, Zaventem, tel: 723 8050.
United Airlines, 350 Avenue Louise, tel: 713 3600 or at the airport: 753 2680.
Virgin Express, there is no office in Brussels you can visit, but contact them by phone on: 752 0505, or web: www.virgin-express.com

BY ROAD

Belgium is criss-crossed by international motorways which are toll-free.

Coach services depart daily from London's Victoria Coach Station and are operated by:
Eurolines, tel: 0990 980980.
Anglia Lines, tel: 01582 451777
The journey takes about 8 hours. There is a credit card booking line at the coach station, tel: 0171 730 3499.

Distances to other European cities:
Amsterdam 211 km (131 miles)
Paris 309 km (192 miles)
Calais 200 km (125 miles)
Cologne 220 km (136 miles)
Ostend 114 km (70 miles)
Luxembourg 216 km (134 miles)

BY RAIL

Trains from Paris take 1 hour 25 minutes; from Cologne 2 hours; from Amsterdam 2 hours 40 minutes.

International trains stop at all the city's main rail stations, which are Brussels North (Nord), Brussels Central (Centrale) and Brussels South (Midi).

International rail information is available in Brussels on tel: 555 2525.

P&O European Ferries in London, (tel: 0990 980980), or National Rail Enquiries (tel: 0345 484950) are reliable sources of information about boat trains to Brussels from the UK.

EuroTunnel has shuttle trains with a capacity of 120 cars, which take about 10 minutes to load. Vehicles are carried by train through the tunnel between Folkestone in Kent and Nord-Pas de Calais in

Public Holidays

1 January	New Year's Day
March/April	Easter Monday
1 May	Labour Day
May	Ascension Day
	Whit Monday
21 July	National Day
15 August	Assumption
1 November	All Saints' Day
11 November	Armistice Day
25 December	Christmas Day

If any of these holidays happen to fall on a Sunday, the following Monday is taken off.

France. The fare varies greatly depending on the time of travel; night or early morning crossings are the cheapest. Booking is not essential; but recommended during peak times. Enquiries in UK, tel: 0990 353535.

Eurostar train services run from London (Waterloo) via Ashford and Lille to Brussels Midi and take 2 hours 40 minutes. There are up to 12 trains a day between the hours of 6am and 7pm. For reservations and information, tel: 0990 186186. The Eurostar number is Brussels is: 525 9292.

BY SEA

Ferry services between the UK and Belgium are operated by:
P&O North Sea Ferries between Hull and Zeebrugge, tel: 01482 377177.
P&O European Ferries between Dover and Calais and Zeebrugge, tel: 0990 980980.

Tourist Offices Abroad

Canada: Belgian Tourist Office, PO Box 760, succursale NDG, Montreal, Quebec H4A 3S2, tel: 514 484 3595, fax: 514 489 8965.
France: Office Belge de Tourisme, 21, Boulevard des Capucines, 75002 Paris, tel: 01 47 42 41 18, fax: 01 47 42 71 83, web: www.belgique-tourisme.net
Germany: Belgisches Verkehrsamt, Berliner Allee 47, 40212

Düsseldorf, tel: 0211 86 48 40, fax: 0211 13 42 85, web: www.belgien-turismus.net
Italy: Ufficio Belga per il Turismo, Piazza Velasqua 5, 20122 Milano, tel: 02 86 05 66, fax: 02 87 63 96, web: www.belgio-turismo.net
Netherlands: Belgisch Verkeersbureau, Kennemerplein 3, 2011 MH Haarlem. Tel: 023 534 4434, fax: 023 534 2050, web: www.belgie-toerisme.net
Scandinavia: Belgian Tourist Office for the Nordic Countries, Nyropsgade 47, 1602 Copenhagen V, tel: 033 939=03 57/8, fax: 033 93 48 08, web: www.belgium-tourism.net
United Kingdom: Belgian Tourist Office, 31 Pepper Street, London E14 9RW, tel: 0171 458 2888 (premium rate call), fax: 0171 458 2999, web: www.belgium-tourism.net
United States: Belgian Tourist Office, 780 Third Avenue, New York 10027, tel: 212 758 8130, fax: 212 355 7675, web: www.visitbelgium.com

Practical Tips

Business Hours

There are no laws governing the closing times of shops in Belgium. Most businesses maintain hours between 9am and 6pm; supermarkets and local grocery stores often keep their doors open until 9pm. Some shops close for a lunch break from noon–2pm.

On Fridays many larger stores and supermarkets in Brussels are open until 8 or 9pm. A few night shops are open around the clock. Apart from those in the city centre, the vast majority of shops close on Sundays and holidays.

Banks

All banks in Belgium will exchange foreign money. Most open 9am–4pm Monday–Friday, with some closing for lunch between noon and 2pm.

Tipping

You're not obliged to leave a tip in Belgium. Nevertheless, in the cinema, for example, it is wise to pay BF20 for the programme if you wish to avoid an altercation with the usherette. Tips are already included in hotel room prices, but a small tip when you depart is always appreciated.

In lavatories where there is an attendant, it is customary to leave between BF10 and 15.

Media
NEWSPAPERS & MAGAZINES
Because Belgium is composed of three different language communities, you'll find numerous newspapers. The three most important French newspapers are the *Le Soir, La Libre Belgique* and *La Dernière Heure*. The three most widely distributed Dutch papers are the *Het Laatste Nieuws, De Standaars* and *De Morgen*. *Grenz-Echo* is the major German newspaper.

The weekly English language newspaper, *The Bulletin*, keeps the many thousand members of the international community in Brussels informed and up-to-date regarding what is going on in Belgium.

Foreign newspapers and magazines can be purchased at bookshops throughout the city.

RADIO & TELEVISION
Aside from the many local stations in Belgium, there are also some national radio stations: RTBF for Walloons, BRT for Flemings and the BRF for those who speak German. RTBF and BRT share the television monopoly. In addition, in practically all areas of the country it is possible to receive a huge range of foreign stations by cable. BBC Radio 4 is clearly audible on long wave.

Post & Telecoms
POSTAL SERVICES
The post office located at the South Railway Station is open every day around the clock. Other post offices are open between 9am and 5pm and are closed on weekends as well as holidays. The main office in the city centre is located in the Anspach Centre above de Brouckère Métro station. Some shops which sell postcards also sell stamps.

TELEGRAMS
Telegrams can be sent by calling the number 1225, or through the reception at your hotel.

TELEPHONE
The dialling code for Brussels is 02. Current calling rates can be found posted in all telephone booths; booths from which it is possible to make long-distance calls to other

countries are marked with international flags. If you want to place a call outside Belgium, first dial 00, then the country code, and finally the number of the party you wish to contact (delete the zero in the area code). Public phone boxes take BF20 coins, or phonecards, which are available from bookshops, newsagents and kiosks.

Tourist Offices in Brussels

Brussels Tourist and Information Office, Brussels Town Hall, Grand' Place, 1000 Brussels, tel: 513 8940, fax: 514 4538, theatre and concert booking service 0800 21221, e-mail: tourism.brussels @tib.be. Open: summer: daily 9am–6pm; winter: 10am–2pm; closed Sundays in January and February.
Belgian Tourist Office, 61 Rue du Marché-aux-Herbes, 1000 Brussels, tel: 504 0390, fax: 504 0270. Open: November to April Monday–Saturday 9am–6pm, Sunday 9am–1pm; May, June, September, October daily 9am–6pm; July and August daily 9am–7pm.
Belgian Tourist Reservations, 111/4 Boulevard Anspach, 1000 Brussels, tel: 513 7484, fax: 513 9277. Hotel reservation service.

Business Information
CHAMBERS OF COMMERCE
Brussels Chamber of Commerce, 500 Avenue Louise, 1050 Brussels, tel: 648 5002, fax: 640 9328.
British Chamber of Commerce, 15 Rue d'Egmont, 1000 Brussels, tel: 540 9030, fax: 512 8363, e-mail: office@britcham.be, web: www.britcham.be.

EUROPEAN UNION OFFICES
The main buildings housing the office of the European Union institutions are located to the east of the city centre around the Rond Point Schuman.

Emergency Numbers

Ambulance: 100
Fire brigade: 100
Police: 101
Red Cross: 105
Doctors on emergency call: 479 1818 and 648 8000

Until the Berlaymont re-opens, the main **European Commission** building is at 45 Avenue d'Auderghem, tel: 299 1111. The postal address is: 200 Rue de la Loi, 1049 Brussels.
To arrange a visit to the Commission, write at least two months in advance to the Head of the Visitors' Service, European Commission, 120 Rue de Trèves - 05/45, 1049 Brussels
You'll find the EU **Council of Ministers** in the Justus Lipsius building at 175 Rue de la Loi, tel: 285 6111.
The controversial new **European Parliament** building is at 43 Rue Wiertz, 1000 Brussels, tel: 284 3453.
Guided tours to the Council and Parliament are also possible, but for groups only, by written request several weeks in advance. Call one of the above numbers for details.

CONFERENCES
The Brussels Tourist Information Association (TIB) maintains a special service providing information on all conference facilities and events: **Bruxelles Congrès asbl**, 6 Rue du Musée, 1000 Brussels, tel: 549 5050, fax: 549 5059.

Embassies

Australia: 6 Rue Guimard, tel: 286 0500.
Canada: 2 Avenue de Tervuren, tel: 741 0611.
Germany: 190 Avenue de Tervuren, tel: 774 1911
Ireland: 89 Rue Froissart, tel: 230 5337.
United Kingdom: 85 Rue d'Arlon 85, tel: 287 6211.
USA: 25 Boulevard du Régent, tel: 508 2111.

Emergencies
CHEMISTS
After regular business hours and during holidays you will find the name and address of the nearest chemist on night-duty posted at all chemists.

DOCTORS & HOSPITALS
Visitors from EU countries should obtain a form E111 before leaving home. This entitles them to some free treatment, but does not cover all eventualities. Treatment must be paid for and the cost recovered when you return home. All visitors are advised to take out private medical insurance.

Lost & Found

There is a Lost & Found office for items lost at Brussels airport, tel: 753 6820; to recover belongings left on an aeroplane, tel: 723 3929 8am–4pm; to retrieve lost luggage tel: 723 6011.
For articles lost or left behind on a train, tel: 555 2525, or enquire at the nearest train station.
Otherwise items left on trams, buses or the Métro may turn up at the STIB Lost Property Office, located at 15 Avenue de la Toison d'Or, tel: 513 2394.
Lost items may also be reported to the police inspector's office in the relevant commune, or at the police headquarters at 30 Rue du Marché au Charbon (in the city centre), tel: 517 9611.

Getting Around

On Arrival

Brussels lies at the centre of Belgium and the motorways radiate from the capital outwards into the surrounding country. A motorway (the Ring) runs around the outside of the city, giving vehicles easy access into as well as around the city. There is also an inner ring road encircling the city centre.

The following is a list of distances from Brussels to the main Belgian towns. Where towns have both Flemish and French names, the local names is given first:

Antwerpen/Anvers 48 km (30 miles)
Brugge/Bruges   97 km (61 miles)
Charleroi   61 km (38 miles)
Ghent/Gand   55 km (34 miles)
Liège/Luik   94 km (59 miles)
Mechelen/Malines 27 km (17 miles)
Mons/Bergen   67 km (42 miles)
Namur/Namen   63 km (39 miles)
Oostende   114 km (71 miles)
Tournai/Doornik 86 km (54 miles)

A frequent train service (every 20 minutes) connects the airport with Brussels' main railway stations from about 5.30am– midnight. The journey takes 20 minutes.

Public Transport

BY AIR
From Zaventem Airport it is possible to fly to various cities within the country. However, because of its relatively small distances involved, train or road are usually more efficient.

BY RAIL
There are six railway stations in Brussels:

Gare du Nord (North Station), Rue du Progrès.
Gare Centrale (Central Station), located underground at the Boulevard de l'Impératrice.
Gare du Midi (South Station), Rue de France.
Quartier Léopold, Place du Luxembourg.
Schaerbeek, Place Princessè Elisabeth (for car/sleeper trains to Spain and the south of France).
Schuman, Rond Point Schuman (serves the European institutions for passengers from outlying districts).

These railway stations are connected to one another by the Métro. Further information and tickets for the National Belgian Railways (Chemins de Fer Belges) are available in the booking halls at all the city's railway stations. For all national and international information, tel: 555 2525.

BY BUS, TRAM AND METRO
Brussels has a well-developed and extensive Métro network, complemented by bus and tram routes. You can recognise Métro stations by the "M" sign (a white "M" against a blue background). Bus stops are marked with red and white, tram stops with blue and white signs. At bus or tram stops sporting a sign saying *sur demande*, it's necessary to motion for the vehicle to halt and pick you up.

Bus, tram and Métro information is available from STIB at 15 Avenue de la Toison d'Or, tel: 515 2000, as well as at Porte de Namur, Rogier and Midi Métro stations, tel: 515 2000, fax: 515 3285.

There are several different types of tickets issued, including single-journey tickets, multi-journey tickets for five or 10 rides, and a 24-hour ticket, good for all trams, buses and Métros within the city centre.

Passengers caught riding without a valid ticket by the frequent, roaming controls are required to pay a hefty fine, which accumulates daily if not paid on the spot.

TAXIS
Taxis are plentiful in Brussels but cannot be hailed in the street. There are many taxi ranks in the town centre: outside the European institutions, hotels and railway stations, on Boulevard Anspach and Place de l'Agora. Alternatively, they can be ordered from the following companies:
Autolux, tel: 411 1212
Taxis Bleus, tel: 268 0000
Taxis Verts, tel: 349 4949
Taxis Orange, tel: 349 4343
Any complaints should be addressed to the Service Régional des Taxis et Limousines, tel: 204 2111 or 0800/14795.

Private Transport

BY CAR
In Belgium the maximum speed limit in built-up areas is 50 kph (31 mph), and on country roads 90 kph (56 mph). On motorways and dual carriageways this limit rises to 120 kph (75 mph). The use of both front and back seat belts is mandatory.

In general, the "priority to the right" rule applies to most situations, meaning that the vehicle to your right usually has the right of way, unless the road is marked with an orange diamond-shaped sign. If you have priority, take it – otherwise the driver behind you may go straight into the back of your car.

It is illegal for children under the age of 12 to sit in the front passenger seat if there is room in the back seat. Motorcyclists and moped riders are obliged by law to wear helmets and parking is not permitted in places where the curb is marked with a yellow stripe.

Hazard triangles must be carried in the vehicle at all times. Trams always have the right of way. Foreigners caught defying traffic regulations are required to pay any fines incurred on the spot.

Breakdown Services
Touring Secours, tel: 233 2211/ 070 344 777.
RACB, tel: 078 152 000.

Automobile Clubs

Royal Automobile Club de Belgique (RACB)
Rue d'Arlon 53, 1040 Brussels, tel: 287 0900.
Touringclub Royal de Belgique (TCB)
Rue de la Loi 44–46, 1000 Brussels, tel: 233 2211, 513 8240.

Car Hire

There are several car hire firms in Brussels; most have an office in town and a branch at the airport.
Airport Cars, 98 Diegemstraat, Zaventem, tel: 725 7653, fax: 725 3389.
Avis, 107 Rue du Colonel Bourg, tel: 730 6211, web: www.avis.com
Budget, at the airport tel: 753 2170, fax: 721 1970; 327B Avenue Louise tel: 646 5130, fax: 646 2721.
Europcar, at the airport tel: 721 0592, international tel: 348 9212.
Hertz, at the airport tel: 720 6044, town centre tel: 513 2886.

Travelling By Bicycle

Cycling in the city centre can be a hair-raising experience. Although there are plenty of cycle lanes, car drivers are not always considerate of other road users, so always be on your guard.

Outside of town, however, it's a different story. The flat landscape is ideal and country folk are far more cycle-friendly. The SNCB operate a *Train + Vélo* scheme to 35 destinations in Belgium, many of them easily accessible from Brussels. The reasonable price covers both train ticket and hire of touring cycles or mountain bikes. Bikes must be returned to the station where you hired them. The brochure entitled *B-Excursions* gives all the details, and is available from the tourist office on the Grand' Place or from main railway stations.

Where to Stay

Hotels

Visitors to Brussels will find a large selection of hotel accommodation in every price range. Many of the larger hotels offer special bargain rates for weekend stays. Hotels must post their room rates at the reception desk and are permitted to charge only these prices on your final bill.

In the city's official hotel guide you will find a complete list, including addresses and prices, of the 120 or so hotels in the city. This guide is available at the Tourist Offices on Rue du Marché aux Herbes (Grasmarkt) 61 and in the Town Hall (TIB) (*see page 230 for contact details*). It is also possible to book accommodation at both these places. Belgian Tourist Reservations will also book a hotel room for you. They can be contacted at 111 Boulevard Anspach, 1000 Brussels, tel: 513 7484, fax: 513 9277.

THE BEST HOTELS

Amigo
1–3 Rue de l'Amigo
Tel: 547 4747
Fax: 513 5277
e-mail: hotelamigo@compuserve.com
This luxury-class hotel just off the Grand' Place deserves its high reputation and five-star status.
$$–$$$$

Astoria
103 Rue Royale
Tel: 227 0505
Fax: 217 1150
e-mail: info.bxl.astoria@sofitel.be
One of Brussels' most illustrious hotels dating from 1909, with lovely belle époque interior and excellent restaurant. **$$–$$$$**

Brussels Hilton
38 Boulevard de Waterloo
Tel: 504 1111
Fax: 504 2111
A luxury hotel with 4 renowned restaurants, a bar and conference facilities. All rooms have a view of the city and a park. **$$$–$$$$**

Hôtel Métropole
31 Place de Brouckère
Tel: 217 2300
Fax: 218 0220
e-mail: info@metropolehotel.be
An elegant hotel rich in tradition, with high-class restaurant, piano bar and café. Located in the heart of town, with very reasonable weekend rates. **$$–$$$$**

Président World Trade Center
180 Boulevard E. Jacqmain
Tel: 203 2020
Fax: 203 2440
Large 5-star hotel with conference facilities. All rooms have a mini-bar, TV, phone and fax. There is also a fitness centre and sauna. **$$–$$$$**

Sheraton
3 Place Rogier
Tel: 224 3111
Fax: 224 3456
Web: www.sheraton.com/brussels
Modern 5-star hotel in the lower city with two restaurants, a piano lounge, and health and fitness facilities. Breakfast buffet each morning is not included in the room rate. **$$–$$$$**

LUXURY CLASS HOTELS

Bristol Stéphanie
91 Avenue Louise
Tel: 543 3322
Fax: 538 0307
An ultra-modern hotel with an indoor swimming pool on fashionable Avenue Louise. **$$–$$$**

Château du Lac
87 Avenue du Lac
1332 Genval
Tel: 655 7111
Fax: 655 7444
e-mail: cdl@martins_hotels.com
Overlooking the Lac de Genval, a popular beauty spot southeast of Brussels, the Château dates from the 1890s and is a copy of an old abbey. **$$$–$$$$**

Jolly Hotel Atlanta
7 Boulevard Adolphe Max

Tel: 217 0120
Fax: 217 3758
A fine location and a reputation for consistent service are the main attractions of this Italian-owned hotel. **$$–$$$**
Radisson SAS Hotel
47 Rue du Fossé-aux-Loups
Tel: 219 2828
Fax: 219 6262
e-mail: phv@bruzh.rdsas.com
Impeccable top-flight hotel, incorporating part of Brussels' old city wall, featuring a gym, the excellent Sea Grill restaurant, and Henry J Bean's cocktail bar downstairs. **$$–$$$$**
Royal Windsor Hotel
5 Rue Duquesnoy
Tel: 505 5555
Fax: 505 5500
A modern hotel with an old-fashioned sense of style and a location near the Grand' Place. **$$**

GOOD HOTELS

Albert Premier
20 Place Rogier
Tel: 203 3125
Fax: 203 4331
One of the grand old names in Brussels lodging, this hotel is located near the North Railway Station and offers conference facilities and a tavern. **$–$$**
Arenberg
15 Rue d'Assaut
Tel: 501 1616
Fax: 501 1818
Four-star hotel located near the Central Railway Station. **$$–$$$**
Chambord
82 Rue de Namur
Tel: 548 9910
Fax: 514 0847
A comfortable hotel with its own bar, close to the chic Upper City shopping areas. **$–$$**
Diplomat
32 Rue Jean Stas
Tel: 537 4250
Fax: 539 3379
A modern hotel located in the midst of the elegant shopping area along the Avenue Louise. **$$**
Dixseptième
25 Rue de la Madeleine
Tel: 502 5744
Fax: 502 6424

A graceful and elegant hotel close to the Grand' Place, this is one of those places that generates a lot of repeat business thanks to customer loyalty. Early booking is advisable. **$$–$$$**
Kasteel Gravenhof
676 Alsembergsesteenweg
1653 Dworp
Tel: 380 4499
Fax: 380 4060
e-mail: gravenhof@hwv.be
Maybe the nearest thing Brussels has to a Spanish parador, Gravenhof is a lovely old Flemish-style château located not far from Brussels. **$$**

Hotel Price Guide

For a double room including breakfast:
$ = BF1,600–3,500
$$ = BF3,500–7,000
$$$ = BF7,000–10,000
$$$$ = over BF10,000
Where two categories are indicated, the lower of the two is the weekend rate.

Manos
100-104 Chaussée de Charleroi
Tel: 537 9682
Fax: 539 3655
e-mail: manos@pophost.eunet.be
A highly individual and characterful mansion-style hotel near Avenue Louise. **$$$**
Art Hotel Siru
1 Place Rogier
Tel: 203 3580
Fax: 203 3303
Four-star hotel not far from the North Railway Station with restaurant and conference facilities. The rooms have been decorated with works of art by contemporary Belgian artists. **$–$$**
Ramada
38 Chaussée de Charleroi
Tel: 533 6666
202 rooms; all rooms have colour TV, mini-bar, telephone and air-conditioning.
Stanhope
9–13 Rue du Commerce
Tel: 506 9111
Fax: 512 1708

Three former townhouses converted to a hotel situated between the stylish uptown shopping district and the EU institutions, the Stanhope has all the grace of an English country hotel combined with a good city location. **$$$–$$$$**

REASONABLY PRICED HOTELS

Arlequin
17–19 Rue de la Fourche
Tel: 514 1615
Fax: 514 2202
e-mail: arlequin@skynet.be
You only have to step out of the hotel door to be in the heart of Brussels' atmospheric city-centre dining area, the Ilot Sacré. **$–$$**
Agenda Louise
6–8 Rue de Florence
Tel: 539 0031
Fax: 539 0063
A fine small hotel located just off Avenue Louise and close to Place du Châtelain, an area full of trendy bars and restaurants. **$–$$**
De Boeck's
40 Rue Veydt
Tel: 537 4033
Fax: 534 4037
Its big rooms and reasonable prices make this hotel a good bet for budget group travellers. Conveniently located near Place Stéphanie. **$**
Derby
24 Avenue de Tervuren
Tel: 733 7581/0819
Fax: 733 7475
A small budget hotel close to the Cinquantenaire Park. **$**
Congrès
42 Rue du Congrès
Tel: 217 18 90
Fax: 217 1897
Converted from two townhouses, this hotel has comfortable rooms and is located close to Rue Royale and the Botanique. **$**
Grande Cloche
10–12 Place Rouppe
Tel: 512 6140
Fax: 512 6591
Small budget hotel (some rooms without bath) close to the city centre. Save on your hotel bill and book a table at Comme Chez Soi across the square! **$**

Les Bluets
124 Rue Berckmans
Tel: 534 3983
Fax: 534 0970
e-mail: bluets@skynet.be
Small and friendly hotel in a
beautiful 19th-century house
located in a quiet street close to
Avenue Louise. **$**
Pacific
57 Rue Antoine Dansaert
Tel: 511 8459
Highly individualistic – not to say
eccentric – hotel on a chic shopping
street near the Bourse. **$**
Queen Anne
110 Boulevard Emile Jacqmain
Tel: 217 1600
Fax: 217 1838
A business-traveller orientated hotel
in an area of Brussels that may be
looking up after years of steady
decline. It's located just out of the
city centre, but in compensation it's
fairly quiet. **$–$$**
Vendôme
98 Boulevard Adolphe Max
Tel: 227 0300
Fax: 218 0683
Large, modern hotel with good
facilities in downtown Brussels.
$–$$
Welcome
5 Rue du Peuplier
Tel: 219 9546
Fax: 217 1887
A small (6 rooms) hotel near the
Fish Market which prides itself on
its personal service. An excellent
restaurant, La Truite d'Argent, is
attached. **$**

Campsites

There are no camping sites in the
city of Brussels itself. However, the
following three sites are located in
places quite nearby and are within
reach by public transport.
Camping Paul Charles
114 Avenue Albert 1er
1332 Genval
Tel: 653 6215
Open all year round.
Camping de Renipont
7A Rue du Ry Beau Ry
1380 Ohain (near Waterloo)
Tel: 654 0670
Open all year round.

Camping Welcome
104 Kouterstraat
3090 Overijse
Tel: 687 7577
Open April–October.

Bed & Breakfast

For information on staying with
local families, contact the
following:
Bed & Breakfast Taxistop
28 Rue du Fossé aux Loups
1000 Brussels
Tel: 223 2310
Fax: 223 2232
Bed & Brussels
2 Rue G Biot
1050 Brussels
Tel: 646 0737
Fax: 644 0114
e-mail: BnBru@ibm.net
New Windrose
21A Avenue Paul Dejaer
1060 Brussels
Tel: 534 7191
Fax: 534 7192
This organisation also acts as a
contact point for au pair
positions.

Youth Hostels

Auberge de Jeunesse Breugel
2 Rue du Saint Esprit
1000 Brussels
Tel: 511 0436
Fax: 512 0711
e-mail: jeugdherberg.bruegel@ping.be
Conveniently located in the city
centre. close to the Gare Centrale.
Parking for bikes and motorbikes,
24-hour access.
Auberge de Jeunesse Jean Nihon
4 Rue de l'Eléphant
Tel: 410 3858
Fax: 410 3905
e-mail: aj.nihon.yh.inf@infonie.be
This hostel is located slightly out of
town, but has good facilities: bar,
restaurant, garden and barbeque,
laundry and parking. Métro: Comte
de Flandre.
Auberge de Jeunesse Jacques Brel,
30 Rue de la Sablonnière
1000 Brussels
Tel: 218 0187
Fax: 217 2005

e-mail: brel.aj.yh@skynet.be
This youth hostel has 174 beds,
with some facilities for disabled
people. Métro: Botanique
Centre Vincent Van Gogh/CHAB
8 Rue Traversière
Tel: 217 0158
Fax: 219 7995
e-mail: chab@ping.be
A 15-minute walk from the Grand'
Place, this hotel has bar, restaurant
and gardens and also offers
internet access. Métro: Botanique.
Sleep Well
23 Rue du Damier
1000 Brussels
Tel: 218 5050
Fax 218 1313
e-mail: info@sleepwell.be
This modern building in the city
centre has a wide range of facilities
including cybercafé, tourist
information centre, disabled
access. Métro: Rogier.

Where to Eat

What to Eat

The people of Belgium have the reputation of possessing especially fine tastebuds and this fact is attested to by the large number of excellent restaurants, particularly in Brussels. The *Gourmet* dining guide available from the Tourist Information Centre (TIB) on the Grand' Place contains a list of restaurants along with their addresses, hours, prices and particular house specialities. Belgians usually have their lunch sometime between noon and 2 or 3pm; dinner is customarily eaten at any time between 6pm and midnight.

Brussels is especially well-known for its fresh mussels, oysters and lobster. Fish dishes made from sole, cod and turbot are prepared in a variety of tasty ways. *Waterzooi* is a light creamy soup-cum-stew made with either chicken or fish. Beef cooked in beer (*carbonnades flamandes*) is a hearty dish for a cold day. In the autumn, game frequently appears on restaurant menus. Belgian chicory is also very popular, often cooked in the form of a casserole (*chicons au gratin*). Two more delicious dishes are red cabbage prepared in the Flemish style and (in season) asparagus from Mechelen (*asperges à la flamande*). The Belgians also love their steak and chips, and the quality of the meat is generally high.

Beer – and there are over 400 different kinds to choose from! – is the national drink. However, the wine, primarily imported from France, is also recommended.

Brussels' many cafés are really more like pubs where you can drink and get a relatively inexpensive bite to eat – sandwiches *or tartines* (usually an open sandwich made with wholemeal bread). If you can stomach it, the most popular sandwich filling is raw minced beef with various seasonings (*filet américain* or *américain préparé*). Getting a good meal in Brussels is not likely to pose a problem. The city centre is absolutely packed with places to eat and drink.

Price Guide

Average cost of a meal for two including a bottle of wine:

$	=	BF1,200–3,000
$$	=	BF3,000–4,800
$$$	=	BF4,800–7,500
$$$$	=	over BF7,500

Where to Eat

FIRST-CLASS RESTAURANTS

Barbizon
95 Welriekendedreef
3090 Overijse (Jesus-Eik)
Tel: 657 0462
Fine, long-established French restaurant in the pleasant village of Jesus-Eik. Garden open in summer. **$$$$**

De Bijgaarden
20 I. Van Beverendstraat
1702 Groot-Bijgaarden
Tel: 466 4485
Legendary French restaurant on the outskirts of Brussels offering some of the country's very best food in delightful surroundings. **$$$$**

Bruneau
75 Avenue Broustin
Tel: 427 6978
Famous Brussels restaurant specialising in French cuisine. **$$$$**

Claude Dupont
46 Avenue Vital Riethuisen
Tel: 426 0000
One of the country's top restaurants, serving French cuisine in elegant surroundings. Reservations essential. **$$$$**

Comme Chez Soi
23 Place Rouppe
Tel: 512 2921
This is reputedly *the* best restaurant in the whole of Brussels;

a gastronomic paradise with Art Nouveau decor. Book well in advance. **$$$$**

La Maison du Cygne
2 Rue Charles Buls 2 (just off the Grand' Place)
Tel: 511 8244
Superb and sumptuous French restaurant with exceptional wine cellar. Views over the Grand' Place. **$$$**

La Sirène d'Or
1A Place Sainte-Catherine
Tel: 513 5198
Master chef Robert Van Duüren creates divine seafood dishes in one of the best restaurants on the square. **$$–$$$**

La Truffe Noire
12 Boulevard de la Cambre
Tel: 640 4422
Small restaurant specialising in French cuisine; modern surroundings and garden for summer dining. **$$$$**

L'Ecallier du Palais Royal
18 Rue Bodenbroeck
(Place du Sablon)
Tel: 512 8751
Exclusive restaurant which prepares the very best in fish and seafood dishes. **$$$**

Les 4 Saisons
(in the Royal Windsor Hotel)
2 Rue de l'Homme Chrétien
Tel: 505 5100
Refined French cuisine, served along with what the owners claim to be the capital's biggest selection of fine wines. **$$$**

Villa Lorraine
28 Chaussée de la Hulpe
Tel: 374 3163
One of the country's most prestigious restaurants; French cuisine with the accent on fish and seafood; beautiful surroundings. **$$$$**

GOOD RESTAURANTS

Aux Armes de Bruxelles
13 Rue des Bouchers
Tel: 511 5550
This restaurant in the heart of the Ilot Sacré is one of the city's best locations, well respected for its high quality Belgian cuisine at reasonable prices. **$$**

La Belle Maraîchère
11 Place Ste-Catherine
Tel: 512 9759
Country-style decor; the speciality in this well-loved restaurant is seafood. **$$**

Castello Banfi
12 Rue Bodenbroeck
Tel: 512 8794
Chef Breeda Ruane-Kober creates sublime Italian food, which is attentively served in this elegant restaurant on the Place du Grand Sablon. **$$–$$$**

Les Crustacés
8 Quai aux Briques
Tel: 511 5644
Popular restaurant in typical Brussels style specialising in lobster. **$$**

L'Ogenblik
1 Galerie des Princes
Tel: 511 6151
Offers a Parisian-style bistro ambiance, despite its semi-Dutch name ('blink of an eye'). The food is of a high standard, well presented and served by helpful staff. **$$–$$$**

Les Petits Oignons
13 Notre-Seigneur
Tel: 512 4738
Set in a shabby but characteristic part of the Marolles, this 17th-century townhouse is splendidly atmospheric. The welcoming service is matched by fine french cuisine. **$$**

La Quincaillerie
45 Rue du Page
Tel: 538 2553
Perhaps a little too conscious of its own modish good looks, this restaurant in a converted hardware store nevertheless remains perenially popular. Reservations recommended. **$$**

Scheltema
7 Rue des Dominicains
Tel: 512 2084
One of the Ilot Sacré restaurants that has not allowed the easy tourist market to demean its standards of service, quality and price. French and Belgian cuisine, with seafood specialities. **$$**

La Truite d'Argent
23 Quai au Bois à Brûler
Tel: 219 9546
This restaurant has an attractive

19th-century interior, plus a terrace on the old fish market. Owner Michel Smeesters relishes the history and traditions of the place, and his beautifully presented seafood specialities are highly recommended. **$$–$$$**

Au Vieux Saint-Martin
38 Place du Grand Sablon
Tel: 512 6476
High quality brasserie food; the restaurant is decorated with Belgian works of art. **$$**

Price Guide

Average cost of a meal for two including a bottle of wine:
$ = BF1,800–3,000
$$ = BF3,000–4,800
$$$ = BF4,800–7,500
$$$$ = over BF7,500

BISTROS

Bij den Boer
60 Quai aux Briques
Tel: 512 6122
Popular and traditional Brussels bistro on the old fish market serving good value Belgian food. **$**

La Bonne Humeur
244 Chaussée de Louvain
Tel: 230 7169
It may look like a transport caff, but this small family-run restaurant has people queueing in the street to eat the excellent *moules et frites*. Closes at 9.30pm. **$**

Café de la Gare
95 Rue de la Station de Woluwe
Tel: 762 7470
Excellent bistro serving Belgian fare in homely surroundings. Piano player on Saturday nights. **$–$$**

Chez Henri
113 Rue de Flandre
Tel: 219 6415
Just off Place Sainte Catherine, this old restaurant somewhat incongruously serves caviar and lobster in a fish'n'chips style café. Excellent mussels and fish dishes are also on the menu. **$$**

In 't Spinnekopke
1 Place du Jardin aux Fleurs
Tel: 511 8695
One of Brussels' oldest restaurants, which proudly

proclaims its affinity with traditional Belgian beers. **$–$$**

Jacques
44 Quai aux Briques
Tel: 513 2762
One of Brussels' seafood favourites in the old fish market. Reservations advisable. **$–$$**

't Kelderke
15 Grand' Place
Tel: 513 7344
Plain, hearty Belgian fare such as *stoemp*, *carbonnades* and *moules*, served by friendly waiters in a convivial cellar. **$**

Chez Léon
18 Rue des Bouchers
Tel: 511 1415
A Brussels institution since 1893, the chefs serve up thousands of mussels in various guises every day. The quality is always reliable, the service fast but friendly. **$**

A Malte
30 Rue Berckmans
Tel: 537 0991
Café-bistro with a relaxed bohemian atmosphere offering good, reasonably priced food from breakfast until supper. **$**

Aux Marches de la Chapelle
5 Place de la Chapelle
Tel: 512 6891
Housed in a former post-house near the chic Sablon quarter, this superior brassiere has a stylish belle époque interior. It specialises in *plats du terroir* – earthy local dishes. The sole from Zeebrugge is also popular. **$**

La Mirabelle
459 Chaussée de Boondael
Tel: 649 5173
Located near the univeristy campus, this is representative of the good-value restaurants in the area frequented by students and *Bruxellois* in-the-know. Great steaks; garden in summer. **$**

't Misverstand
916 Chaussée d'Alsemberg
Tel: 376 2398
Although it's located to the south of Brussels out in Uccle, this restaurant is well worth the trip for its fine steaks and fish dishes. Lovely garden for dining outside on summer nights. **$–$$**

Le Paon
35 Grand' Place
Tel: 513 3582
The magnificent building dates back to the 17th century, and the food is traditional Belgian. **$$**
Le Pré aux Sources
36 Rue St-Lambert
Tel: 771 4787
This is a delightful restaurant in Woluwe St Lambert offering good traditional bistro food. Terrace in summer. **$**
La Roue d'Or
26 Rue des Chapeliers
Tel: 514 2554
The brasserie decor is a mixture of mirrored art nouveau and homage to René Magritte. Service and atmosphere are familiar and friendly, and the food is great. **$**
Les Salons de l'Atalaïde
89 Chaussée de Charleroi
Tel: 537 2154
Huge bar-restaraunt in a former auction house, with reasonably priced brasserie food served by glamourous waitresses. **$**
Ultieme Hallucinatie
316 Rue Royale
Tel: 217 0614
There are two places to eat at this address, both renowned for their good food and art nouveau surroundings. The restaurant (**$$$**) is in a former masonic lodge; the brasserie (**$**) in a glasshouse.
Vincent
8–10 Rue des Dominicains
Tel: 511 2303
Walk through the kitchens to reach the unusually decorated dining room. The traditional Brussels fare, *moules*, seafood and steaks, is great value for money. **$**

ETHNIC RESTAURANTS
L'Atlantide
73 Rue Franklin
Tel: 736 2002
An excellent choice for lunch in the Schuman area. Authentic Greek dishes such as feta cheese and spinach pasties, aubergines and calamari. **$**
Blue Elephant
1120 Chaussée de Waterloo
Tel: 374 4962
Wonderful Thai food served in

Hotel Restaurants

The following hotel restaurants are highly recommended to all gourmets:
Astoria Hotel
Palais Royal
103 Rue Royale
Tel: 227 0532
French cuisine in beautiful *belle époque* hotel. **$$–$$$**
Château du Lac
Le Trèfle à Quatre
1332 Genval
Tel: 654 0798
Prestigious French restaurant on the banks of the Lac de Genval. **$$$**
Hilton Hotel
La Maison du Boeuf
38 Boulevard de Waterloo
504 1334
Exclusive French restaurant. **$$$$**
Métropole Hotel
Alban Chambon
31 Place de Brouckère
Tel: 217 2300
Excellent French cuisine. **$$$**
Radisson SAS Hotel
Sea Grill
47 Rue du Fossé aux Loups
Tel: 227 3120
Specialises in seafood. **$$$**

sumptuous surroundings by waiters in traditional dress. A real treat. **$$**
Au Bon Coeur
27 Rue J Claes
Tel: 538 9669
Try this cheap and cheerful Greek restaurant near the Gare du Midi for platefuls of delicious ribs grilled with oregano, *salade paysanne*, and chips to die for, all washed down with jugs of dubious plonk. **$**
La Brace
1 Rue Franklin
Tel: 736 5773
The best of the many Italian restaurants on this street in the European quarter; great pasta and pizzas, but the service can be somewhat brusque. **$**
Las Castañuelas
132 Rue Stévin
Tel: 280 0081
A good tapas bar in the Schuman

area. Food is served in the garden in summer. **$**
Kasbah
20 Rue Antoine Dansaert
Tel: 502 4026
A taste of Morocco in downtown Brussels; generous portions served in dimly-lit atmospheric bistro. **$**
King-Hwa
240 Chaussée de Louvain
Tel: 230 1579
Excellent Chinese restaurant in St Josse which offers an enormous choice of dishes from all regions of China. **$**
Pablo's
51 Rue de Namur
Tel: 502 4135
Situated between Porte de Namur and Place Royale, this relaxed Tex-Mex joint does great margaritas and solid food. Occasional live music at weekends. **$**
Passage to India
223 Chaussée de Louvain
Tel: 735 3147
Unpretentious and friendly Indian restaurant, the best of those along this road. **$**
Pastissimo
21 Rue du Berger
Tel: 502 1165
Sophisticated Italian cuisine served in unusual ultra-modern surroundings. **$**
La Porte des Indes
455 Avenue Louise
Tel: 647 8651
High-class Indian restaurant in a beautifully decorated old house. Discreet service from waiters in traditional dress. **$$**
Le Rocher Fleuri
19 Rue Franklin
Tel: 735 0021
Near Rond-Point Schuman in the European Quarter, this Vietnamese restaurant is great value for money and does a delicious all-you-can-eat buffet at lunchtime and evenings. **$**
Sukhothai
135 Avenue d'Auderghem
Tel: 649 4366
Well-established Thai restaurant in the European quarter; good food and friendly service. **$**

Drinking Notes

The Belgians have always been great beer-drinkers. A frothy lambic beer can still conjure up images of a Breughelian banquet while a Trappist ale evokes the jollier side of monastic life. Until 1900 each Belgian village had its own brewery, with 3,000 in Wallonia alone. Today, the number of breweries has fallen to 115, but there are still over 400 different beers to choose from, many still produced by the small breweries. Belgian beer enthusiasts can choose the likes of Mort Subite (sudden death) or Verboden Vrucht (forbidden fruit). While Ghent's Stropken (literally "noose") is a tangy brew named after a humiliating event in 1453 when Philip the Good commanded the city burghers to parade with nooses around their necks.

Belgian beers encompass light, refreshing *bières blanches* such as Hoegaarden to potent Trappist ales, including the renowned Chimay. The tangy flavour of a *blanche* comes from such spicy additions as orange peel and coriander. More of an acquired taste are the cherry-flavoured Kriek and sparkling raspberry-flavoured Framboise – the rosé of beers. Lambic beer has no yeast added, and ferments spontaneously. Belgium is the only place in the world where such fermentation takes place. Gueuze, a Brussels beer made by combining five or six lambics, is a cider-like concoction known by connoisseurs as the champagne of beers.

Of the standard lagers, although Stella Artois may be the most famous, the other common brands, Maes and Jupiler, are just as good.

Trappist beers are made by monks and lay brothers who follow the ancient monastic brewing traditions. Only six Cistercian abbeys in the world have the right to term their beer Trappist, and five of these are in Belgium: Orval, Rochefort, Westmalle, Chimay and Westvleteren. Chimay, the "Burgundy of Belgium", is the best-known beer, produced according to a secret monastic recipe in Hainaut

and matured in the bottle. At 7% proof Chimay rouge is the least strong of the beers – even so, the monks claim to dilute it before serving it with their daily lunch.

Orval Abbey is home to 25 contemplative monks who have chosen to live in silence and solitude. Theirs is a fruitier brew than the strong Sint Sixtus Abdij beers from Westvleteren, near Ypres (Ieper).

The Rochefort brewery was originally founded in 1595 near Namur, but the current brewery dates from 1899. It produces a powerful, dark, chocolatey brew. Westmalle Abbey, in Antwerp province, has produced a rich, sweetish, malty beer since 1836.

Culture

The daily newspapers contain information about entertainment in Brussels. Visitors can reserve tickets for the opera, concerts and theatre productions at the Brussels Tourist Information Centre (TIB) at the Grand' Place, tel: 0800/21221.

In Brussels there are theatres which perform dramatic pieces in both French and Dutch. There is a lively English-language theatre scene, with groups specialising in Shakespeare, Irish and American drama and comedy. Check *The Bulletin* for details of future events.

Most of the important concerts take place in the Palais de Beaux Arts. Opera and ballet productions are performed at the Théâtre Royale de la Monnaie (the National Opera House), the most famous stage in Brussels. Aside from these large venues, there is a host of smaller theatres which stage less mainstream productions. Puppet shows played out in the Brussels dialect have been performed at the Toone Puppet Theatre since 1830.

Theatres

The city offers a wide selection of productions at the following venues:
Beursschouwburg
Rue Auguste Orts
Tel: 513 8290
Halles de Schaerbeek
22a Rue Royale
Tel: 218 2107
Koninklijke Vlaamse Schouburg
146 Rue de Laeken
Tel 217 6937
Théâtre de la Balsamine
1 Avenue Félix Marchal
Tel: 735 6468
Théâtre des Martyrs
22 Place des Martyrs
Tel: 223 3208

Théâtre National
Place Rogier
Tel: 203 5303
Théâtre Royal des Galeries
32 Galerie du Roi
Tel: 512 0407
Théâtre Royal du Parc
3 Rue de la Loi
Tel: 511 4149
Théâtre Toone VII
21 Petite Rue des Bouchers
Tel: 511 7137
Théâtre Varia,
78 Rue du Sceptre
Tel: 640 8258 or 0900/00600

Music & Ballet

Ancienne Belgique
110 Boulevard Anspach
Tel: 548 2424
Le Botanique
236 Rue Royale
Tel: 226 1211
Cirque Royal
81 Rue de l'Enseignement
Tel: 218 20 15.
Forest National
36 Avenue du Globe
Tel: 340 2211 or 0900/00991
Halles de Schaerbeek
31 Rue Royale Ste-Marie
Tel: 070/345678
Palais des Beaux-Arts
23 Rue Ravenstein
Tel: 507 8200
Théâtre Royal de la Monnaie
Place de la Monnaie
Tel: 229 1211

Museums

A huge variety of objets d'art, machines and curiosities are housed in over 70 museums in Brussels, many of them interesting buildings in their own right.

Most museums are open daily except Monday, from 10am–5pm and offer reduced entrance fees to groups, children, senior citizens, etc.

There are museums all over the city catering for every taste, from art and architecture to chicory, nesting boxes and sewers. The following is a list of some of the more important museums:

Album
25 Rue des Chartreux
Tel: 511 9055
A small hands-on museum looking at the history of Brussels and Belgium through photos, books and videos and covering subjects such as the monarchy, cinema, beer and the comic strip. Open: daily except Tuesday 1-7pm
Autoworld
11 Parc du Cinquantenaire
Tel: 736 4165
The vehicles on display here date from between about 1886 and 1970; many are part of the 800 or so magnificent cars belonging to Belgian collector Ghislain Mahy. Open: 1 October–31 March: daily 10am–5pm; 1 April–30 September daily 10am–6pm.
Bibliotheca Wittockiana
21 Rue de Bémel
Tel: 770 5333
This is both a museum of the history of bookbinding and a 3,000-volume library, with sections on genealogy and heraldry. Open: Tuesday–Saturday 10am–5pm.
Centre Belge de la Bande Dessinée
(Comic Museum)
20 Rue des Sables
Tel: 219 1980
A wonderful museum, devoted to one of Belgium's passions. It is housed in a magnificent house designed by Horta. Fun and enjoyment for both the young and the young at heart (*see page 82*). Open: Tuesday–Sunday 10am–6pm.
La Maison Brueghel (Breughel's House)
132 Rue Haute
1000 Brussels
Tel: 503 4268
The house of Pieter Brueghel the Elder, containing a display of paintings, documents and keepsakes of this famous painter who died in Brussels in 1569. Open: groups by written request only from 1 April to 31 October.
Musée Bruxellois de la Gueuze
(Beer Museum)
56 Rue Gheude (Anderlecht)
Tel: 521 4928
Here you can witness gueuze beer being brewed (from end October to end March) on original 19th-century

machinery from a recipe handed down from generation to generation. Guided tours and, of course, tastings are available. Open: Monday–Friday 8.30am–5pm Saturday 10am–5pm.
Musée Charlier (House of Guillaume Charlier)
16 Avenue des Arts
Tel: 218 5382/220 2819
This villa, part of which was designed by Art Nouveau architect Victor Horta, is now a showcase for many forms of decorative arts. The absence of labelling preserves the feeling of a real home. In the house are also paintings by Ensor and Meunier, among others. Open: Monday 10am–5pm, Tuesday–Thursday 1.30–5pm, Friday 1.30–4.30pm.
Musée David et Alice van Buuren (David and Alice van Buuren Museum)
41 Avenue Léo Errera
Tel: 343 4851
A wonderful collection of paintings, sculpture and objet d'art, both ancient and modern, displayed in the beautiful art deco house of a wealthy collector, which is surrounded by extensive gardens. Open: Sunday 1–6pm, Monday 2–6pm; gardens open daily 2–6pm.
Musée de la Brasserie (Museum of Brewing)
10 Grand' Place
Tel: 511 4987
The history, theory and techniques of beer brewing in Belgium. Open: daily 10am–5pm.
Musée de la Résistance (Resistance Museum)
14 Rue Van Lint
Tel: 522 4051
Exhibits depicting the Belgian resistance against the occupying forces of World Wars I and II. Open: Monday, Tuesday, Thursday, Friday 9am–noon and 1pm–4pm.
Musée de la Ville de Bruxelles: Maison du Roi et Hôtel de Ville
(City of Brussels Museum: King's House and Town Hall)
Grand' Place.
Tel: 279 4355
This is the essential museum covering the archaeological, historical and cultural development

Cinemas

Some foreign-language films in Brussels are dubbed, but most of them are also shown in the original language, with Dutch and French subtitles. If that's what you're after, look for the letters **VO STB** (*version originale, sous-titres bilingues*).

The city's cinemas are located in two main areas: in the Lower City, around Place de Brouckère:

Kladaradatsch Palace
85 Boulevard Anspach
Tel: 501 6776
Web: www.kladaradatsch.be
Arty cinema which opened for the 1999 Brussels Film Festival on the site of the city's first moviehouse. Bar and restaurant attached.

UGC/De Brouckère
38 Place de Brouckère
Tel: 0900/10440
Large, mainstream cinema with 8 screens.
In the Upper City near the Porte de Namur and the Avenue de la Toison d'Or:

UGC Toison d'Or
8 Avenue de la Toison d'Or
Tel: 0900/10440
Cinema with 11 screens on two adjoining sites.

Vendôme
18 Chaussée de Wavre
Tel: 502 3700
Five-screen cinema 5 minutes' walk from the Porte de Namur.

Two other cinemas:
Actor's Studio
16 Petite Rue des Bouchers
Tel: 512 1696
Small moviehouse with bar showing less mainstream films and some not on general release.

Kinepolis
Bruparck
Tel: 474 2600
Huge cinema in the Brupark leisure complex, with 26 screens and a giant IMAX wrap-around theatre.

---

of the city. In the **Maison du Roi** There are collections of paintings, tapestries, porcelain and pottery, as well as Manneken Pis' wardrobe. Open: Monday–Friday 10am–12.30pm and 1.30–5pm (4pm between 1 October and 31 March); Saturday and Sunday 10am–1pm. Opposite, at the **Hôtel de Ville**, visitors can view the reception rooms and offices of the councillors, which are hung with priceless woven tapestries from Brussels, dating from the 16th, 17th and 18th centuries. Open: daily by guided tour only (available in several languages).

Musée des Chemins de Fer Belges (Belgian Railway Museum)
Gare du Nord
76 Rue du Progrès
Tel: 224 6279
An exhibition of some 30 Belgian locomotives and coaches, the earliest dating from 1835. Open: Monday–Friday and the first Saturday in the month 9am–4.30pm.

Musée des Enfants (Children's Museum)
15 Rue du Bourgmestre
Tel: 640 0107
An altogether fascinating hands-on museum for children, designed to make education fun. Open: Wednesday, Saturday and Sunday and school holidays 2.30–5pm.

Musée des Postes et des Télécommunications (Postal Museum)
40 Place du Grand Sablon
Tel: 511 7740 (post); 511 9830 (telecommunications)
An extensive collection of stamps from Belgium and elsewhere. In addition, the evolution of post and telecommunication systems is explained along with a display of various equipment and postmen's uniforms. Hours: Tuesday–Saturday 10am–4.30pm.

Museum des Sciences Naturelles de Belgique (Belgian Museum of Natural Sciences)
260 Chaussée de Wavre
Tel: 627 4211
Large collections of minerals, fossils and skeletons, including the famous Bernissart iguanodons and an Arctic and Antarctica section, which provide an insight into mineralogy, zoology and evolution. Open: Tuesday–Friday 9.30am–4.45pm; Saturday and Sunday 10am-6pm.

Musée du Cinéma (Cinema Museum)
9 Rue Baron Horta
Tel: 507 8370
Fascinating collection for film buffs, including equipment from the era of silent movies (with piano accompaniment) and a revolving programme of films highlighting different genres. Open: daily 5.30–10.30pm; by appointment Tuesday–Friday 10am–5pm.

Musée du Jouet (Toy Museum)
24 Rue de l'Association
Tel: 219 6168
An interactive museum and playroom containing thousands of toys from 1830 to the present day. Open: daily 10am–12.30pm and 2–6pm.

Musée du Livre et Cabinets de Donations) (Book Museum and Donation Rooms)
4 Boulevard de l'Empereur
Tel: 519 5357
A selection of diverse manuscripts, prints and book covers which afford an overview of the history of books from antiquity up until the present time. Open: Monday, Wednesday, Saturday 2–4pm.

Musée du Théâtre Royal de Toone - Fondation Toone VII (Toone Theatre Museum)
21 Petite Rue des Bouchers
Impasse Schuddeveld
Tel: 511 7137 or 217 0464
The Toone Marionette Theatre has been keeping Brussels' oral tradition alive for generations. On display is an assortment of old puppets, posters and manuscripts relating to the theatre's history. Open: only during intermissions of peformances, which take place Tuesday–Saturday at 8.30pm.

Musée Horta (Horta Museum)
25 Rue Américaine

Tel: 543 0490
The beautiful house and studio of architect and initiator of Art Nouveau in Belgium, Victor Horta (1861–1947), is a museum in itself and also contains exhibits on his best known architectural achievements. Open: Tuesday–Sunday 2–5.30pm.

Musée Instrumental (Museum of Musical Instruments)
New England building
Place Royale
Tel: 545 0130
This museum is due to re-open in 2000 in new premises, which will display to full effect its remarkable collection of 6,000 musical instruments. Contact the Tourist Office or ring the above number for details of the re-opening.

Musée Juif de Belgique (Jewish Museum of Belgium)
74 Avenue de Stalingrad
Tel: 512 1963
This museum chronicles the history of Judaism generally as well as that of the Belgian Jews, and is also a showcase for contemporary Jewish art. Open: Monday–Thursday noon–5pm, Sunday 10am–1pm.

Musée René Magritte
135 Rue Esseghem
Tel: 428 2626
A museum in the northern suburb of Jette opened in 1999 to celebrate the life and works of the father of Belgian Surrealism. Open: Wednesday–Sunday 10am–6pm.

Musée Royal de l'Afrique Centrale (Royal Museum of Central Africa)
13 Leuvensesteenweg
Tervuren
Tel: 769 5211
This beautiful building on the edge of Tervuren park houses a broad collection of artefacts and stuffed animals reflecting central African culture and natural history, and recalling Belgium's colonial days. Contemporary environmental issues are also addressed. Open: Tuesday–Friday 10am–5pm; Saturday and Sunday 10am–6pm.

Musée Royal de l'Armée et d'Histoire Militaire (Royal Army and Military History Museum)
Parc du Cinquantenaire
Tel: 734 5252

Extensive collection of weapons and armaments from the 7th to the 18th centuries. In the aviation section there's a large hall full of planes illustrating the history of military aviation and parachuting from 1912 to the present day. Open: Tuesday–Sunday 9am–noon and 1–4.45pm.

Musées Royaux d'Art et d'Histoire (Royal Museums of Art and History)
Parc du Cinquantenaire
Tel: 741 7211
This impressive museum offers a kind of grand overview of world history and civiliation. There are works from Roman, Greek and Egyptian antiquity; relics from the Roman and Frankish eras in Belgium, as well as sections on the European decorative arts and non-European civilisations. Open: Tuesday–Friday 9.30am–5pm; weekends and public holidays 10am–5pm.

Musées Royaux des Beaux-Arts (Royal Museum of Fine Arts: Museum of Early Art and Museum of Modern Art)
3 Rue de la Régence
Tel: 508 3211
Brussels' best and one of the most famous art museums in the world, with an enormous collection. The **Musée d'Art Ancien** lays the emphasis on paintings, but there are also graphics and sculpture, all dating from the 15th–18th centuries. Art treasures from the 19th and 20th centuries are on display in the **Musée d'Art Moderne**, and feature many Belgian artists, including the a large collection of works by Surrealist René Magritte. Open: Tuesday–Sunday 10am–5pm, closed Mondays and public holidays.

Musée Wiertz (Wiertz Museum)
62 Rue Vautier
Tel: 648 1718
A fascinating glimpse into the work of the Romantic artist Antoine Wiertz, who used this studio from 1846 until his death in 1865. Open: Tuesday–Sunday 10am–noon and 1–5pm, closed public holidays and alternate weekends.

Attractions

For Children

Apart from some of the museums, cinemas and sporting activities, the following attractions should appeal especially to kids:

Atomium
Boulevard du Centenaire
Tel: 474 8977/04
This symbol of Brussels was built for the 1958 World Exhibition and represents an atom in the form of an iron crystal molecule, enlarged 165 billion times. The lower level houses a changing programme of exhibitions on various subejcts. Panoramic views are to be had from the upper spheres. Open: April–August daily 9am–8pm; September–March daily 10am–6pm.

Bruparck
This entertainment complex just next to the Atomium should amuse the kids for several hours. It includes the multi-screen cinema **Kinepolis**, the **Village**, a selection of shops and restaurants, as well as **Mini-Europe**, where you can do a whistlestop tour of all of Europe's famous landmarks in miniature. Opening times vary: winter 9.30am–5pm; summer 9.30–8pm plus late opening on weekend nights. Tel: 474 1311 for exact times. There's also **Océade**, a water funpark with all the usual slides and wave pools. It is open all year round at varying times; tel: 478 4320 or 478 4944 for details.

Children's Zoos
There are two in Brussels. One is just north of the city centre: Ferme du Parc Maximilien, 21 Quai du Batelage, tel: 201 5609. The other is in the southern suburb of Uccle: Ferme Modèle d'Uccle, 93 Vieille

Rue du Moulin, tel: 374 1896.
Labyrinthes de Q-Zar
Boulevard de l'Empereur
Tel: 512 0874
Laser-gun fun daily from 2pm,
Sundays from 10am.
Plankendael
Leuvensesteenweg 582
2812 Muizen - Mechelen
Tel: (015) 414 921
A short drive out of Brussels, this is
a large animal park, with most of
the animals surrounded by
greenery, plus a mini-farm and
adventure playground.
UGC/De Brouckère
38 Place de Brouckère
Tel: 0900/10440
On Saturday at 9.30am, children
are amused with a suitable film,
leaving adults free to watch the
movie of their choice.
Walibi
This is Belgium's biggest and best
theme park featuring a range of
white-knuckle rides and other
amusements. Open: Easter and
June–September: daily 10–6pm
(7pm July and August). At other
times of year, ring (010) 421 500
or 421 717 for exact opening
hours. The adjacent **Aqualibi** is
great for hours of watery fun:
slides, chutes, jacussi. Open: as for
Walibi, but the phone number is
different: tel (010) 414 466 or 421
515. If travelling by train, enquire at
the station for group tickets and/or
combined train-and-Walibi tickets at
a reduced rate.

City Tours

Guided tours are offered by the
following companies:
ARAU
55 Boulevard Adolphe Max
Tel: 219 3345
Fax: 219 8675
Organises tours in English on urban
architecture and history, departing
from outside the Hôtel Métropole.
Brussels by Water
2bis Quai des Péniches
Tel: 203 6406
Fax: 420 5921
Boat trips around the city's
waterways for groups and
individuals.

**Cellule Patrimoine de la Ville de
Bruxelles**
6 Boulevard Anspach
Tel: 279 3010
Created to protect the city's
architectural heritage, this
department publishes leaflets with
detailed information on Brussels'
buildings and suggests walks to
discover them.
Chatterbus
12 Rue des Thuyas
Tel: 673 1835
Fax: 675 1967
Tours on foot and by bus for adults
and children.
De Boeck's
8 Rue de la Colline
Tel: 513 7744
Fax: 502 5869
Daily tours by bus around the city,
also to Ghent, Antwerp and
Waterloo.
Hélitour
40 Avenue J Wybran
Tel: 361 2121
Fax: 360 2770
See Brussels by helicopter.
Pro Vélo
13–15 Rue de Londres
Tel: 502 7355
Fax: 502 8641
Cycling organisation which runs
guided bike tours through the city
and rents out bikes to groups and
individuals.

Outside the City Centre

Tervuren is only 13 km (8 miles)
away from Brussels. It is well worth
your while to pay a visit to Tervuren
Park, Hubertus Chapel (dating from
the 17th century), and especially
the Royal Museum of Central Africa
(Musée Royal de l'Afrique Centrale),
which includes a collection of items
from Belgium's past as a colonial
power. From Tervuren you can also
walk or cycle through the lovely
Forêt de Soignes.
   St Peter's Church (dating from
the 15th century) and the House of
Erasmus, both located in
Anderlecht, also draw their share of
visitors each year.
   A few kilometres north of
Brussels is **Grimbergen Abbey**,

source of the strapping Trappist
Grimergen beers, which are sold in
the café. The abbey was founded in
1128, but the present church dates
from the 17th century. It has a
particularly fine interior, including
delicately chiselled carvings and a
number of Flemish old masters.
   Northwest of Brussels is **Ghent**.
Built over the waterways of the Leie
and the Schedlt, Ghent's historical
centre of meandering alleyways and
elegant buildings is surrounded by a
vibrant city of industry and maritime
trade. It is the capital of the
province of East Flanders and for
centuries has been the focal point
of the Flemish nationality. There are
many historic buildings to see as
you stroll around the pleasantly
relaxed streets.
   Lying just 50km (30 miles) to the
north of Brussels, **Antwerp** has
much to offer the visitor. It is
Europe's largest port, a diamond
centre, an industrial nucleus, the
city of Rubens, as well as a haven
for gourmets and an elegant
shopping centre. The lovely old city
features the largest and most
beautiful Gothic church in Belgium,
the Grote Markt with its Town Hall.
Also of interest are the zoo and the
Jewish quarter close to the main
railway station.
   Between Antwerp and Brussels is
the small town of **Mechelen**. Its
Rombout Church has a 100-metre
(330-ft) high tower and a famous
carillon. The Town Hall at the Grote
Markt, Palace of Justice and Church
of St John are all interesting places
to visit.
   Southeast of Antwerp, the town
of **Lier** is known mainly for two of its
citizens: the author and painter
Felix Timmermans, and Louis
Zimmer, who constructed the first
astronomical clock. The
Timmermans-Opsomer House and
the Zimmer Tower, the Town Hall
(Hôtel de Ville), the Church of St
Gommarus and the Wuyts van
Campen-Caroly Museum are all
worth visiting. Belgium's best-
preserved Beguine Convent is
located in Lier.
   The university city **Louvain**
(**Leuven**) is also just a short jaunt

from Brussels. Be sure to take a stroll through the big market which takes place at the Town Hall (Hôtel de Ville) and St Peter's Church. The university was established in 1425.

The most frequently visited tourist attraction in Brabant is the site of Napoleon's downfall, **Waterloo**, with its museums and visitor's centre commemorating the famous battle.

The old weavers' town of **Nivelles** is 35 km (22 miles) south of Brussels. Its Abbey of St Gertrude, was founded in the 7th century and is the oldest monastery in Belgium. The Tour de Jean de Nivelles, where a famous bronze figure sounds out the hour every hour, has become the symbol of the town.

A short excursion to the ruins of the 12th-century Cistercian abbey of **Villers-la-Ville**, located east of Nivelles, is also interesting.

In the pilgrims' city **Halle** 15 km (9 miles) from Brussels, you will find a great variety of art treasures housed in the Notre Dame Basilica.

The abundance of parking places in **Huizingen** make it easy for visitors to leave their cars and step out for a relaxing walk in the 91-hectare (225-acre) park and gardens. Not too far away you'll come across **Beersel**, a medieval moated castle.

Festivals

Festivals & Exhibits

Brussels has a lively festival calendar. The following events take place at roughly the same time each year:

JANUARY
Automobile Exhibition at Heysel held every two years
Brussels International Film Festival at the Palais des Congrès, 3 Coudenberg

FEBRUARY
Mardi Gras, Brussels' premier horse-racing event held at Sterrebeek Hippodrome
Antiques Trade Fair held at the Palais des Beaux Arts
Batibouw, ideal homes exhibition at the Parc des Expositions, Heysel

MARCH
Salon des Vacances, the holiday, tourism and leisure fair at the Parc des Expositions, Heysel
International Book Fair at the Palais des Congrès, 3 Coudenberg

APRIL
Serres Royales free visits to the spectacular royal greenhouses from late April to early May on the Royal Estate in Laeken

MAY
Serres Royales as above
Queen Elisabeth International Music Competition prestigious musical event alternating between singing, violin and piano, held in the Palais des Beaux Arts
Jazz Rallye live jazz at cafés and on outdoor stages throughout the city
Brussels 20 km run, starting at the Parc du Cinquantenaire

JUNE
Re-entactment of the Battle of Waterloo large-scale and popular event held every five years (2000, 2005)
Couleur Café World Music festival in the Tour et Taxis complex, Rue Picard

JULY
Ommegang Originally a religious procession dating back to the 14th century, today a carnival-like parade held during the first week of July on the Grand' Place.
Brosella Folk and Jazz Festival held in mid-July at the Théâtre de Verdure in Osseghem
National Day celebrated on 21 July with processions in the city centre and fireworks and festivities in the Royal Park
Royal Palace open for visits from 21 July to the end of August
Foire du Midi a large, annual funfair near Midi Railway Station runs for about a month from mid July
Sundays in the Bois de la Cambre classical and jazz concerts from 11am–1pm throughout July and August
Drive-in Cinema every weekend night in front of the Cinquantenaire arch throughout July and August

AUGUST
Sundays in the Bois de la Cambre as above
Drive-in Cinema as above
Foire du Midi as above
Planting of the Meiboom ("Tree of Joy") the planting of the Meiboom tree on 9 August is preceded by a folkloric ritual and procession from Rue des Sables to the Grand' Place
Carpet of Flowers every two years (2000, 2002) the Grand' Place is covered in a wonderful display of flowers

SEPTEMBER
Ivo Van Damme Memorial athletics meeting in Heysel stadium in the first week of September
Brussels Marathon starting at the Parc du Cinquantenaire
Brueghel Festivities held in the middle of the month in Rue Haute, in honour of the great local artist

OCTOBER
Audi Jazz Festival concerts at venues throughout the city from mid-October to mid-November

NOVEMBER
Audi Jazz Festival as above

DECEMBER
Brussels International Horse Show at Heysel Exhibition Centre
Christmas Market craft stalls on the Place du Grand Sablon
Crib and Christmas Tree Display on the Grand' Place

Nightlife

For a city full of bureaucrats, Brussels' nightlife is livelier than you might expect, and undoubtedly lubricated by the absence of licensing laws. Although night spots tend to change hands frequently, the listings which follow are well-established, popular places which stay open well past midnight. Areas to head for at night include: Place de la Bourse and the surrounding area, Place St Géry and the streets radiating from it; Rue du Marché aux Charbon, and Place du Châtelain off Avenue Louise.

The bars and discos located in the Lower City are generally, but not always, more relaxed than those in the Upper City, where prices are higher, and the clientele pays more attention to dressing stylishly. This applies particularly to venues in the expensive hotels.

Discos rarely open their doors much before 10pm.

Nightclubs and Discos

Bazaar
63 Rue des Capucins
Tel: 511 2600
This bar-disco-restaurant serves good food at very reasonable prices until midnight. On Friday and Saturday there is dancing on different floors, depending on your taste in music.

Cartagena
Tel: 502 5908
70 Rue du Marché au Charbon
Only hot-blooded Latin types need apply – along with any cool northerners whose blood could use a little extra heat.

Le Fool Moon
126 Quai de Mariemont
Tel: 410 1003
Located near the canal in Brussels' old industrial zone of Molenbeek, this fashionable venue is open on Saturdays for concerts, jazz, funk and hip-hop. Métro: Gare de l'Ouest.

Le Garage
18 Rue Dusquenoy
Tel: 512 6622
This nightclub appears to have lost its appeal to Brussels' ultra-chic crowd. Nonetheless its location near the Grand'Place ensures it remains a popular disco with tourists and is usually crowded. Sunday evenings are for gays only.

Mirano Continental
38 Chaussée de Louvain
Tel: 218 5772
This is one of the smartest dance-venues in town, where the young and hip can admire each other – and themselves, of course.

Tour & Taxis
5 Rue Picard
Fashionable bar-disco in the enormous old customs house to the north of Place Rogier. Métro: Ribeaucourt or Belgica.

Late-night Restaurants

Ateliers de la Grande Ile
33 Rue de la Grande Ile
Tel: 512 8190
Large Russian restaurant with bohemian atmosphere; a great place to quaff large quantities of vodka till 2am. A gypsy orchestra provides the music.

Le Campus
437 Avenue de la Couronne
Tel: 648 5380
As its name suggests, popular with students, but also with anyone who fancies steak or spaghetti in the middle of the night. Open from mid-morning to 5am.

Cap de Nuit
28 Vieille Halle-aux-Blés
Tel: 512 9342
Inexpensive restaurant specialising in steak, open all night till 6.30am during the week and 8am at weekends.

La Grande Porte
9 Rue Notre Seigneur
Tel: 512 8998
A real gem, tucked away in a side street off the Sablon. A small bistro

with eccentric decor serving traditional Belgian cuisine. You can eat outside when the weather permits. Open till 2am

Le Mozart
541 Chaussée d'Alsemberg
Tel: 344 0809
Popular restaurant specialising in

Jazz

L'Archiduc
6 Rue Antoine Dansaert
Tel: 512 0652
Ultra-cool jazz bar with live music on Sunday afternoons. Good selection of Belgian beers.

Le Cercle
20–22 Rue Sainte Anne
Tel: 514 0353
A small and intimate venue just off the Sablon featuring live jazz (as well as a wide range of other types of music).

Pinte d'Argent
11 Place des Bienfaiteurs
Tel: 241 0314
Informal jazz bar with free live music every night at 8pm.

Preservation Hall
3 Rue de Londres
Tel: 511 0304
This is a smoky and crowded venue with lots of atmosphere. Its programme changes frequently but the quality is always high and it occasionally features musicians from its famous namesake in New Orleans.

Sheraton Brussels Airport
Zaventem
Tel: 724 1000
Jazz brunches on Sunday, from noon–3pm.

Sounds
28 Rue de la Tulipe
Tel 512 9250
Well-established jazz club, where the live music usually starts around 10pm.

Travers
11 Rue Traversière
Tel: 218 4086
Tucked away in St Josse, this is a tiny club with a friendly atsmophere focusing on modern jazz.

French cuisine and steaks, which is open till 4am during the week and 5am on the weekend.

Ultime Atome
4 Rue St-Boniface
Tel: 511 1367
Noisy bar-restaurant popular with the young arty crowd, which serves pretty good food from noon till 1am.

Bars

A La Becasse
11 Rue de Tabora
Tel: 511 0006
Traditional Brussels tavern specialising in beer (tastings can be arranged), popular with students.

Belgica
Rue du Marché au Charbon
One of Brussels best known and popular gay bars; very friendly and always busy.

Beursschouwburg
22 Rue A Orts
Tel: 513 8200
Just across the road from the Bourse, the unpromising yellow façade opens into a stylish and spacious bar, popular with young Flemish people.

Au Bon Vieux Temps
12 Rue du Marché aux Herbes
Tel: 217 2626
One of the city centre's brown cafés with a homely atmosphere selling good beer.

Le Corbeau
18–20 Rue Saint Michel
Tel: 219 5246
Lively and convivial bar just off Rue Neuve, where you can drink a yard of Belgian ale from a *chevalier* (a large glass on a wooden frame), preferably without spilling a drop.

La Fleur en Papier Doré
53–55 Rue des Alexiens
Tel: 511 1659
Located on the edge of the Marolles district, this is a quaint, quiet tavern, once the headquarters of the Belgian Surrealist movement and is still popular with arty types.

Goupil le Fol
22 Rue de la Violette
Tel: 511 1396
Sink into the enormous sofas in the recesses of this dimly-lit bar on several floors of a rambling old town

house. Not far from the Grand' Place and open until late into the night.

Mappa Mundo
26 Rue du Pont de la Carpe
Tel: 514 3365
Friendly and trendy bar with good food on the Place St Géry, the centre of the city's nightlife for the young and hip.

La Mort Subite
7 Rue Montagne-aux-Herbes Potagères
Tel: 513 1318
A favourite haunt of *Bruxellois* young and old, good beers and snacks. The service can be leisurely to say the least, but relax and enjoy the ambiance.

P.P. Café
28 Rue Van Praet 28
Tel: 514 2562
Lively bar-restaurant with 1930s decor. Good food is served in a series of rooms which lead into the Kladaratsch cinema on Boulevard Anspach.

Au Soleil
86 Rue du Marché au Charbon
Tel: 513 3430
Fashionable bar-café with typical art nouveau interior, on a street full of good bars and teeming with life on a Saturday night.

Cabaret

Black Bottom
1 Rue du Lombard
Tel: 511 0608
Small, raffish and atmospheric, this Parisian-style club offers piano cabaret. The compères Jerry and Martigny keep things moving in a languid sort of way.

Chez Flo
25 Rue au Beurre
Tel: 513 3152
Transvestite cabaret show just off the Grand' Place (two performances per night with dinner at weekends).

Sport

Spectator

CYCLING

The most popular sport in Belgium is cycling. You'll find avid cyclists everywhere, despite the fact that traffic in Brussels is chaotic and drivers more or less inconsiderate. Bicycle racing also enjoys widespread popularity – as evidenced by the sheer number of spectators who come out to cheer.

HORSE RACING
Hippodrome de Boitsfort
51 Chaussée de la Hulpe
1180 Brussels
Tel: 672 1484
Sterrebeek
43 Avenue du Roy de Blicquyln
1933 Sterrebeek
Tel: 767 5475

SOCCER
Heysel Stadium,
135 Avenue du Marathon
1020 Brussels.
Royal Daring THCM
1 Avenue du Château
1080 Brussels
Tel: 414 2916
Royal Union Saint-Gilloise
223 Chaussée de Bruxelles
1190 Brussels
Tel: 344 1656

Participant

There are sporting and recreational centres located in all the different districts of Greater Brussels, where non-members will find plenty of opportunities to work up a sweat. The selection of available activities runs the gamut from bowling to ice-skating, soccer, golf, mini-golf, roller-skating, tennis, swimming and squash. Check the Yellow Pages of

the phone directory for details. Avid cycling fans can rent bicycles all over the country (*see Getting Around, page 232*).

BOWLING
There are two bowling alleys in the city centre, both of which are generally open from mid-afternoon until after midnight:
Bowling Crosly Brunswick
43 Qui au Foin
Tel: 217 2801
Bowling Crosly Empereur
36 Boulevard de l'Empereur
Tel: 512 0874

GOLF
There are many golf courses in and around Brussels. Contact the Fédération Royale Belge de Golf, 110 Chaussée de la Hulpe, 1170 Brussels, tel: 672 2389, fax: 672 0897.

ICE-SKATING
The opening hours vary throughout the year and are generally longer during school holidays. Check exact times before setting out.
Poseidon
4 Avenue des Vaillants
Tel: 762 1633
Forest National
36 Avenue du Globe
Tel: 345 1611/376 1067

RIDING
Horse-riding is very popular in the many parks and wooded areas in the Brussels region. Information can be found in the Yellow Pages, or contact the Fédération Royale Belge des Sports Equestres, 156 Avenue Houba de Strooper, 1020 Brussels. tel: 478 5056. Two established stables:
L'Etrier
19 Champ du Vert Chasseur
Tel: 374 2860/3870
Centre Equestre de la Cambre
872 Chaussée de Waterloo
Tel: 375 3408

ROLLER SKATING
Le Gymnase
1 Chemin du Gymnase
Bois de la Cambre
Tel: 649 70002

Open-air rink, closed in winter.
Patinoire du Heysel
134 Avenue de Madrid
Tel: 426 3804
Open-air rink.

RUGBY
Brussels British Rugby Football Club
15 Spechterstraat
3078 Everberg
Tel: 759 7402

SOCCER
Fédération Belge de Football
145 Avenue Houba de Strooper
1020 Brussels
Tel: 477 1211
Brussels United Football Club
Contact Tony Reynolds:
reynolds.a.1@pg.com

SPORTS CENTRES
The following sports centres offer a wide range of facilities for both indoor and outdoor activities:
Forêt de Soignes
2057 Chaussée de Wavre
Tel: 672 2260
Heysel
135 Avenue de Marathon
Tel: 479 3654
Neder-over-Heembeek
99 Petit Chemin Vert
Tel: 268 2633
Omnisport
120 Rue de Lombartzyde
Tel: 268 0043
Palais du Midi
3–9 Rogier van der Weyden
Tel: 279 5954
Woluwe
87 Avenue E Mounier
Tel: 762 8522

SWIMMING POOLS
The 19 Brussels communes all operate public sports centres which have swimming pools as well as a wide range of sporting facilities, including tennis, squash and badminton courts, gyms, keep fit and martial arts courses:
Boitsfort
60 Avenue L. Wiener
Tel: 675 4899
Brussels
28 Rue du Chevreuil
Tel: 511 2468

Ixelles
8–10 Rue de la Natation
Tel: 511 9084
Etterbeek
69–71 Rue des Champs
Tel: 640 3838
Evere
260 Avenue des Anciens
Combattants
Tel: 247 6320
Ganshoren
10 Place Reine Fabiola
Tel: 427 3191
Heysel
Océade (Bruparck)
Tel: 478 4320/4944
Laeken
73–89 Rue Champ de l'Eglise
Tel: 425 5712
Molenbeek
93 Rue Van Kalck
Tel: 410 0803
Schaarbeek
Neptunium
Place Houffalize
Tel: 215 7424
Saint-Gilles
38 Rue de la Perche
Tel: 539 0615
Saint-Josse
23–27 Rue St-François
Tel: 217 3941
Woluwe St-Lambert
2 Avenue des Vaillants
Tel: 771 6655
Woluwe St-Pierre
2 Avenue Salomé
Tel: 762 1275
Uccle
1 Square De Fré
Tel: 374 9005

FITNESS CENTRES

American Gym
144 Boulevard Général Jacques
Tel: 640 5992
European Athletic City
25A Avenue Winston Churchill
Tel: 345 3077
John Harris Fitness
7th floor of SAS Hotel
Rue du Fossé aux Loups
Tel: 219 8284
Winners
13 Rue Bonneels
Tel: 280 0270

Shopping

Where to Shop

There are numerous areas in Brussels where you can shop to your heart's content. In the Lower City you'll find plenty of shops at the Place de Brouckère, the Place de la Monnaie, along the Boulevard Anspach (predominantly fashion boutiques and book stores), and in the shopping complex City 2, located on Rue Neuve. The smaller galleries off Rue Neuve, for example the Passage du Nord and the Galerie du Centre, have a wide range of unusual shops. The Rue au Beurre is good for food and gift shops. The Rue du Midi is another well-known shopping beat, where there are quite a few art supply shops and music stores.

One of the best places to go window shopping is in the glass-roofed arcades of the famous Galeries Saint Hubert, which was constructed in 1847, the first covered shopping mall to be built in Europe.

Rue Antoine Dansaert is the place to find ultra-fashionable and expensive boutiques.

Fancy shops with internationally recognised designer names are concentrated in the Upper City around the Place Louise and along the Avenue Louise, Porte de Namur, while the Chaussée d'Ixelles is slightly more downmarket. The most chic arcades are located in the Upper City as well. You'll find both the Galerie Espace Louise and the Galerie Louise at the Place Louise; while the Galeries de la Toison and the Galerie d'Ixelles are located at Porte de Namur. These arcades lead one into the other, forming a huge glittering labyrinth where you can shop till you drop.

What to Buy

Brussels is known for its fine chocolate, beer, crystalware, diamonds and the world-famous Brussels lace. You'll find souvenir shops just about everywhere tourists tend to visit: around the Grand' Place, by the Manneken Pis, near the stock exchange and opera house.

Foreigners have the advantage of being able to purchase items without paying VAT.

Bookshops

FNAC
City 2, Rue Neuve
Good section of books in several languages, as well as CDs, maps, concert tickets, photography.
Sterling Books
Rue du Fossé aux Loups
English bookshop.
Waterstones
71 Boulevard Adolphe Max
A good branch of the large British bookshop chain.

Markets

There are several different markets in Brussels well worth visiting for their local colour. Take a stroll through the Flower and Bird Market on Saturday and Sunday mornings at the Grand' Place, the Flea Market which operates daily at the Place du Jeu de Balle, or the Antique Market on weekends at the Place du Grand Sablon. The Sunday morning market at the Gare du Midi is a lively and colourful place to seek out bargains. (*See also the chapter on the markets on page 129.*)

Language

French Pronunciation

Learning the pronunciation of the French alphabet is a good idea. In particular, learn how to spell out your name.

a=ah, **b**=bay, **c**=say, **d**=day, **e**=er, **f**=ef, **g**=zhay, **h**=ash, **i**=ee, **j**=zhee, **k**=ka, **l**=el, **m**=em, **n**=en, **o**=oh, **p**=pay, **q**=kew, **r**=ehr, **s**=ess, **t**=tay, **u**=ew, **v**=vay, **w**=dooblahvay, **x**=eex, **y**=ee grek, **z**=zed

Even if you speak no French at all, it is worth trying to master a few simple phrases. The fact that you have made an effort is likely to get you a better response, even though many Francophone Belgians speak English. Remember to emphasise each syllable, but not to pronounce the last consonant of a word as a rule (this includes the plural "s") and always to drop your "h"s. Whether to use "vous" or "tu" is a vexed question; increasingly the familiar form of "tu" is used by many people. However it is better to be formal, and use "vous" if in doubt. It is very important to be polite; always address people as Madame or Monsieur, and address them by their surnames until you are confident first names are acceptable. When entering a shop always say, "*Bonjour Monsieur/ Madame*," and "*Merci, au revoir*," when leaving.

French Words & Phrases

How much is it?	*C'est combien?*
What is your name?	*Comment vous appelez-vous?*
My name is...	*Je m'appelle...*
Do you speak English?	*Parlez-vous anglais?*
I am English/ American	*Je suis anglais/ americain*
I don't understand	*Je ne comprends pas*
Please speak more slowly	*Parlez plus lentement, s'il vous plaît*
Can you help me?	*Pouvez-vous m'aider?*
I'm looking for...	*Je cherche*
Where is...?	*Où est...?*
I'm sorry	*Excusez-moi/ Pardon*
I don't know	*Je ne sais pas*
No problem	*Pas de problème*
Have a good day!	*Bonne journée!*
That's it	*C'est ça*
Here it is	*Voici*
There it is	*Voilà*
Let's go	*On y va/Allons-y*
See you tomorrow	*A demain*
See you soon	*A bientôt*
Show me the word in the book	*Montrez-moi le mot dans le livre*
At what time?	*A quelle heure?*
When?	*Quand?*
What time is it?	*Quelle heure est-il?*
yes	*oui*
no	*non*
please	*s'il vous plaît*
thank you	*merci*
(very much)	*(beaucoup)*
you're welcome	*de rien*
excuse me	*excusez-moi*
hello	*bonjour*
OK	*d'accord*
goodbye	*au revoir*
good evening	*bonsoir*
here	*ici*
there	*là*
today	*aujourd'hui*
yesterday	*hier*
tomorrow	*demain*
now	*maintenant*
later	*plus tard*
right away	*tout de suite*
this morning	*ce matin*
this afternoon	*cet après-midi*
this evening	*ce soir*

On Arrival

I want to get off at...	*Je voudrais descendre a...*
Is there a bus to the Grand' Place?	*Est-ce qui'il y a un bus pour la Grand' Place?*
What street is this?	*A quelle rue sommes-nous?*
Which line do I take for...?	*Quelle ligne dois-je prendre pour...?*
How far is...?	*A quelle distance se trouve...?*
Validate your ticket	*Compostez votre billet*
airport	*l'aéroport*
train station	*la gare*
bus station	*la gare routière*
Metro stop	*la station de Métro*
bus	*l'autobus*
bus stop	*l'arrêt*
platform	*le quai*
ticket	*le billet*
return ticket	*billet aller-retour*
hitchhiking	*l'autostop*
toilets	*les toilettes*
This is the hotel address	*C'est l'adresse de l'hôtel*
I'd like a (single /double) room	*Je voudrais une chambre (pour une/deux personnes)...*
...with shower	*avec douche*
...with bath	*avec salle de bain*
...with a view	*avec vue*
Does that include breakfast?	*Le prix comprend-il le petit déjeuner?*
May I see the room?	*Je peux voir la chambre?*
washbasin	*le lavabo*
bed	*le lit*
key	*la clé*
elevator	*l'ascenseur*
air conditioned	*climatisé*
swimming pool	*la piscine*

On the Road

Where is the spare wheel?	*Où est la roue de secours?*
Where is the nearest garage?	*Où est le garage le plus proche?*
Our car has broken down	*Notre voiture est en panne*
I want to have my car repaired	*Je veux faire réparer ma voiture*

It's not your right of way	Vous n'avez pas la priorité
I think I must have put diesel in the car by mistake	Je crois que j'ai mis le gasoil dans la voiture par erreur
the road to...	la route pour...
left	gauche
right	droite
straight on	tout droit
far	loin
near	près d'ici
opposite	en face
beside	à côté de
car park	parking
over there	là-bas
at the end	au bout
on foot	à pied
by car	en voiture
town map	le plan
road map	la carte
street	la rue
square	la place
give way	céder le passage
dead end	l'impasse
no parking	stationnement interdit
motorway	l'autoroute
toll	le péage
speed limit	la limitation de vitesse
petrol	l'essence
unleaded	sans plomb
diesel	le gasoil
water/oil	l'eau/l'huile
puncture	un pneu crevé
bulb	l'ampoule
wipers	les essuies-glace

Shopping

Where is the nearest bank/ post office?	Où est la banque/ poste la plus proche?
I'd like to buy	Je voudrais acheter
How much is it?	C'est combien?
Do you take credit cards?	Est-ce que vous acceptez les cartes de crédit?
I'm just looking	Je regarde seulement
Have you got?	Avez-vous...?
I'll take it	Je le prends
I'll take this one/ that one	Je prends celui-ci/celui-là
What size is it?	C'est de quelle taille?
Anything else?	Avec ça?

Market shopping

In a market prices are usually by the kilo or by the piece, that is, each item priced individually. Usually the stall holder (marchand) will select the goods for you. Sometimes there is a serve yourself system – observe everyone else! If you are choosing cheese, for example, you may be offered a taste to try.

size (clothes)	la taille
size (shoes)	la pointure
cheap	bon marché
expensive	cher
enough	assez
too much	trop
a piece of	un morceau de
each	la pièce (e.g. ananas, Bfr 75 la pièce)
bill	la note
chemist	la pharmacie
bakery	la boulangerie
bookshop	la librairie
library	la bibliothèque
department store	le grand magasin
delicatessen	la charcuterie/le traiteur
fishmongers	la poissonerie
grocers	l'épicerie
tobacconist	le tabac
market	le marché
supermarket	le supermarché
junk shop	la brocante

Sightseeing

town	la ville
old town	la vieille ville
abbey	l'abbaye
cathedral	la cathédrale
church	l'église
town hall	l'hôtel de ville/la mairie
nave	la nef
stained glass	le vitrail
staircase	l'escalier
tower	la tour
walk	le tour
country house/ castle	le château
Gothic	gothique
Roman	romain
Romanesque	roman

museum	le musée
art gallery	la galerie
exhibition	l'exposition
tourist information office	l'office du tourisme/le syndicat d'initiative
free	gratuit
open	ouvert
closed	fermé
every day	tous les jours
all year	toute l'année
all day	toute la journée
to book	réserver

Dining Out

Table d'hôte (the "host's table") is one set menu served at a set price. Prix fixe is a fixed price menu. A la carte means dishes from the menu are charged separately.

breakfast	le petit déjeuner
lunch	le déjeuner
dinner	le dîner
meal	le repas
first course	l'entrée/les hors d'oeuvre
main course	le plat principal
made to order	sur commande
drink included	boisson comprise
wine list	la carte des vins
the bill	l'addition
fork	la fourchette
knife	le couteau
spoon	la cuillère
plate	l'assiette
glass	le verre
napkin	la serviette
ashtray	le cendrier

BREAKFAST & SNACKS

baguette	long thin loaf
pain	bread
petits pains	rolls
beurre	butter
sel/poivre	salt/pepper
sucre	sugar
confiture	jam
oeufs	eggs
...à la coque	boiled eggs
...au bacon	bacon and eggs
...au jambon	ham and eggs
...sur le plat	fried eggs
...brouillés	scrambled eggs
tartine	bread and butter
yaourt	yoghurt
crêpe	pancake
croque-monsieur	ham and cheese

	toasted sandwich
croque-madame	...with a fried egg on top
galette	type of pancake
quiche	tart of eggs and cream with various fillings
quiche lorraine	quiche with bacon

MAIN COURSES
la viande/meat

bleu	very rare
saignant	rare
à point	medium
bien cuit	well done
grillé	grilled
agneau	lamb
andouille/ andouillette	tripe sausage
bifteck	steak
boudin	sausage
boudin noir	black sausage
boudin blanc	white sausage
blanquette	stew of veal, lamb or chicken with creamy egg sauce
à la bordelaise	beef with red wine and shallots
à la Bourguignonne	cooked in red wine, onions and mushrooms
brochette	kebab
caille	quail
canard	duck
carbonnade	casserole of beef, beer and onions
carré d'agneau	rack of lamb
cassoulet	stew of beans, sausages, pork and duck
cervelle	brains (food)
châteaubriand	thick steak
choucroute	Alsace dish of sauerkraut, bacon and sausages
confit	duck or goose preserved in its own fat
contre-filet	cut of sirloin steak
coq au vin	chicken in red wine
côte d'agneau	lamb chop
dinde	turkey
entrecôte	beef rib steak
escargot	snail
faisan	pheasant
farci	stuffed
faux-filet	sirloin

feuilleté	puff pastry
foie	liver
foie de veau	calf's liver
foie gras	goose or duck liver pâté
cuisses de grenouille	frog's legs
grillade	grilled meat
hachis	minced meat
jambon	ham
langue	tongue
lapin	rabbit
lardon	small pieces of bacon, often added to salads
magret de canard	breast of duck
médaillon	round piece of meat
moelle	beef bone marrow
navarin d'agneau	stew of lamb with onions, carrots and turnips
oie	goose
perdrix	partridge
petit-gris	small snail
pieds de cochon	pig's trotters
pintade	guinea fowl
porc	pork
pot-au-feu	casserole of beef and vegetables
poulet	chicken

First Courses

An amuse-bouche, amuse-gueule is an appetizer, something to "amuse the mouth", served before the first course.

assiette anglaise	cold meats
potage	soup
poussin	young chicken
rognons	kidneys
rôti	roast
sanglier	wild boar
saucisse	fresh sausage
saucisson	salami
veau	veal
viande	meat

poission/fish

anchois	anchovies
anguille	eel
bar (or loup)	sea bass
barbue	brill

belon	Brittany oyster
bigorneau	sea snail
bercy	sauce of fish stock, butter, white wine and shallots
brandade	salt cod puree
cabillaud	cod
calmars	squid
colin	hake
coquillage	shellfish
coquilles Saint-Jacques	scallops
crevette	shrimp
daurade	sea bream
flétan	halibut
fruits de mer	seafood
hareng	herring
homard	lobster
huître	oyster
langoustine	large prawn
limande	lemon sole
lotte	monkfish
morue	salt cod
moule	mussels
moules marinières	mussels in white wine and onions
oursin	sea urchin
poissons	fish
raie	skate
saumon	salmon
thon	tuna
truite	trout

legumes/vegetables

ail	garlic
artichaut	artichoke
asperge	asparagus
aubergine	eggplant
avocat	avocado
bolets	boletus mushrooms
céleri remoulade	grated celery with mayonnaise
champignon	mushroom
cèpe	boletus mushroom
chanterelle	wild mushroom
cornichon	gherkin
courgette	zucchini
chips	potato crisps
chou	cabbage
chou-fleur	cauliflower
concombre	cucumber
cru	raw
crudités	raw vegetables
épinard	spinach
frites	chips, French fries

In the Café

Settle the bill when you leave; the waiter may leave a slip of paper on the table to keep track of the bill.

gratin dauphinois	sliced potatoes baked with cream
haricot	dried bean
haricots verts	green beans
lentilles	lentils
maïs	corn
mange-tout	snow pea
mesclun	mixed leaf salad
navet	turnip
noix	nut, walnut
noisette	hazelnut
oignon	onion
panais	parsnip
persil	parsley
pignon	pine nut
poireau	leek
pois	pea
poivron	bell pepper
pomme de terre	potato
pommes frites	chips, French fries
primeurs	early fruit and vegetables
radis	radish
roquette	arugula, rocket
ratatouille	Provençal vegetable stew of aubergines, courgettes, tomatoes, peppers, olive oil
riz	rice
salade Niçoise	egg, tuna, olives, onions and tomato salad
salade verte	green salad
truffe	truffle

FRUITS/FRUIT

ananas	pineapple
cavaillon	fragrant sweet melon
cerise	cherry
citron	lemon
citron vert	lime
figue	fig
fraise	strawberry
framboise	raspberry
groseille	redcurrant
mangue	mango
mirabelle	yellow plum
pamplemousse	grapefruit

pêche	peach
poire	pear
pomme	apple
raisin	grape
prune	plum
pruneau	prune
reine-claude	greengage

SAUCES/SAUCES

aïoli	garlic mayonnaise
béarnaise	sauce of egg, butter, wine and herbs
forestière	with mushrooms and bacon
hollandaise	egg, butter and lemon sauce
lyonnaise	with onions
meunière	fried fish with butter, lemon and parsley sauce
meurette	red wine sauce
Mornay	sauce of cream, egg and cheese
Parmentier	served with potatoes
paysan	rustic style, ingredients depend on the region
pistou	Provençal sauce of basil, garlic and olive oil;
provençale	sauce of tomatoes, garlic and olive oil
papillotte	cooked in paper

DESSERTS/PUDDINGS

Belle Hélène	fruit with ice cream and chocolate sauce
clafoutis	baked pudding of batter and cherries
coulis	purée of fruit
gâteau	cake
île flottante	whisked egg whites in custard sauce
crème anglaise	custard
pêche melba	peaches with ice cream and raspberry sauce
tarte tatin	upside-down tart of caramelised apples

crème caramel	caramelised egg custard
crème Chantilly	whipped cream
fromage	cheese
chèvre	goat's cheese

BOISSONS/DRINKS

coffee	café
...with milk or cream	au lait or crème
...decaffeinated	déca/décaféiné
...black/espresso	noir/express
...American filtered	filtre
tea	thé
...herb infusion	tisane
...camomile	verveine
hot chocolate	chocolat chaud
milk	lait
mineral water	eau minérale
fizzy	gazeux
non-fizzy	non-gazeux/plat
fizzy lemonade	limonade
fresh lemon juice served with sugar	citron pressée
fresh squeezed orange juice	orange pressée
full (e.g. full cream milk)	entier
fresh or cold	frais, fraîche
beer	bière
...bottled	en bouteille
...on tap	à la pression
...from the barrel	au fût
pre-dinner drink	apéritif
white wine with cassis: black-currant liqueur	kir
kir with champagne	kir royale
with ice	avec des glaçons
neat/dry	sec
red	rouge
white	blanc
rose	rosé
dry	brut
sweet	doux
sparkling wine	crémant
house wine	vin de maison
Where is this wine from?	De quelle région vient ce vin?
pitcher	carafe/pichet
...of water/wine	d'eau/de vin
half litre	demi-carafe
quarter litre	quart
mixed	panaché
after dinner drink	digestif
cheers!	santé!

Useful Phrases

Help!	Au secours!
Stop!	Arrêtez!
Call a doctor	Appelez un médecin
Call an ambulance	Appelez une ambulance
Call the police	Appelez la police
Call the fire brigade	Appelez les pompiers
Where is the nearest telephone?	Où est le téléphone le plus proche?
Where is the nearest hospital?	Où est l'hôpital le plus proche?
I am sick	Je suis malade
I have lost my passport/purse	J'ai perdu mon passeport/porte-monnaie
How do I make an outside call?	Comment est-ce que je peux téléphoner à l'extérieur?
I want to make an international (local) call	Je voudrais une communication pour l'étranger (une communication locale)
What is the dialling code?	Quel est l'indicatif?
I'd like an alarm call for 8 o'clock tomorrow morning	Je voudrais être réveillé à huit heures demain matin
Who's calling?	C'est qui a l'appareil?
Hold on, please	Ne quittez pas s'il vous plaît
The line is busy	La ligne est occupée
I must have dialled the wrong number	J'ai dû faire un faux numéro
tasting	la dégustation
organic	biologique
flavour	le parfum
basket	le panier
bag	le sac
What do you recommend?	Que'est-ce que vous recommandez?
Do you have local specialities?	Avez-vous des spécialités locales?
I am a vegetarian	Je suis végétarien

I am on a diet	Je suis au régime
I'd like to order	Je voudrais commander
That is not what I ordered	Ce n'est pas ce que j'ai commandé
Is service included?	Est-ce que le service est compris?
May I have more wine?	Encore du vin, s'il vous plaît?
Enjoy your meal	Bon appetit!

Numbers

0	zéro
1	un/une
2	deux
3	trois
4	quatre
5	cinq
6	six
7	sept
8	huit
9	neuf
10	dix
11	onze
12	douze
13	treize
14	quatorze
15	quinze
16	seize
17	dix-sept
18	dix-huit
19	dix-neuf
20	vingt
30	trente
40	quarante
50	cinquante
60	soixante
70	septante
80	quatre-vingts
90	nonante
100	cent
200	deux cents
500	cinq cents
1000	mille
1,000,000	un million

The number 1 is often written like an upside-down V, and the number 7 is crossed.

Seasons

spring	le printemps
summer	l'été
autumn	l'automne
winter	l'hiver

Months

January	janvier
February	février
March	mars
April	avril
May	mai
June	juin
July	juillet
August	août
September	septembre
October	octobre
November	novembre
December	décembre

Days of the Week

Days of the week, seasons and months are not capitalised in French.

Monday	lundi
Tuesday	mardi
Wednesday	mercredi
Thursday	jeudi
Friday	vendredi
Saturday	samedi
Sunday	dimanche

Saying the Date

12th August 1999	le douze août, mille neuf cent nonante-neuf

Flemish Words & Phrases

How much is it?	Hoeveel is het?/ Hoeveel kost dat?
What is your name?	Wat is u naam?
My name is...	Mijn naam is ... Ik heet ...
Do you speak English?	Spreekt u Engels?
I am English/ American	Ik ben Engelsman/ Amerikaan
I don't understand	Ik begrijp het niet
Please speak more slowly	Kunt u langzamer praten, alstublieft
Can you help me?	Kunt u mij helpen?
I'm looking for...	Ik zoek...
Where is...?	Waar is...?
I'm sorry	Excuseer/Pardon
I don't know	Ik weet het niet
No problem	Geen probleem
Have a good day!	Prettige dag nog!
That's it	Precies
Here it is	Hier is het
There it is	Daar is het
Let's go	Laten we gaan/ We zijn weg
See you tomorrow	Tot morgen
See you soon	Tot straks!
Show me the word in the book please	Toon mij het woord in het boek, alstublieft

At what time?	Hoe laat?
When	Wanneer?
What time is it?	Hoe laat is het?
yes	ja
no	neen
please	alstublieft
thank you	dank u
(very much)	(wel)
you're welcome	graag gedaan
excuse me	excuseer/ pardon
hello	hallo
goodbye	tot ziens!
good evening	Goeden avond!
here	hier
there	daar
today	vandaag
yesterday	gisteren
tomorrow	morgen
now	nu
later	later
right away	direct/onmiddellijk
this morning	vanmorgen
this afternoon	deze namiddag
this evening	vanavond

On the Road

Where is the spare wheel?	Waar is het reservewiel?
Where is the nearest garage?	Waar is de dichtstbijzijnde garage?
Our car has	Onze auto is in

On Arrival

I want to get off at...	Ik wil uitstappen in....
Is there a bus to the Grote Markt?	Is er een bus naar de Grote Markt?
What street is this?	Welke straat is dit?
Which line do I take for...?	Welke lijn moet ik nemen voor...?
How far is...?	Hoe ver is...?
Validate your ticket	Stempel uw ticket af
airport	de luchthaven
train station	het station
bus station	het busstation
Metro stop	de metrohalte
bus	de bus
bus stop	de bushalte
platform	het perron
ticket	het ticket

return ticket	een ticket retour
hitchhiking	liften
toilets	de toiletten
This is the hotel address	Dat is het adres van het hotel
I'd like a (single/double) room...	Ik wil graag een kamer (voor een/ twee personen)
...with shower	...met douche
...with bath	...met bad
...with a view	...met zicht
Does that include breakfast?	Is het ontbijt inbegrepen?
May I see the room?	Mag ik de kamer zien?
washbasin	de wastafel
bed	het bed
key	de sleutel
elevator	de lift
air conditioning	airconditioning

broken down	panne
I want to have my car repaired	Ik wil mijn auto laten herstellen
It's not your right of way	U heeft geen voorrang
I think I must have put diesel in the car by mistake	Ik denk dat ik per ongeluk diesel in mijn auto heb gedaan
the road to...	de straat naar...
left	links
right	rechts
straight on	rechtstreeks
far/near	ver/nabij
opposite	tegenover
beside	naast
car park	de parkeerplaats
over there	daar
at the end	aan het eind
on foot	te voet
by car	met de auto
town map	het stadplan
road map	de (land)kaart
street	de straat
square	het plein
give way	geef voorrang
dead end	doodlopende straat
no parking	verboden te parkeren
motorway	de autosnelweg
toll	de tol
speed limit	de snelheids- beperking
petrol	de benzine
unleaded	loodvrij
diesel	de diesel
water/oil	water/olie
puncture	een lekke band
bulb	de lamp
wipers	ruitewissers

Shopping

Where is the nearest bank/ post office?	Waar is de dichtstbijzijnde bank (het dichtstbijzijnde postkantoor)?
I'd like to buy...	Ik zou graag ... kopen
How much is it?	Hoeveel is het?/ Hoeveel kost dat?
Do you take credit cards?	Neemt u cretiet karten?
I'm just looking	Ik kijk alleen maar
Have you got?	Hebt u...?
I'll take it	Ik neem het
I'll take this	Ik neem dit/deze

one/that one	
What size is it?	Welke maat is het?
Anything else?	Iets anders?
size	de maat
cheap	goedkoop
expensive	duur
enough	genoeg
too much	te veel
a piece	een stuk
each	per stuk
bill	de rekening
chemist	de apotheek
bakery	de bakkerij
bookshop	de boekhandel
delicatessen	delicatessen
library	de bibliotheek
department store	het warenhuis
fishmongers	de viswinkel
grocery	de kruidenier
tobacconist	de tabakwinkel
markets	de markt
supermarket	de supermarkt
junk shop	curiosa/ antiquiteiten
tasting	proeven
organic	biologisch
flavour	het aroma/de smaak
basket	de mand
bag	de zak

Sightseeing

town	de stad
old town	de oude stad
abbey	de abdij
cathedral	de kathedraal
church	de kerk
keep	de slottoren
mansion	het hotel
hospital	het ziekenhuis
town hall	het stadhuis
nave	het schip
stained glass	het glasraam
staircase	de trap
tower	de toren
walk	de tour
country house/ castle	het kasteel
Gothic	Gotisch
Roman	Romaans
Romanesque	Romaans
museum	het museum
art gallery	de galerij
exhibition	de tentoonstelling
tourist information	het bureau voor toerisme (VVV)

office	
free	gratis
open	geopend
closed	gesloten
every day	iedere dag
all year	het hele jaar
all day	de hele dag
swimming pool	het zwembad
to book	reserveren/ boeken

Dining Out

breakfast	het ontbijt
lunch	lunch/middageten
dinner	diner/avondeten
meal	de maltijd
first course	het voorgerecht
main course	het hoofdgerecht
made to order	op bestelling
drink included	dranken inbegrepen
wine list	de wijnkaart
the bill	de rekening
fork	de vork
knife	het mes
spoon	de lepel
plate	het bord
glass	het glas
napkin	het servet
ashtray	de asbak
I am a vegetarian	Ik ben vegetarier
I am on a diet	Ik volg een dieet
What do you recommend?	Wat beveelt u aan?
Do you have local specialities?	Heeft u specialiteiten van de regio?
I'd like to order	Ik wil bestellen
That is not what I ordered	Dit is niet wat ik besteld heb
Is service ncluded?	Is de dienst inbegrepen?
May I have more wine?	Mag ik nog een beetje wijn?
Enjoy your meal	Smakelijk!

BREAKFAST & SNACKS

boter	butter
boterham	bread with butter
brood	bread
broodjes	rolls
croque-monsieur	ham and cheese toasted sandwich
croque-madame (met een spiegelei)	... with a fried egg on top
eieren	eggs

...zachtgekookt	boiled eggs
...met spek	bacon and eggs
...met ham	ham and eggs
...spiegelei	fried eggs
...roerei	scrambled eggs
honig	honey
jam	jam
pannekoek	pancake
peper	pepper
quiche	tart of eggs and cream with various fillings
quiche lorraine	quiche with bacon
stokbrood	long thin loaf
yoghurt	yoghurt
zout	salt
zuiker	sugar

FIRST COURSE

charcuterie	cold meats
soep	soup

MAIN COURSES
vlees/meat

biefsteak	steak
bladerdeeg	puff pastry
brochette	kebab
carbonnade	casserole of beef, beer and onions
chateaubriand	thick steak
coq au vin	chicken in red wine
eend	duck
eendenborst	breast of duck
entrecote	beef rib steak
escargot	snail
everzwijn	wild boar
fazant	pheasant
foie gras	goose or duck liver pâté
gans	goose
gebraad	roast
gegrild	grilled
gegrild vlees	grilled meat
gehakt	minced meat
gestoofd vlees	beef stew with red wine, onions and tomatoes
gevuld	stuffed
goedgebakken	well done
ham	ham
hersens	brains (food)
kalfslever	calf's liver
kalfsvlees	veal
kalkoen	turkey
kikkerbillen	frog's legs
kip	chicken
konijn	rabbit
kuiken	young chicken

kwartel	quail	rog	skate
lam	lamb	saus van stokvis,	sauce of fish
lamskotelet	lamb chop	schelvis/stokvis	stock, butter,
lendestuk	sirloin	boter, witte wijn	white wine and
lendebiefstuk	cut of sirloin	en sjalotten	shallots
	steak	schaaldier	shellfish
lever	liver	sint-jakobsschelp	scallops
medaillon	round piece of	tonijn	tuna
	meat	zeebaars	sea bass
niertjes	kidneys	zeeslak	sea snail
parelhoen	guinea fowl	zeebrasem	sea bream
patrijs	partridge	zeevruchten	seafood
pens	sausage	zeeëgel	sea urchin
petit-gris	small snail	zalm	salmon
ragot	stew of veal, lamb		
	or chicken with	**Groenter/Vegetables**	
	creamy egg sauce	aardappel	potato
rundvlees in rode	beef in red wine	ajuin/ui	onion
wijn met wortelen,	with carrots,	artisjok	artichoke
uien en	onions and	asperge	asparagus
champignons	mushroom	aubergine	eggplant
saignant	rare	augurk	gherkin
saucijs	fresh sausage	avocado	avocado
spek	small pieces of	biet	turnip
	bacon, often	bloemkool	cauliflower
	added to salads	boon	dried bean
stoofpot	casserole of beef	champignon	mushroom
	and vegetables	cantharel	wild mushroom
svarken	pork	(dooierzwam)	
tong	tongue	chips	potato crisps
varkenspoten	pig's trotters	courgette	zucchini
witte pens	white pudding	erwt	pea
worst/salami	salami	frieten/patat	chips, French
zuurkool	duck or goose		fries
in eigen vet	preserved in its	gemengde sla	mixed leaf salad
ingemaakt vlees	own fat	groene bonen	green beans
zwarte pens	black pudding	groene sla	green salad
		hazelnoot	hazelnut
vis/fish		komkommer	cucumber
ansjovis	anchovies	kool	cabbage
calamares	squid	linzen	lentils
daurade	sea bream	look	garlic
forel	trout	mais	corn
garnaal	shrimp	noot/walnoot	nut, walnut
gezouten	salt cod puree	paprika	bell pepper
griet	brill	peterselie	parsley
haring	herring	peulvruchten	snow pea
heilbot	halibut	pijnpitten	pine nut
kabeljouw	cod	prei	leek
koolvis	hake	radijs	radish
kreeft	lobster	rauw	raw
langoestine	large prawn	rijst	rice
limande	lemon sole	roquette	arugula, rocket
lot	monkfish	salade	raw vegetables
mossel	mussels	salade Niçoise	egg, tuna, olives,
mosselen in wijn	mussels in white		onions and
en uien	wine and onions		tomato salad
oester	oyster	selder in	grated celery with
paling	eel	remouladesaus	mayonnaise

spinazie	spinach
truffel	truffle
witte peen	parsnip

Vruchter/Fruit

aalbes	redcurrant
aardbei	strawberry
ananas	pineapple
appel	apple
citroen	lemon
(wijn)druif	grape
framboos	raspberry
grapefruit	grapefruit
kers	cherry
limoen	lime
mango	mango
mirabel	yellow plum
perzik	peach
peer	pear
pruim	prune
vijg	fig

Sauzer/Sauces

béarnaise	sauce of egg,
	butter, wine and
	herbs
eieren en kaas	egg and cheese
hollandaise saus	egg, butter and
	lemon sauce
landelijk (van de	rustic style,
streek)	ingredients
	depend on the
	region
looksaus	garlic mayonnaise
met uien	with onions
meunière	fried fish with
	butter, lemon and
	parsley sauce
provencalse saus	Provençal sauce
van	of basil, garlic
knoflook, basili-	and olive oil
rode wijn saus	red wine sauce
saus met	with mushrooms
champignons en	and bacon
spek	

Puddings

Belle Hélène	fruit with ice
	cream and
	chocolate sauce
caramelcreme	caramelised egg
	custard
coulis	puree of fruit
custardpudding	custard

gebak	cake
geitenkaas	goat's cheese
kaas	cheese
pêche melba	peaches with ice cream and raspberry sauce
slagroom	whipped cream
tarte tatin	upside-down tart of caramelised apples

Dranken/Drinks

after dinner drink	Ipousse-café
beer	bier
...bottled	op fles
...on tap	van het vat
coffee	koffie
...with milk or cream	met melk of room
...decaffeinated	decafeine
...black/espresso	zwart/espresso
...American filtered	filterkoffie
dry	brut
fizzy lemonade	limonade
fresh lemon juice	vers citroensap
fresh orange juice	vers sinaasappelsap
fresh or cold	koud
full (e.g. full cream milk)	volle melk
half litre	halve liter
hot chocolate	warme chocolademelk
house wine	huiswijn
milk	melk
mineral water	mineraalwater
...fizzy	spuitwater/Spa rood
...non-fizzy	plat water/ Spa blauw
neat	sec
pitcher	karaf
...of water/wine	water/wijn
pre-dinner drink	aperitief
quarter litre	kwart liter
red	rood
rose	rose
sparkling wine	schuimwijn
sweet	zacht
tea	thee
...herb infusion	kruidenthee
...camomile	kamille
white wine with cassis: black-currant liqueur	kir

white	wit
with ice	met ijs

Useful Phrases

Help!	Help!
Call a doctor	Bel een dokter
Call an ambulance	Bel een ziekenwagen
Call the police	Bel de politie
Call the fire brigade	Bel de brandweer
Where is the nearest telephone?	Waar is de dichtstbijzijnde telefoon?
Where is the nearest hospital?	Waar is het dichtstbijzijnde ziekenhuis?
I am sick	Ik ben ziek
I have lost my passport/purse	Ik ben mijn paspoort/ portemonnee kwijt/verloren
How do I make an outside call?	Hoe krijg ik een buitenlijn?
I want to make an international (local) call	Ik wil naar het buitenland bellen
What is the dialling code?	Wat is het zonennummer/ landnummer?
I'd like an alarm call for 8 o'clock tomorrow morning	Ik wil om 8 uur gewekt worden
Who's calling?	Met wie spreek ik?
Hold on, please	Blijf aan de lijn,alstublieft
The line is busy	De lijn is in gesprek
I must have dialled the wrong number	Ik heb een verkeerd nummer gedraaid

Months

January	januari
February	februari
March	maart
April	april
May	mei
June	juni
July	juli
August	august(us)
September	september
October	oktober
November	november
December	december

Seasons

Spring	de lente
Summer	de zomer
Autumn	de herfst
Winter	de winter

Days of the Week

Monday	maandag
Tuesday	dinsdag
Wednesday	woensdag
Thursday	donderdag
Friday	vrijdag
Saturday	zaterdag
Sunday	zondag

Numbers

0	nul
1	één
2	twee
3	drie
4	vier
5	vijf
6	zes
7	zeven
8	acht
9	negen
10	tien
11	elf
12	twaalf
13	dertien
14	veertien
15	vijfteen
16	zestien
17	zeventien
18	achttien
19	negentien
20	twintig
30	dertig
40	veertig
50	vijftig
60	zestig
70	zeventig
80	tachtig
90	negentig
100	honderd
200	tweehonderd
500	vijfhonderd
1000	duizend

Further Reading

General

Civilisation by Kenneth Clark, Penguin. Insightful commentaries on the major works of the Flemish Masters.

The Sorrow of Belgium by Hugo Claus, Viking. A novel charting the effects of the Nazi occupation of Flanders through the eyes of a young boy.

From Van Eyck to Bruegel by Max J. Friedlander, Phaidon. Definitive account of the Flemish Masters.

A New Guide to the Battlefields of Northern France and the Low Country by Michael Glover, Michael Joseph.

Battlefields of the First World War by T.&V. Holt, Pavilion.

History of the Belgians by A. de Meeiis. A colourful and wide-ranging history of the Belgians.

Bruegel by Gregory Martin. An introduction to the works of Pieter Bruegel.

The Renaissance and Mannerism Outside Italy by Alastair Smart.

Defiant Dynasty: The Coburgs of Belgium by Theo Aronson. A gossipy history of the kings of the House of Saxe-Coburg-Gotha from 1831 to 1950.

Twelve Cities by John Gunter. Includes an essay on the temperament of Brussels and its citizens.

The Low Countries: 1780–1940 by E.H. Kossman. A thorough history.

Online

For a complete listing of Belgian sites on the Internet, see:
http://www.online.be/

Other Insight Guides

Nearly 200 Insight Guides cover the world, complemented by more than 100 Insight Pocket Guides and 100 Insight Compact Guides.

In more than 300 pages, **Insight Guide: Belgium** covers in comprehensive detail every aspect of the country: history, culture, people and places. It's the ideal companion.

For those on a tight schedule, **Insight Pocket Guide: Brussels** sets out carefully crafted itineraries designed to make the most of your visit. It contains recommendations from a local expert and comes with a full-size fold-out map showing the itineraries.

Insight Compact Guides to **Belgium**, **Bruges** and **Brussels** are ideal on-the-spot reference guides – in essence, mini-encyclopedias. Highly portable, each is packed with detailed text, photography and maps, all meticulously cross-referenced for ease of use.

ART & PHOTO CREDITS

Photography by
Afrika Museum, Tervuren 48
**Archiv für Kunst and Geschichte,
Berlin** 28, 29, 30, 34, 35, 50
Auschwitz-Stiftung, Antwerp 54, 55
Bodo Bondzio Cover, 3, 14/15, 22,
88L, 93, 138/139, 160, 170, 174,
183, 184, 221, 222
**(c) 1967 Carlsen Verlag/
Castermann** 82, 83
Henning Christoph/Fotoarchiv 68,
69, 70, 71, 141, 188, 213, 217
**(c) 1990 Cosmopress, Genf
(Switzerland)** 75
Hartmut Dierks 132
dpa 62
Wolfgang Fritz 9, 18/19, 26, 27,
36/37, 40, 41, 42, 43, 56/57, 60,
61, 67, 87, 94, 98/99, 100/101,
115, 116, 118, 120, 124, 125,
126, 129, 143L, 151, 156/157,
158/159, 171, 175, 182, 191,
200, 202, 204, 224
Gil Galvin 72, 89, 133, 134L,
134R, 135, 136, 218L, 218R, 219,
223
Inbel, Brussels 194/195, 196, 198
**Institut Belge d'Information et de
Documentation, Brussels** 45, 46L,
46R, 52, 53

Jochen Keute 64, 73, 84/85,
112/113, 165, 186/187
Ingeborg Knigge 20/21, 44, 58,
59, 65, 66, 86, 91, 92 96/97,
104, 114, 117, 119, 121, 122,
123, 128, 130, 131, 137, 142,
143R, 144, 145, 146/147, 148,
150, 152L, 152R, 162, 163, 166,
167, 168, 169, 172/173, 177,
178, 180, 189, 190, 192, 193,
205R, 210/211
Thomas Mayer/Fotoarchiv 70,
102/103, 127, 155, 161,
208/209, 214, 215, 216
Wolfgang Schmerfeld 156
**(c) Stiftung Studienbibliothek zur
Geschichte der Arbeiterbewegung,
Zurich (Switzerland)** 76
Süddeutscher Verlag, Munich 47
(c) 1990 VG Bild-Kunst, Bonn 81
Topham Picture Source 38
Stephan Wiener 79, 88R, 95, 140,
164, 176, 179, 181, 205L

Map Production
Berndtson & Berndtson
© 1999 Apa Publications GmbH & Co.
Verlag KG (Singapore branch)

Index

Numbers in italics refer to photographs